D0805709

DRINKING BEHAVIOR AMONG SOUTHWESTERN INDIANS

DRINKING BEHAVIOR AMONG SOUTHWESTERN INDIANS

AN ANTHROPOLOGICAL PERSPECTIVE

Editors
Jack O. Waddell
Michael W. Everett

Collaborators

Donald N. Brown
Richard Cooley
Fernando Escalante
Maurice Miller
Don Ostendorf
Martin Topper
Ron Wood

THE UNIVERSITY OF ARIZONA PRESS
TUCSON, ARIZONA

About the editors

Jack O. Waddell, professor of anthropology, joined the faculty of the Department of Sociology and Anthropology, Purdue University in 1966, after receiving his Ph.D. in anthropology from the University of Arizona. Dual degrees in anthropology and sociology have sharpened his focus in ethnographic studies. Most of his research has focused on ethnic peoples of the southwest, particularly the Papagos. He has done field work among them during the 1960s and 1970s. His main research emphases have been in Papago economic adjustments, Papago drinking behavior, and contemporary ritual life in Papago society. These interests have extended to other indigenous populations in the western hemisphere as well as to global comparative ethnology.

Michael W. Everett became Director, Tribal Health Authority, White Mountain Apache Tribe, White River, Arizona, in 1975. Prior to this he was assistant professor of anthropology at Northern Arizona University. He received his Ph.D. in anthropology from the University of Arizona in 1970. He has had a long-standing research interest in health, illness, suicide, homicide, alcoholism, and other stresses among southwest Native American populations, especially Western Apaches. In addition, he has maintained an active involvement in manpower training of Native American health workers. A number of scholarly articles reflect these academic and applied concerns.

THE UNIVERSITY OF ARIZONA PRESS

Copyright © 1980
The Arizona Board of Regents
All Rights Reserved
Manufactured in the U.S.A.

Library of Congress Cataloging in Publication Data

Main entry under title:

Drinking behavior among southwestern Indians.

    Includes bibliographies and index.
    1. Indians of North America—Southwest, New—Liquor problem.   I. Waddell, Jack O., 1933–   II. Everett, Michael W.   III. Brown, Donald Nelson, 1937–
[DNLM: 1. Alcohol drinking.   2. Anthropology, Cultural —United States.   3. Indians, North American—United States. WM274.3 D781]
E78.S7D74   1979   362.2′92   79-16379

ISBN 0-8165-0676-0
ISBN 0-8165-0615-9 pbk.

To Richard Cooley
whose health failed while he was working
to resolve Native American alcohol problems

Contents

Illustrations

Tables

Preface

We first conceived the idea to bring together a collection of ethnographic studies on Native American drinking shortly after the two of us met for the first time. Everett had just completed his doctoral field research among the Western Apache and Waddell had just returned from doing field research among Papagos. We had each done long-term field research wherein alcohol use was the central problem for investigation, not just another thread in that "thing of threads and patches" called culture.

Naturally, we spent many good times comparing our research experiences and findings once we became acquainted; and this led us to communicating with other ethnographic researchers who might possibly have done extensive work in the ethnography of drinking. As always, both our list of possible contributors and our general idea of including several types of Native American societies grew idealistically large. In actuality, our final list of contributors depreciated considerably due to one of three factors:

1. the potential contributor had collected some data on Indian drinking but in no way would it be considered an exhaustive ethnographic effort;
2. the potential contributor indeed did seem to have extensive ethnographic data on drinking but was committed to other projects and therefore could not contribute at the time; and
3. the potential contributor was in the midst of a research project that appeared to provide extensive ethnographic data but was not ready to contribute at the time.

These circumstances also operated together to limit our geographical focus. An earlier plan conceived of including cases throughout North America, but for more obvious reasons this was unwise because it invited too broad a range of studies, some ethno-historical or survey-type rather than ethnographic. It eventually occurred to us that we had forgotten some important parts of our "methods" training under Edward H. Spicer. We finally realized that the method of controlled comparison, with emphasis upon comparison among societies sharing the

[ix]

same historical area, was the best approach. With this in our minds, we concentrated on recent ethnographic works in the Greater Southwest that focused on drinking behavior. We wanted to include some Mexican, Yuman, Piman, Shoshonean, Pai, etc. representation but because of the reasons mentioned above, we were not able to extend ourselves as much as we had hoped.

We finally settled on the studies that are included in this volume. In spite of our original hope that the book could incorporate more cases for greater variation, the four studies included can be fit into a rationale for valid comparison in that they represent some of the significant variance necessary for undertaking comparisons of any kind. And each study can also be evaluated on its own merits as well.

We hope that in bringing this volume together we can contribute to a better understanding of both academic and applied problems related to the cultural use of alcohol among Native Americans.

JACK WADDELL
MICHAEL EVERETT

Acknowledgments

We must pay many tributes as editors. First, of course, the patience of our main contributors has been exceptional in that they have waited a long time, wondering if their editors would ever see this project through. We thank them for this as well as for their acknowledgment of our capacity as editors to render any portion of their contributions into an overall fit with our main idea.

Material of this kind also depends a great deal on the understanding of Native Americans, both those who comprised our sources of information and those who may read and react to what we have done. Our intentions have been to report accurately and fairly, and in an ethically responsible manner. We do not claim immunity from error or misconception. In fact we would welcome any such corrections or alternative explanations. To all who have aided us in gathering data, some of it extremely sensitive to ethical consideration, and to those who might be so kind as to study our material and react to it, we are and will continue to be extremely appreciative.

A work of this kind is also a work of production. Marshall Townsend, Director of the University of Arizona Press, has been continuously supportive while always maintaining demanding professional standards along the way. His detailed and critical communications at various stages of consideration have been welcome and refreshing as we have moved along in the project. Our gratitude to him, his excellent staff of editors, particularly Lydia Burton and Elizabeth Shaw, and the unknown reviewers who were called upon to critique our manuscripts must be expressed here. The reviewers especially have been immensely helpful in the expanding, adding, deleting, revising, and rearranging that has continously been going on. They have helped us to see what we could not or did not see about our writing that made it less than what it should be. Many issues were raised that prompted much thought and reworking. Whether or not we have responded to all of their advice and criticism, they have played an invaluable role in this final project, which we hope is not really final.

Ms. Catherine Alexander deserves special consideration in these acknowledgments for the many hours of typing and retyping that have gone into this volume. In addition to her tasks as a part-time administrative secretary and a part-time emergency medical technician, she set aside additional hours in order to see that this manuscript was typed. She deserves a special kind of thanks.

General Introduction

Michael W. Everett

"Firewater" is the perennial Native American burden, not only for the problems it actually causes but also for those it is presumed to precipitate. The myth that "Indians can't hold their liquor" has so dominated Anglo-Indian affairs that contemporary Native Americans, from traditionalists to young militants, view alcohol and drinking as the major culprits in the "breakdown" of the "old ways." Tribal leaders and health officials enthusiastically join professionals, missionaries, traders, and teachers in decrying the consequences of alcohol abuse. Yet the "Indian problem" persists—and worsens almost daily. Figures published by the U.S. National Institute of Mental Health in 1973 show 1) that alcohol related mortality rates for Native Americans are four to five times greater than comparable rates for all "races," 2) that two-thirds of the alcohol deaths for Indians result from cirrhosis of the liver, and 3) that arrest rates for alcohol-related offenses are twelve times greater for Indians than non-Indians. (Waddell, ····)

In response to this worsening situation with alcohol-related homicide, accidents, suicides, illness, school drop-out rates, and so on, alcohol has received the highest priority in Native American community health and social service programs (U.S. Public Health Service 1969). Because of the influence of agencies like the American Indian Commission on Alcoholism and Drug Abuse and the National Indian Board on Alcoholism and Drug Abuse, a significant amount of money was budgeted for alcoholism programs. In Arizona, the state Department of Health Services provided some funding for 17 different Indian alcoholism programs. Halfway houses and recovery centers are becoming standard components in such programs. Several university programs have developed special Indian alcoholism training projects (e.g. the University of Utah Western Region Indian Alcoholism Training Center). And the National Institute on Alcohol Abuse and Alcoholism (NIAAA) is preparing to provide up to one million dollars in funding for a three-western state Indian alcoholism training program.

Yet in the almost bandwagon atmosphere that prevails, one issue becomes increasingly obscured: What is the character of the phenomenon in question? What is this thing called "Indian drinking"? Scanty biomedical research suggests only that Native American drinkers may exhibit some metabolic rate differences in comparison to non-Indian drinkers (e.g. Fenna and others 1971; Lieber 1972; Hanna 1976). Also it may be that Disulfiram (Antabuse) treatment routines are affected by such poorly understood physiological variables as skin pigmentation. At the moment, therefore, it appears that "Indian drinking" is, at least biomedically speaking, hardly distinctive or unique. However, psychosocial or sociocultural studies, of which there are an abundance, tend not to support this proposition (see e.g. Popham and Yawney 1967).

The comparative method has been used by investigators in pursuit of valid cross-cultural generalizations about drinking and drunkenness, both descriptively and analytically (e.g. Child and others 1965; Schaefer 1974, 1976). These studies focus on Native American culture in general (e.g. Dozier 1966; Lurie 1971; Westermeyer 1974; Littman 1970), on distinctive tribal clusters (e.g. Lemert 1954, 1958; Levy and Kunitz 1971), on single cultures (e.g. Whittaker 1963; Devereux 1948; Hamer 1965), on reservation environments (e.g. Heath 1964; Curley 1967), on urban environments (e.g. Westermeyer 1972a; Graves 1970; Waddell 1973), on historical variables (e.g. Daily 1968, nd; Kunitz and others 1971; Savard 1968), and on economic variables (e.g. Collins 1970; Robbins 1973). In their efforts to contrast Native American drinking with non-Indian drinking, these investigators provide further support for the validity of Keller's Law on the Oddities of Alcoholics: "The investigation of any trait in alcoholics will show that they have either more or less of it" (Keller 1972:1147).

However, two common themes are evident in the majority of these and other studies. The first is that "Indian drinking" *is* somehow different from non-Indian drinking. The second is that "Indian drinking," despite all of its abuses and problems, has a number of positive aspects that are often ignored or denied. Two now-classic studies and a 1974 publication amply illustrate these propositions and the apparently unintended consequences of their widespread acceptance.

In 1954, sociologist Edwin Lemert published his comprehensive treatise on Indian drinking among Northwest Coast tribes, including Salish, Nootka, and Kwakiutl (Lemert 1954). Intensive fieldwork formed a solid foundation for Lemert's generalizations on drinking functions and "dysfunctions" among these Native Americans. These people had virtually no contact with beverage alcohol prior to European intrusion. As their traditional behavior came increasingly under attack from outside forces, these groups retaliated by using alcohol to revitalize leadership patterns, beliefs regarding social status, and ritual. Lemert also notes the absence of addictive drinking and social rejection among his informants. After contrasting the Northwest Coast with Mojave and Chamula data, he concludes by reemphasizing the positive values of "intoxication and pathological drinking" in acculturation situations.

In 1969, MacAndrew and Edgerton, a psychologist and an anthropologist, published *Drunken Comportment,* their careful review of cross-cultural literature on drunkenness. Filled with ethnographic and historical detail, it argues in general and for Native Americans in particular that, contrary to "conventional wisdom," drunkenness only precipitates disinhibitions within culturally allowable limits, that intoxicated individuals behave differently under different social circumstances, that drunkenness constitutes a kind of "time-out" during which the clock of social responsibility is temporarily halted, and that some troublesome individuals are "ineligible" for the "time-out excuse" of intoxication. Thus, Indian drunkenness becomes 1) a positive mechanism for social integration which cannot operate in more heterogeneous societies and 2) an effective strategy for coping with acculturation problems due to external intrusion into native culture.

The most recent publication on "Indian drinking" is a 1974 case study of that title by the anthropologist-physician team, Jerrold Levy and Stephen Kunitz. Based on over five years intensive research, this work focuses on Navajo drinking, and to a lesser extent Hopi and White Mountain Apache drinking, in contrast to "Anglo American theories" of drinking and drunkenness (Levy and Kunitz 1974). The authors ask a question that they say is ignored in other research: "Is Indian drinking best explained by considering it as a retreatist or escapist response to social disintegration, or by viewing it as serving ends that are compatible with preexisting and persisting tribal institutions and values" (p.3)?

After examining patterns of alcohol related homicide, suicide, and cirrhosis, Levy and Kunitz conclude that 1) "... patterns of deviance are largely explainable in terms of social type" (p.106); 2) "... the stability of rates and the persistence of patterns of suicide and homicide over long periods indicate that neither increased acculturation nor increased alcohol use have been the major factors influencing these types of social deviance" (p.106); and 3) "... the prevalent style of Navajo

xvi   *Native American Drinking*

drinking differs considerably from that displayed by White Americans both in regard to overt behavior and in the nature of the involvement with alcohol'' (p.173).

Now, in view of the popular concern for the "Indian problem," the nagging question all this research raises is simple and obvious: "If Indian drinking is somehow distinctive, are these differences relevant to solutions for problem drinking and alcoholism?" The problem, of course, is that much of the research not only does not focus on the practical issue of treatment for and prevention of alcohol problems, but it also strongly implies that these are not necessary because of the "positive functions" of drinking and drunkenness. A corollary to this proposition is that continued acculturation and adoption, whether forcible or not, of non-Indian ways and values will inevitably mitigate these positive effects and bring about circumstances appropriate to the alcohol rehabilitation strategies proposed by non-Indian benefactors.

There is hardly any agreement, however, as to precisely how this process will work, whom it will affect, where it will occur, or how rapidly it will take place. MacAndrew and Edgerton (1969:164) argue that a truly accurate understanding of drunken behavior is only possible through an appreciation of the different *meanings* attached to this conduct in different societies. Yet Levy and Kunitz (1974:184) contend that "the pattern of alcohol use differs, depending on degree of acculturation. To be like a white man means, in part, drinking like one." For Minnesota Chippewas, Westermeyer (1972b) suggests that this process is a voluntary and calculated one, used by Native Americans to their own advantage in coping with stress from living in a non-Indian world, a notion supported by Lurie (1971). But Everett and others (1973) argue that Indian alcoholism programs and the operating standards upon which they are based are too often merely reflections of Euro-American definitions, expectations, and perspectives, adopted by Native American communities for their economic value (e.g. in providing jobs) rather than to meet locally defined needs. Further problems are pointed out by Levy and Kunitz (1974; Kunitz and Levy nd) when they note that 1) most Navajo alcohol programs are based on an alien definition of alcoholism as a disease and that 2) Navajo paraprofessional workers, because of their nontraditional status, are inclined to label traditional forms of (drinking) behavior as "deviant" and attempt to hasten the adoption of relevant perceptions and values.

The Native American alcoholism programs that have developed out of this combination of native and non-native perceptions and values seem to share three common characteristics. First, where staff training is available, it tends to focus on regional or national *forms* but not *meanings* of Native American cultures in relation to alcoholism models (e.g. University of Utah School of Social Work 1972; University of California at Santa Cruz nd). Second, where staff members or administrators are involved, there is often an abiding concern for an appreciation of the particular cultural configurations of the Indian *community* but not of the individual *client* (e.g. Ferguson 1968, 1970; Savard 1968; Gracia 1973; Shore and Von Fumetti 1972). Finally, Native American staff personnel are used on the assumptions that 1) this in itself constitutes local community involvement for the program, 2) local people can help to establish better rapport and community relations for the program, and 3) recovered or stabilized Indian drinkers can be more effective in relating to local alcohol experiences of clients in the program and of problem drinkers in the community (e.g. Shore and Von Fumetti 1972).

It should be noted, however, that not all Native American approaches to alcoholism and problem drinking fit this description. Interestingly, the most notable exceptions are "spiritual" and emphasize the development and use of local cultural resources. The Native American Church, whose sacrament is peyote, has long been recognized as an effective strategy for alcohol rehabilitation (Roy 1973). Fundamentalist Christianity, with appropriate modifications, has also proven markedly successful in the treatment of alcohol problems (Hippler 1973; Everett 1974). In each case, an alternative approach to both Euro-American medical and psychosocial models has demonstrated its viability for some segments of the Native American population. Culture-specific approaches, like the use of Native American medical practitioners (e.g. Montana Indian Commission on Alcoholism and Drug Abuse 1973) and the implementation of a decentralized, local community model, including native healers (Navajo Nation Health Authority 1975), may well reveal new insights for the treatment of Native American problem drinking and alcoholism.

Yet, based on the discussion above, it is our contention that theories and research methodologies have contributed little to an understanding of the *meanings* of Native American drinking practices and even less to the development of effective treatment and prevention strategies for Indian alcoholism and problem drinking. Some would argue that this is an inherent defect in the so-called "scientific method." We do not believe this, and the present volume is an effort to demonstrate the useful application of culturally meaningful research techniques toward a practical understanding of that vague phenomenon, "Indian drinking."

The intent, organization, and content of this volume reflects our firm belief that a systematic comparison of culturally meaningful descriptions and explanations of drinking, as they are used locally, can make significant practical contributions to the self-management of problem drinking by Native Americans themselves.

For our comparison of culture-specific perspectives of drinking, we have chosen four Native American groups in the southwestern United States. The method of "controlled comparison" was first developed there by Eggan (1954) because of the ease by which historical and environmental variables could be isolated in the pursuit of cultural variation. Spicer (1962) and others (e.g. Kirchhoff 1954) have also considered the Southwest to be a distinct cultural entity. Finally, at the time this project began, those investigators engaged in current research on Indian drinking and amenable to our proposed approach (papers in Part Two by Waddell, Brown, Topper, and Everett) were working in the Southwest. The paper in Part One by Waddell on historical roots of Native American drinking in the Southwest further demonstrates the value of this "controlled comparison" focus.

For our research methodology, we have modified an approach developed and refined by Frake (1964a, 1964b), Metzger (1963), and Siverts (1973) and utilized most notably by Spradley (1970) in his work with "urban nomads." The basic scheme of this strategy is the use of native language and English vernacular forms to describe the cognitive categories, perceptions, plans, and rules that participants themselves use in scheduling activities from one environment to another. Thus, not only do these accounts hope to reflect accurate descriptions of cultural "reality," but they also hope to make more explicit how and why things happen as they do. Using this approach, each paper in Part Two deals with a different topic in relation to drinking: Waddell on urban social relationships and cultural values among Papagos, Brown on the disruptiveness of community life at Taos Pueblo, Topper on status dramatization among youthful Navajos, and Everett on categories of propriety and impropriety among White Mountain Apaches.

For a practical application of these culturally meaningful data to alcohol treatment and prevention programs, we have selected three related approaches. In Part Two, each author offers an appraisal of the practical relevance of his research. Part Three attempts to develop the notion that non-Indian perspectives on Indian drinking can be combined with Indian and health practitioner perspectives to produce valuable insights into community alcohol problems and their solution. Escalante, a Yaqui sociologist, interprets his own experiences in light of the research carried out and theories of Native American drinking promulgated by non-Indians. The selections by Cooley, Miller and Ostendorf, and Wood offer three additional perspectives by those directly involved in Indian programs. They raise a number of practical issues in Native American alcoholism program development and management.

In Part Four we seek to set forth some tentative conclusions derived from the four case studies, the perspectives of Indian and/or health personnel, and other studies on Indian and non-Indian alcohol use and abuse. Conclusions about the value of culture-specific studies to the building of culturally meaningful helping programs will be stated in the final chapter, with the hope they will be of some practical utility for workers in the field.

It is our belief that the approach endorsed here is useful and appropriate for a meaningful and practical understanding of "Indian drinking" and its abuses. The forms and meanings it entails derive from specific Native American communities themselves rather than from outside interests. In trying to represent as accurately as possible the perceptions and viewpoints of native individuals, we have had to resolve the problem as to how this can best be done. In some instances we have tried to utilize native language terminologies to capture the essence of native meanings and their proximate English renderings. More often, informant statements have been elicited in English since among all four tribal groups bilingualism, in a wide range of proficiency, is a common phenomenon. Nonetheless, it should be kept in mind that for a large number English is, at best, a second language. While it may be necessary to negotiate in English daily, it is not their first language. Hence, when our contributors deem it necessary to employ native statements in direct quote form in order to represent as closely as possible their original intent, it has been necessary to paraphrase some of these remarks into a more standard prose rather than in the more vernacular form as they were rendered by informants. If programs work because native views are considered and if the same programs help Native Americans to find meaningful solutions to their own drinking problems, then they can be adopted. If they do not work, they should be modified or discarded. In the process, local community self-confidence, self-determination, and trained manpower development—rather than continued Indian dependency—are actively encouraged and promoted.

While there is much legitimate interest in drinking in general and in Indian drinking as a special kind of social phenomenon, the intention of this volume is much more modest. We choose to look at a specific culture area, sampling only some of the intercultural and intracultural variation by looking at a few very select southwest Native American examples. And since we have practical aims in view, we think it appropriate to include the perspectives of Native American health workers, including Native Americans themselves, even though they couch their concerns in a different kind of discourse. It is, after all, the local community of practitioners and the Native American communities themselves that must and should judge the value of our approach. We want to reflect the local views, for it is not so much, as MacAndrew and Edgerton (1969:173) conclude, that people deserve the kind of drunken behavior they allow, but rather, it is as Russell Means (Ahrens 1973:69) put it: "There is a word that is prevalent in the Indian world that has much more meaning than how Webster's dictionary defines it. That word is respect—respect for your brother's vision."

REFERENCES CITED

Ahrens, H. C.
  1973   Russell Means, Sign of Unrest. *Youth* **24,** No. 11, November.
Child, I. L., M. K. Bacon, and H. Barry, III
  1965   A Cross-Cultural Study of Drinking, I. *Quarterly Journal of Studies on Alcohol* Supplement No. 3.
Collins, T. W.
  1970   Economic Change and the Use of Alcohol Among American Indians. MS, Paper presented at 69th Annual Meeting of American Anthropological Association.
Curley, R. T.
  1967   Drinking Patterns of the Mescalero Apache. *Quarterly Journal of Studies on Alcohol* **28**:116–31. New Brunswick.
Daily, R. C.
  1968   The Role of Alcohol Among North American Indian Tribes as Reported in the Jesuit Relations. *Anthropology* **10**:46–57.
  nd   Three Phases of Explosive Intoxication Among Northeastern Indians. MS, Florida State University.
Devereux, G.
  1948   The Function of Alcohol in Mojave Society. *Quarterly Journal of Studies on Alcohol* **9**:207–51.
Dozier, E. P.
  1966   Problem Drinking Among American Indians: The Role of Sociocultural Deprivation. *Quarterly Journal of Studies on Alcohol* **27**: 72–87.
Eggan, F.
  1954   Social Anthropology and the Method of Controlled Comparison. *American Anthropologist* **56**:743–63.

Everett, M. W.
1974   Theory and Practice in the Ethnography of Problem Drinking. MS, Paper presented at Annual Meeting of Society for Applied Anthropology. Boston.
Everett, M. W., M. R. Endfield, and J. Cruz
1973   Cowboys, Indians, and "Alcoholism": White Mountain Apache Solutions to Problem Drinking. MS, Paper presented at 72nd Annual Meeting of American Anthropological Association. New Orleans.
Fenna, D., L. Mix, O. Schaefer, and J. A. L. Gilbert
1971   Ethanol Metabolism in Various Racial Groups. *Canadian Medical Association Journal* **105**:472–5.
Ferguson, F. N.
1968   Navajo Drinking: Some Tentative Hypotheses. *Human Organization* **27**:159–67.
1970   A Treatment Program for Navajo Alcoholics. *Quarterly Journal of Studies on Alcohol* **31**:898–919.
Frake, C. O.
1964a Notes on Queries in Ethnography. *American Anthropologist* **66**:132–45.
1964b How to Ask For A Drink in Subanun. *American Anthropologist* **66**:127–32.
Gracia, M. F.
1973   Analysis of Incidence of Alcoholic Intake by Indian Population to One State of U.S.A. (Montana), In Relation to Admissions to a Psychiatric Hospital for Treatment and Hospitalization. MS, paper presented at 9th International Congress of Anthropological and Ethnological Sciences. Chicago.
Graves, T. D.
1970   The Personal Adjustment of Navajo Indian Migrants to Denver, Colorado. *American Anthropologist* **72**:35–54.
Hamer, J. H.
1965   Acculturation Stress and the Functions of Alcohol Among the Forest Potawatomi. *Quarterly Journal of Studies on Alcohol* **26**:285–302.
Hanna, J. M.
1976   Ethnic Groups, Human Variation, and Alcohol Use. In *Cross-Cultural Approaches to the Study of Alcohol: An Interdisciplinary Perspective*, edited by Michael Everett, Jack Waddell, and Dwight Heath. The Hague: Mouton.
Heath, D. B.
1964   Prohibition and Post-Repeal Drinking Patterns Among the Navajo. *Quarterly Journal of Studies on Alcohol* **25**:119–35.
Hippler, A. E.
1973   Fundamentalist Christianity: An Alaska Athabascan Technique for Overcoming Alcohol Abuse. *Transcultural Psychiatric Research Review* **10**:173–9.
Keller, M.
1972   The Oddities of Alcoholics. *Quarterly Journal of Studies on Alcohol* **33**:1147–48.

Kirchhoff, P.
1954   Gatherers and Farmers in the Greater Southwest: A Problem in Classification. *American Anthropologist* **56**:529–56.
Kunitz, S. J. and J. E. Levy
nd   Changing Ideas of Alcohol Use Among Navajo Indians. MS, University of Rochester.
Kunitz, S. J., J. E. Levy, C. L. Odoroff, and J. Bollinger
1971   The Epidemiology of Alcoholic Cirrhosis in Two Southwestern Indian Tribes. *Quarterly Journal of Studies on Alcohol* **32**:706–20.
Lemert, E. M.
1954   Alcohol and the Northwest Coast Indians. *University of California Publications in Culture and Society* **2**:313–406.
1958   The Use of Alcohol in Three Salish Indian Tribes. *Quarterly Journal of Studies on Alcohol* **19**:90–107.
Levy, J. E. and S. J. Kunitz
1971   Indian Reservations, Anomie, and Social Pathologies. *Southwestern Journal of Anthropology* **27**:97–128.
1974   *Indian Drinking: Navajo Practices and Anglo-American Theories.* New York: John Wiley and Sons.
Lieber, C.
1972   Metabolism of Ethanol and Alcoholism: Racial and Acquired Factors. *Annals of Internal Medicine* **76**:326–7.
Littman, G.
1970   Alcoholism, Illness, and Social Pathology Among American Indians in Transition. *American Journal of Public Health* **60**:1769–87.
Lurie, N. O.
1971   The World's Oldest On-Going Protest Demonstration: North American Indian Drinking Patterns. *Pacific Historical Review* **40**:311–32.
MacAndrew, C. and R. B. Edgerton
1969   *Drunken Comportment: A Social Explanation.* Chicago: Aldine.
Metzger, D.
1963   Drinking Performances in Aguacatenango. MS, Doctoral Dissertation, University of Chicago.
Montana Indian Commission on Alcoholism and Drug Abuse
1973   Montana State Indian Plan on Addiction. MS, Billings, Montana.
Navajo National Health Authority
1975   Traditional Healing Ways Applied to Navajo Alcoholism and Drinking Problems. MS, St Michaels, Arizona.
Popham, R. E. and C. D. Yawney
1967   Culture and Alcohol Use: A Bibliography of Anthropological Studies. *Addiction Research Foundation Bibliographic Series No. 1.* Toronto.
Robbins, R.
1973   Alcohol and the Identity Struggle: Some Effects of Economic Change on Interpersonal Relations. *American Anthropologist* **75**:99–122.

Roy, C.
1973   Indian Peyotists and Alcohol. *American Journal of Psychiatry* **130**:329–30.

Savard, R. J.
1968   Effects of Disulfiram Therapy on Relationships Within the Navajo Drinking Group. *Quarterly Journal of Studies on Alcohol* **29**:909–16.

Schaefer, J. M.
1974   A Methodological Review of Holocultural Studies on Drunkenness. International Studies Association Comparative Interdisciplinary Studies Section, *Working Paper No. 18*. Pittsburgh.
1976   Drunkenness and Culture Stress: A Holocultural Test. In *Cross-Cultural Approaches to the Study of Drinking: An Interdisciplinary Perspective*, edited by Michael Everett, Jack Waddell, and Dwight Heath. The Hague: Mouton.

Shore, J. H. and B. Von Fumetti
1972   Three Alcohol Programs for American Indians. *American Journal of Psychiatry* **128**:134–8.

Siverts, H. (ed.)
1973   *Drinking Patterns in Highland Chiapas*. Oslo: Universitetsforlaget.

Spicer, E. H.
1962   *Cycles of Conquest: The Impact of Spain, Mexico, and the United States on the Indians of the Southwest, 1533–1960*. Tucson: University of Arizona Press.

Spradley, J. P.
1970   *You Owe Yourself A Drunk: An Ethnography of Urban Nomads*. Boston: Little Brown and Co.

U.S. National Institute of Mental Health
1973   *Homicide, Suicide, and Alcoholism Among American Indians*. Washington: Government Printing Office.

U.S. Public Health Service
1969   *Report to the Indian Health Service Task Force on Alcoholism*. Washington: Health Services and Mental Health Administration.

University of California at Santa Cruz
nd   Indian Counselor's Training Design on Alcoholism. MS, Santa Cruz, California.

University of Utah School of Social Work
1972   Western Region Indian Alcoholism Training Center Information Brochure. Salt Lake City.

Waddell, J. O.
1973   "Drink, Friend!" Social Contexts of Convivial Drinking and Drunkenness Among Papago Indians in an Urban Setting. In *Research on Alcoholism: Clinical Problems*. Proceedings of the First Annual Alcoholism Conference of the National Institute on Alcohol Abuse·and Alcoholism, Morris Chafetz. Department of Health, Education, and Welfare Publication HSM 73-9074. Washington: U.S. Government Printing Office.

Westermeyer, J.
    1972a   Chippewa and Majority Alcoholism in the Twin Cities: A Comparison. *Journal of Nervous and Mental Disease* **155**:322–7.
    1972b   Options Regarding Alcohol Use Among the Chippewa. *American Journal of Orthopsychiatry* **42**:398–403.
    1974   Alcoholism. In Indian Mental Health, edited by M. Beiser. *Psychiatric Annals* **4**, No. 9.
Whittaker, J. O.
    1963   Alcohol and the Standing Rock Sioux Tribe, II. Psycho-Dynamic and Cultural Factors in Drinking. *Quarterly Journal of Studies on Alcohol* **24**:80–90.

PART ONE

Historical Antecedents

Introduction

The major emphasis in this collection of essays on Native American drinking is on contemporary patterns. Many historical and structural reasons can be accounted for in explaining the current social fact that much Indian drinking is like chronic drinking elsewhere in contemporary America. The fact that most U.S. cities and towns are the end products of frontier-settlement beginnings, whether Spanish or northern-European initially, underlies some of the convergence in drinking styles. As frontier settlements, based on combinations of subsistence farming, herding, and surface mining, evolved into regional towns with regional economies, differentially linked to growing national and international market economies, the settlements came to be dominated by commercial and mercantile interests. The growth of cosmopolitanism in territorial towns brought numerous subsidiary businesses bent on ''making it'' among the growing numbers of emigrant citizens.

Among the commercial interests, both legally and illegally manifest, was the liquor and beer industry, ranging from large wholesale distributions to local consumer distribution in bars and illegal back-alleys. Much ''time out'' or recreational activity in the growing towns centered in bars, saloons, cantinas, or in public places, where people from diverse folk backgrounds (farmers, cattlemen, miners, military men, etc.) indulged in their ways while cosmopolitan elites (businessmen, professionals, educators, etc.) from eastern towns and cities indulged in their ''more civile'' ways. The buildup of commercial activities in the town centers not only challenged or depleted rural subsistence economies; it also fostered the familiar urban profile of extremely contrasting styles of life, the business and professional elite and the increasing urban proletariate being drawn from marginalized rural areas.

There were opposing moralities, leading to efforts to legislate and enforce civic morality. Thus, marginal peoples, especially Indians, received special attention. Since Indians were potentially, if not actually,

a threat to the civil order and since they were thought to become raven-
ous with the slightest amount of alcohol, special prohibitions were
established regarding the sale of intoxicants to them. And all Indians
were treated as if they were uniformly alike! Yet liquor was so much a
part of the commercial picture; illegal activity thrived and the illegal
sales and distribution had an unquestionable impact on establishing the
manner in which Native Americans came to acquire and consume
alcohol.

But it was not only frontier models for drinking, nor the attraction to
commercial towns, nor the institution of prohibition that provided a
common base for Native American behavior. Their special status as
native occupants of land increasingly desired by non-Indians and the
benevolent or expediency concerns of non-Indian elites to see Indians
"civilized" brought native populations under institutional management
in religion, health, economics, politics, education, and occupation.
This was a "total institution" involvement that did much to foster a
"generalized Indian" profile.

Through the years of this total institutional dependency, native value
systems, social structures, and lifestyles underwent rapid and differential change. Along with other social forces in American life, it helped to
promote cultural alienation through ecological displacement, new forms
of social differentiation and schism, and competing ideologies. Some
social sectors developed at the expense of other sectors, and the majority (not all) of Native American people were "trapped" in the social
margins, having only limited access to the "mainstream" of economic,
educational, political, and social institutions. Their attachments to marginal lands, their access to certain religious institutions, and their dependency on government institutions for health services, limited
technological training and special education, all worked together to
generate certain commonalities in cultural personality for
"generalized" Indians. The social margins, whether in towns, on farms
and ranches, or on reservations, engendered certain coping
strategies—rules for successfully behaving within these margins and
ways of adaptively accommodating these social margins to the
mainstream institutions, to which they did not have direct access. Some
aspects they shared with and even modeled after other marginal
peoples.

In short, because of the many historical and social trends briefly
alluded to above, it may seem that the most efficient way of dealing
with the problem of Indian drinking would be to isolate the common

foundations of their experience, not as specific tribal peoples but as a class of especially marginalized people along with other people from a variety of ethnic backgrounds.

Granted, there is much in favor of the argument that some Papagos drink much like some Pueblos who drink much like some Navajos who, in turn, drink much like some Apaches, who drink like some other Indians, who drink like some other non-Indians, etc. Also, there is not just one kind of Papago drinking any more than is there one kind of American drinking; there is much variation within a single population. The complexity of the picture presented above would insist on this.

In acknowledging all of this, it would be sheer delusion to suppose that indigenous societies, in their coping strategies, have not maintained continuity with past traditions. In spite of the credibility of there being a "generalized Indian" or a generalized social margin shared with non-Indians, it still means something to be a Papago, a Tiwa, a Navajo, an Apache. It is true not only in a cultural sense but in terms of more particularistic local histories relative to each other and to outsiders. Not all Papagos, Tiwa, Navajos, or Apaches are equally influenced by whatever has been continuous in their separate traditions but there *are* separate traditions and it seems most necessary to consider differential responses to alcohol in the light of their different histories.

We choose to make the point of different historical profiles by emphasizing the variations in aboriginal cultural usages of intoxicants. It is deemed significant for the contemporary studies in Part Two to understand each of the cases in terms of their comparative aboriginal and early contact histories. This chapter is intended to provide this perspective.

1

The Use of Intoxicating Beverages Among the Native Peoples of the Aboriginal Greater Southwest

Jack O. Waddell

This collection of ethnographic studies on drinking among select Southwestern Indian societies has as its major focus the range of variation in patterns of current alcohol use. It is therefore of extreme importance to look at the entire Greater Southwest[1] in ethno-historic perspective in order to establish the presence or absence of intoxicating beverages among the people distributed throughout this vast region of the North American mainland. More important than a simple trait distribution of native beverages, that is, whether beverages were present or absent, is a discussion of the variable cultural contexts in which native beverages were employed. Hence, it is of concern that we not only isolate the particular native beverages and their social and cultural usages, but that we account for variations in the patterns and why these variations might be so. Questions must therefore be raised about the

---

[1] I use the term "Greater Southwest" in the same sense that Haury (1954) and others use the term, knowing that in using it I perpetuate a geo-bias. I could very well use a more encompassing or neutral term, such as "Greater Southwest United States-Northwest Mexico," to accommodate the Mexican bias but for the sake of economy the latter notion has to be implied in my choice of the term used.

historical relations and cultural contacts among these peoples. Further, certain complexes of cultural traits revolving around intoxicants diffused together to lay a basic substratum of culture, helping to distinguish some groups in the Greater Southwest from other groups lacking these complexes. Demonstration of these relations should cast some light on the similarities and variations in drinking patterns among the contemporary native groups that receive major attention in this volume.

THE GREATER SOUTHWEST
AS A CULTURE AREA

Within the Greater Southwest area, which also includes a vast portion of upper northwestern Mexico comprising the states of Sonora, Chihuahua, Sinaloa, Durango, and Nayarit as well as the United States southwest, there are a number of regional cultures. Kirchhoff (1954:530) argues that these regional cultures are not just theoretical constructs but "living realities," temporally and spatially limited phenomena, which change in both content and organization over time while maintaining the basic integral features that identify them. The cultures included in this volume seem to comprise but a few of a much larger and more widely scattered complex of specific cultures throughout "Oasis America" (Kirchhoff 1954:533). Among the peoples included in this book, the Kiowa-Tanoan Tiwa at Taos and the Uto-Aztecan Papago are parts of that extensive sweep of Aztecan Tanoan (Voeglin and Voeglin 1966) speakers belonging to the farming cultures of the Greater Southwest (Kirchhoff 1954:546), or what have been referred to as "ranchería" (Spicer 1962:12) or "rancho" (Kennedy 1963:620). On the other hand, the Western Apache and Navajo Na-Dene or Athapascans (Voeglin and Voeglin 1966) rightfully belong to the hunting-gathering cultures (Kirchhoff 1954-542), although Kirchhoff includes the Navajo with the farmers on the basis of their extensive associations with the Pueblos. Because of the Puebloan influence, Spicer (1962:14) calls them agricultural band people to distinguish them from band people who did not practice any agriculture. For our purposes, these four societies provide us a very good combination of societies to compare because two are aboriginally farming cultures while two are aboriginally hunting-gathering cultures, the former linked to the cultures of the south, the latter to the cultures of the north.

The River and Desert Pueblos and the River Pima and the Desert Papago are all linguistically related and very similar adaptively from the standpoint of their intercultural relations. Their language affinity places them together historically and their adaptive technologies to farming, whether irrigation or dry-field flooding, plus a number of shared traits (Kirchhoff 1954:549; Underhill 1954:651ff) place them together culturally. On the other hand, the Navajo and their close relatives the Western Apache, historically and linguistically unrelated to the Tanoans and Pimans, penetrated the Southwest from the north and, with their instrusions, came to share, in differing ways, some of the traits of the farming peoples among whom they are scattered. These Athapascans appear to have eventually displaced some of these farming settlements or promoted their movements into more compact settlements (Underhill 1954:652).

The River Pueblos and Pimans are the northern-most extensions of the farming cultures of the Sinaloan, Sonoran, and Sierran provinces (Beals 1932:147) that were in both the pre-Hispanic and post-Hispanic flow of culture from the south. While I do not want to argue for any particular routes of diffusion in this study, Underhill's suggestion (1954:650) that one route or stream of Mexican influence up the Río Grande and then west to Zuni and the Hopi villages makes sense, as I will discuss later. Swadesh's linguistic evidence (1964:550) may render further support to this idea. While many cultural influences possibly came via this course, the use of intoxicating beverages as a part of agricultural rituals does not appear to be among them.

We can further subscribe to the well-founded notion that Mexican influences also spread northward through the Sinaloan and Sonoran provinces to such people as the Pima-Papago, where a more continuous distribution of the use of native intoxicants in ceremonies can be traced. The alcohol-intoxication-community ritual complex is more closely associated with the farming cultures rather than the hunting cultures. This certainly is true for the Pima-Papago. On the other hand, the River Pueblos also belong to the farming cultures but there is some question as to whether they had the alcohol-intoxication-community ritual complex, although they do have the agricultural, community ritual dimension. It is from this latter nonalcoholic-intoxication-community ritual complex that the Navajo pattern apparently emerged. Navajos came to be more closely and continuously influenced by their Pueblo farming neighbors than the Western Apaches.

In the case of the Western Apache, where there does appear to be some support for aboriginal usage of native intoxicants, drinking seems to be largely secular. Beverages were used to engage social and kinship relations rather than to invoke rain for their fields. The same may be said to be true for the Zuni, who had very elaborate ceremonies relating to agriculture (Driver 1969:110). The pattern makes sense for the Western Apache, given the limited development of agriculture. But why the

Zuni, if true, bypassed the ceremonial intoxicants in their farming technology poses a different problem.

ALCOHOL AND RITUAL INTOXICATION
IN THE GREATER SOUTHWEST

The Nahua: Early Settlers

The use of intoxicating beverages in agricultural ceremonies among native cultures of the Mexican Northwest-American Southwest dates back well before the Spanish Conquest. It is quite clear that ritual use of native intoxicants in agricultural ceremonies is a part of the larger Mesoamerican cultural pattern since the use of alcoholic intoxicants among native peoples north of the Greater Southwest has not been established (Driver 1969:109–11).

Starting first with the heartland of the Mesoamerican pattern, the early Nahuas settling in the Valley of Mexico elevated the maguey plant to a position of divine eminence and a multiplicity of satisfactions was obtained from this plant. As Goncalves de Lima (1956:16) notes, the importance that these precursors to the Aztec empire gave to the products of the maguey can be seen from the elaborate attention they gave to the maguey varieties themselves. There were from fourteen to sixteen Nahua designations for the varieties of maguey. Besides being used for rope and twine, containers and clothing, or for mortifying the flesh in penance rituals, the maguey was used for satisfying both thirst and hunger. The nutritional and therapeutic properties of pulque, the mild wine produced from the liquid sap of the maguey, have long been recognized. It was also useful in many cases as an excellent diuretic and effective combatant of certain intestinal disorders (Goncalves de Lima 1956:16).

Vaillant says that "not only was this pulque used both as a tipple and a ceremonial intoxicant, but it had an important nutritive effect as well in counterbalancing the lack of greens in the Mexican diet" (1962:106). Studies have shown that pulque provides considerable vitamin B and C and other minerals which prevent certain dietary deficiencies that might otherwise result (Anderson 1946:888).

The formulas and mechanics for producing pulque are likely quite ancient as well as pervasive throughout the vast area where maguey is found. They unquestionably predate the Classic (A.D. 300–600) and Post-Classic (A.D. 900–1200) developments in spite of the mythical credit given to the Post-Classic Toltecs. When the Nahua entered the

Valley of Mexico in the 13th century A.D. as a hunting and collecting people, it is rather certain that both they and the earlier residents of the Valley already had knowledge of and made use of *Ochtli* or pulque. When the Nahua consolidated their empire a couple of centuries after their humble arrival into the Valley of Mexico, it is likely that they gradually came to adopt the strong sanctions against the intemperate use of the beverage as their predecessors had done.

As the Aztec empire pushed outward in its military expansion in the 15th century, sobriety obviously became a very important value comparable to our own civilization's concerns for sobriety. But *Ochtli* also maintained its cultic value in both myth and ritual. The goddess of pulque, *Mayahuel,* and the chief of the pulque gods, *Ometochtli* or Two Rabbit, were among an array of gods that invested the beverage with its sacred character. Various styles of drunkenness were recorded, with four hundred rabbits representing complete drunkenness and fifteen or twenty rabbits representing sociability. Many public ceremonial events were dedicated to these gods (Vaillant 1962:145–6). The events were on such a large scale and the knowledge of pulque so widespread that drunkenness came under rigid state regulation in the period preceding the arrival of the Spanish conquerors.

> Drunkenness was a serious crime except on prescribed ceremonial occasions. Social disapproval, public disgrace, even death by stoning or beating, were penalties suffered by the intemperate. However, the old of both sexes, who had fulfilled their tribal obligations, were allowed great latitude in their potations (Vaillant 1962:99).

All Aztec pulque ceremonies were closely supervised by officials. Anyone breaking the sanctions was severely penalized. Sahagún wrote that no one in the young men's house was to drink the wine until he was mature. Even then he was to hide himself well and not drink before others. The quantity he was to take was to be small (Sahagún 1957:57). Father Sahagún also noted that there were always two separate meals, one without pulque for the young, and one with a small amount of pulque for the elders only. Hence, ceremonial intoxication was allowable among the Aztecs while carefully regulated social drinking among adults of the family was common. In the latter case, drunkenness was permitted only for the venerable aged.

Similar traits in modified variations can be traced among a variety of tribes distributed to the north and west of the Valley of Mexico, in the area from which the Nahua wandered into the valley in the 13th century. This area was known in early legendary annals as the "land of the

Chichimecs'' and the Nahua wanderers may well have been the "Chichimec of Aztlán" (Wolf 1959:130). Most of these Chichimecan tribes to the north and west are linguistically related to the Nahua, all belonging to the Uto-Aztecan family along with the northwest groups that will shortly be discussed. The Nahua or Aztec myths spoke of their ancestors as giant peoples that came into the land as a crude, cruel, and spirited people given to much intoxication and drunkenness with the juice of the maguey (Goncalves de Lima 1956:27).

The Hopi pueblos of the Kiowa-Tanoan family of the same Aztec-Tanoan phylum to which the Uto-Aztecan languages belong, lie on the extreme north of the Greater Southwest area being considered here. Hopi myth, according to Waters (1972:68–69), has Hopi ancestors on a series of migrations, including a visit to the Mysterious Red City of the South or *Palátkwapi*, which impresses Waters as possibly being the ruins of Casas Grandes in Chihuahua, Mexico. Willey (1966:237), in noting the southern influences into the Hohokam Colonial Period (A.D. 500–900) among the pre-Pima of southern Arizona, suggests that the Chalchihuites prehistoric culture of Durango and Zacatecas may have been the primary source for the waves of several varieties of Classic Mexican traits that made their way into the culture of the ancestors of the Pimans. According to Willey (1966:239), Casas Grandes was too far east to have served as a source of ideas making their way into Hohokam, but the remarkably Anasazi-like buildings and pottery may provide some support to Waters' interpretation of Hopi myth.

We have here a suggestion of two possible routes of culture contact; one, northwestward from Chalchihuites through the area inhabited by the Tepehuan, Tarahumara, Cahitans and Pimans and; two, northeastward from Casas Grandes up to the Río Grande to the Eastern Pueblos. This may be important, not because we need a fictive origin for the ceremonial use of intoxicants, but because there seem to be two different patterns that distinguish the northwestern Uto-Aztecans from the northeastern Tanoans and other Pueblos.

Driver (1969:110) mentions that the Zuni, and perhaps the Keresan Pueblos also, knew fermented drinks prior to direct European contact, as did the Apache and Yuman peoples north of the Pimans, but the usage seems to have been social and entirely secular, having little or no part in agricultural ritual. In tracing the trait of ceremonial drinking of intoxicants, Beals notes that

the problem of intoxicating liquors and their distribution is of great interest as presenting a trait of undoubted wide American distribution

... The agave was the overwhelming favorite for the manufacture of such drinks but other materials such as maize were used. Apparently drinking always, or practically always, had ceremonial significance (Beals 1932:105).

Beals' study reveals that ceremonial drunkenness and the production of intoxicating beverages show virtual correspondence in distribution. The diffusion of this trait-complex is considered by Beals to be rather recent but he does not suggest just how recent. He thinks that if it is proven that the Cahitan tribes (Yaqui, Mayo, etc.) are intrusive into their northern Sinaloan/southern Sonora areas, their use of intoxicants would render strong support to this theory of correspondence in distribution (Beals 1932:133). According to Swadesh (1964:550–1), the antecedents to the modern Uto-Aztecan languages may have been clustered in the American Southwest about 1000 B.C., spreading southward from that time. This would probably be an acceptable limit to what Beals might have meant by recent, that is, an intrusion by Cahitan groups into their present areas sometime since the beginning of the Christian era.

The Pimans

Tracing the presence of ceremonial intoxication among the tribes of this Greater Southwest area is built on evidence suggested by lexicostatistics, archaeology, trait-complex distributions, native legend, and early Spanish documentation. The Piman area, according to Swadesh, may have been the center of Uto-Aztecan spread to the south. The Pimans also constitute the northern border of this northwestern extension of ceremonial drinking stemming from Mesoamerica. The Upper Pimans occupied the high basins of northern Sonora and southern Arizona, while the Lower Pimans settled in the warm river valleys of southern Sonora. The Papago are included in the Upper Piman group. Their tribal locations, as well as all of the northwestern Mexico and southwestern United States tribes discussed in this survey, can be seen in Figure 1.1.

The Papago relied significantly on the mesquite bean, pitahaya fruit, tuna or prickly pear, sahuaro cactus and other wild fruits, plants, and seeds (Castetter and Bell 1942:41) but they also depended on small-scale, dry-field farming. Both the Papago and their close relatives, the Gila River Pimas near present day Phoenix, Arizona, had a regular ritual, held at the time of the giant cactus harvest (sahuaro), which was the beginning of the Piman new year. Sometime in late June the Papago-Pima gathered the fruit of the sahuaro cactus, a wild plant,

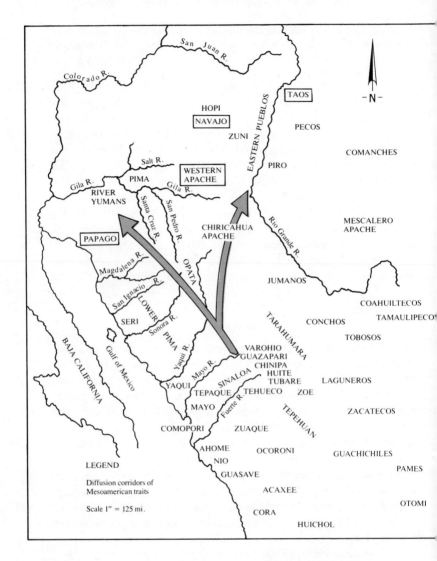

*Figure 1.1   Map of aboriginal tribes of the Greater Southwest,
            showing their distribution about the time of European
            contact, circa A.D. 1700*

fermented it to yield a mildly intoxicating beverage, and drank it in great quantities as a means of inducing rain, so necessary for their small summer fields of corn, beans, and melons, domesticated plants (Castetter and Bell 1942:222–3). The yearly ritual is still held in a number of Papago villages today (see Waddell 1976).

Captain Manje, in his account of his adventures in the lands of the Pimans, noted small settlements of Indians who cultivated no lands, at least at the seasons and locations he observed them. He recorded that they ate the roots of wild potatoes and sought the fruit of the pitahaya in its season (Manje 1954:10). Near the San Ignacio River in southern Sonora he observed the Indians of Pitiquin, probably Lower Pimans, whom Captain Manje (1954:11) noted as being both hunters and cultivators. Later, in his account of northern or upper Sonora, he wrote of some Indians, living on "sterile" lands, called "papabotas" or "bean eaters." The principal harvest of these people was the wild javapi bean but pitahayas, tunas, and other fruit-bearing plants were utilized (Manje 1954:236).

Father Luis Velarde of the Jesuits, writing about the Pimas prior to their conversion, observed:

> They [Pimans] are not accustomed to the excesses of other tribes [presumably those to the south] ... The reason they are more temperate than the others, I believe, is because these Indians live free from drunkenness more so than others. Only during the season of the pitahaya, in such localities where it may be found, do they happen to make wine out of it. This might last them two or three days. They do not use it to the excess that the other nations do (Manje 1954:245).

Bancroft (1882:550) notes that while a number of plants such as agave, maize, pitahaya, aloe, mescal, tuna, and wild grapes were used for making intoxicating liquors, the Pima were, with few exceptions, temperate in their drinking. The Pima and Maricopa, he further notes, macerated the fruit of the pitahaya, a species of cactus, dried it in the sun, mixed it with water, and let it ferment. This was, according to Bancroft at least, a highly intoxicating drink on which the Pima-Maricopa got drunk once a year. The ceremony lasted for a week or two at a time but it was customary for them to take turns getting drunk. One third of the party indulged at one time while the other two thirds took care of them and kept order.

It is clear that among the Pimans as well as Opatans, who will not be discussed in this survey because they are very close to the Pimans (Kirchhoff 1954:550), wines were made from wild plants to be used in agricultural ceremonies to produce rain. The wild plant, from their collecting and hunting economy, seems to mediate the domestic agricultural part of the economy through the action of the ceremonial wine.

The Cahitans

There were numerous tribes extending south from the area of the Seri in western Sonora along the western slope of the Sierra Occidental, running to the Gulf of California, down into what is now northern Sinaloa. The Cahita, also grouped under the terms Yaqui and Cinaloa or Sinaloa, were located in villages along the middle and lower portions of the valleys of the Yaqui, Mayo, and Fuerte rivers, which extended from the Gulf of California upland to the sierras and the land of the Tarahumara. These Cahitan tribes are variously referred to in historical accounts as the Yaqui, Mayo, Tehueco, Zuaque, Ahome, Guasave, Comopori, Sinaloa, Zoe, Tepaque, Ocoroni, Nio, and many others (see Figure 1.1).

Pérez de Ribas (1944a:278) speaks of the four principal "nations"; the Sinaloa, who dwelt at the source of the river in the highlands, the Tehuecos, who lived about 15 miles below the Sinaloa, the Zuaques, a fierce and rebellious group living on the lower river, and the Ahomes, who lived closest to the sea, on the lowest reaches of the Fuertes River. Pérez de Ribas (1944a:366–7) speaks of the Comopori as being the most barbarous of all the Sinaloan tribes and mentions also the Huite, Chinipas, Guazaparis, and other mountain peoples. The latter group may be more closely allied with the Tarahumaras to the east. He comments on the nature of drunkenness among the Chinipas.

For the Cahitan area generally, Beals related that

> intoxicating fermented liquors were made for many ceremonies. Liquor was most often made of baked agave heart mashed in water, but the fruit of the prickly pear tuna, pitahaya, maize, and mesquite beans, either grounded or toasted, and other unspecified plants were employed. The favorite liquor, however, was made from honey. For the three months the cactus fruits were ripe the Guasave were said to be in a continual state of drunkenness (Beals 1943:20).

Pérez de Ribas (1944a:127), describing the people of the villages in the Sinaloa mission province, tells of how these Indians used a kind of wild plant "that they call mesquites" for a sweet drink. He goes on to point out how the land abounded with other similar fruitbearing plants. For example, the "planta del mescal," of which there were many kinds, was reported as being widely used. These plants, while they were all first and foremost foodstuffs, also were used for making a variety of wines or fermented beverages (Pérez de Ribas 1944a:127).

During his ministries in the Sinaloa mission, Pérez de Ribas (1944a:120–30) expresses great concern over the common ''vice'' that he found among the Indian people, namely, the vice of drunkenness, which ''they enjoyed day and night.'' He does not report any cases of solitary drinking or familial drinking at meals; all of his references are to the extensive drinking that took place at public ceremonies. Large vessels were filled with the native wine derived from the plants and the large numbers of people that gathered from the surrounding regions drank until the vessels were empty. During these festivities, the whole community was observed to be full of intoxicated Indians. Any of the plants already mentioned could be used to prepare the wines—tuna, pitahaya, mesquite beans, and agave. Their fruits were crushed and thrown into water, after which the mixture would be allowed to ferment for two or three days. Honey liquor was a very popular drink among these people. While intoxication was prevalent during the ceremonies, women and young people could not be allowed to get drunk; this was the province of adult males only, according to Pérez de Ribas (1944a:129–30). This seems to conform to the Mesoamerican pattern that we noted among the Nahua, as reported by Sahagún.

Alegre (1956:426) reports that Father Tapia, on arriving at the village of Ocoroni among the Zuaque, observed the inhabitants as being buried in fantasy and drunkenness. Likewise, Pérez de Ribas (1944a:174) recorded that Father Tapia, despite his zeal for the salvation of the Ocoroni Indians, was able to do nothing among them because of their condition of intoxication.

The Mayo Indians of Sinaloa were very similar in their customs to the other ''nations'' of Sinaloa. They also used intoxicating beverages in dances and ceremonies (Pérez de Ribas 1944b:10). The Hiaqui (Yaqui), it was noted, used the fruit of the *tepeguajes,* or mesquite, that was found in abundance in the area. In their customs the Yaqui were described as being very much like the other tribes of Sinaloa in their use of intoxicating beverages for achieving drunkenness, during which state they would dance with enemy scalps (Pérez de Ribas 1944b:64–5). It seems probable that the Yaqui scalp dance had ritual significance for bringing rains to their fields. Such, at least, was the meaning of taking enemy scalps and the ritual purification that accompanied such ventures among the Papago (Underhill 1969:165).

Father Méndez of the Society of Jesus, ministering among the Zuaques in the mountain village of Nio, recorded that the people there worshipped a "hidden idol," the pitahaya, the delicious fruit from which they also made a strong beverage (Alegre 1956:450). The people from several of these mountain villages in Sinaloa, while they were cultivators of maize, beans and other domestic crops, also made extensive use of the fruits of the tuna, pitahaya, and other plants. They seem to have followed the same ranchería pattern, built upon small-scale agriculture and an extensive use of wild plants and animals, that has been described for many Uto-Aztecan tribes in this vast area up to recent times. In the Sinaloa area of these several Cahitan tribes, the most important plant seems to have been the maguey, from which they derived wines or fermented drinks that were used in their rain ceremonies and celebrations of their war victories. Alegre (1956:350) noted that in these villages, intoxication was not considered a shameful vice but was publicly and commonly authorized throughout the villages. In 1594, while visiting a particular village, it was noticed that the residents were celebrating some unknown fiesta, in which they were submerged in drunkenness (Alegre 1956:425).

These patterns described by the first missionaries to Sinaloa and the Cahitan tribes in the sixteenth century are strikingly similar to the "milder" usages described by Manje for the Pimans in the latter part of the seventeenth century in upper Sonora. There seems little to dispute the notion that this pattern of ceremonial intoxication among the ranchería peoples stems from the same Mesoamerican source, largely Nahua-derived.

The Tarahumarans and Tepehuanes

To the east of the Cahitan tribes, in the present states of Chihuahua and Durango, are the Tarahumara Indians. At the time the Spanish were moving northward, the Tarahumara were likely living in rancherías in the sierras. Thomas and Swanton (1911:8–10) list the Tubare, Chinipa, and Varohio as sub-tribes of the Tarahumara. The Tubare dwelt in the mountains at the headwaters of the Río Fuertes (also called Cinaloa and Zuaque river). The Chinipa were also a mountain people nearby the Tubare. The Varohios occupied the mountainous terrain to the north, between the Mayo and Fuertes rivers.

In a document (Documentos 1857:219) relating to the mission of the "Taraumares," "Tepeauanes," and some other groups (from 1652–1666), there is an account of Indians who made their intoxicating wine from corn, a common trait among them. There is also reference to maguey or mescal, which was considered a very strong drink.

Lumholtz, in his travels among the Tarahumara over 200 years later, had much to say about their corn wine:

> There is only one industry which has a peculiar bearing on the whole life of the Tarahumare, namely the making of beer. Nothing is so close to the heart of the Tarahumare as this liquor, called in Mexican Spanish *tesvino*. It looks like milky water and has quite an agreeable taste ... To make it, the moist corn is allowed to sprout; then it is boiled and ground, and the seed of a grass resembling wheat is added as a ferment. The liquor is poured into large earthen jars made solely for the purpose and it should now stand for twenty-four hours . . . The *tesvino* forms an integral part of the Tarahumare religion. It is used at all its celebrations, dances, and ceremonies (Lumholtz 1902:253).

Tesvino was given to infants with the mother's milk to keep the baby from getting sick. It was applied internally and externally as a remedy for all diseases. Being able to drink *tesvino* at a feast marked the turning point to manhood; a boy became a man when he drank at feasts. Marriages were not legitimate without it and all who attended a fiesta consumed it. *Tesvino* was taken on hunts or fishing trips to ensure luck, and the dead were buried with it. Lumholtz (1902:254) mentions that there was no act of importance that was not connected in some way with the drinking of *tesvino*. A new jar of the beer was never begun without first sacrificing some before the cross, for the gods were thought to be fond of it. Rain could not occur without it, for corn needed rain, and it was corn that made *tesvino*. This was the Tarahumara view of life and *tesvino* was never drunk unless it was for some purpose relating to crops, health, etc.

> To my knowledge, this beer is not known outside of the Tarahumare tribe and their immediate neighbors, the northern Tepehuanes, the Tubare, and some Mexicans in Chihuahua who have also adopted it. It must not be confounded with the well-known Mexican drink, pulque, to which it is superior in flavor (Lumholtz 1902:255–6).

Tesvino was nourishing in its own right and before a Tarahumara partook of it, he abstained from all other food. During all feasts and dances large quantities were consumed, overpowering those who drank it. The *mitotes* or ritual dances of the Tepehuan and the *rutuburi* dances of the Tarahumara to celebrate the three agricultural festivals for rain, green corn, and harvest, all took place while the participants were intoxicated (Lumholtz 1902:330).

The Tarahumara also used maguey in the making of a sweet wine. The liquid extracted from the maguey had the root of the *frijolillo* added as a ferment. *Tshawi* was derived from a variety of agave plant that grew high up on the slopes of the barrancas. Tarahumara tradition proclaimed this plant as the first one God created; the liquor obtained from it was considered indispensable to certain ceremonies. The same complex was found among the neighboring Tepehuanes. The stalk of the maize plant was also used to obtain a wine by means of a fermentation process similar to that used in making maguey wine. Lumholtz (1902:257) found the beverage much more distasteful than *tesvino*.

Many of the customs and usages of *tesvino* as found by Lumholtz have been confirmed by more recent works. Rea (1943:21, 25) reports that tesguino (*tesvino*) is used against witchcraft and is given to little children to keep them safe. At fifteen, young men assume the work of adults and can share the ceremonial intoxication of the elders. On days of particular patron saints, the people celebrate with *tesvino* and *tonari*, native intoxicants. A Mexican pamphlet (Departamento del Trabajo 1936:147) reports that during a ceremony or fiesta, drinking begins with one person and spreads to others of the ranchería until all are participating. During the state of drunkenness, the people, according to the pamphlet, commit many improper acts and even crimes; nevertheless, it seems that they are not stupefied by the *tesvino* as are other peoples drinking similar fermented drinks. The following day there appears to be no great aftereffect. Kennedy (1963) in his more recent field study confirms many of these same observations.

Among the Tarahumara, then, we see some of the same patterns that we have been characterizing as belonging to the alcohol-intoxication-agricultural ritual complex. When the Apache are discussed, it might be kept in mind that their usage of home brew corn beer in social contexts may have a direct linkage to the sierran Tarahumara, with whom many Apachean groups along the "Apache Corridor" (Spicer 1962:237) undoubtedly had first-hand contacts.

The Tepehuanes, who lived south of the Tarahumara in Durango, on the eastern slope of the Sierra Madres, seem to differ very little from the Tarahumara in religion, customs, and other aspects of culture; and it is quite certain that what is known of native intoxicants among the Tarahumara would hold true also for the Tepehuanes. Father Alegre (1956:467) several centuries ago found the habits and customs of the Tarahumara and Tepehuanes very similar to those of all the other tribes of Sinaloa. He provides no details to support this generalization but since the traits mentioned are observable, it can be considered credible that this pattern is widely distributed and generally uniform.

The Acaxee

Beals (1933) includes the Acaxee among those northwestern Mexican tribes who shared what he terms the agricultural-religious complex. The basic source of his information was a letter by a Father Arnaya, written at an uncertain date, as recorded in an archival document (Documentos 1857). In this letter, Father Arnaya spoke of a fiesta or new corn ceremony that was accompanied by dancing and a drinking "orgy" in which all participants became drunk. Pérez de Ribas (1944c:24) spoke of how the Acaxee Indians who sought work on the Spanish haciendas were physically punished to discipline them in overcoming their penchant for drunkenness. In addition to corn beer, the Acaxee enjoyed a smooth wine that they made from honey obtained from the hollows of evergreens (Pérez de Ribas (1944c:110).

These very scanty references from historical sources allow us to see that the Acaxee, possibly including the Tebaca and Sabaibo, belong within the area of this same cultural pattern of ceremonial intoxication. The beverages are similar to those found among the Piman tribes of the Sonoran desert, the Cahitan tribes of Sonora and Sinaloa, and the mountain tribes of Durango and Chihuahua. While there is little detail provided on the nature of these "ceremonies," the kinds of drinks used, the methods of fermentation employed, and their importance in agricultural ritual are all supported by the early documentary sources and later ethnographic descriptions.

The Cora

Father Tello (1891:30) refers to the Cora Indians who lived about fifty leagues (a little over fifteen miles?) from Guadalajara. In his record he notes that the Cora had fiestas that would last as long as their wine *tepachi* lasted. "Mescales" was abundant in the land of the Cora, which, according to Thomas and Swanton (1911:21), was the rugged mountain country in the states of Nayarit and northern Jalisco, near the Río de Jesús María. The Cora cultivated maize from which they derived many foods and beverages (Tello 1891:31). Lumholtz (1902:510) states that a "prominent feature in the elaborate ceremonies of the tribe, connected with the coming of age of boys and girls, is the drinking of homemade mescal." While this drink was most likely a sweet drink and less fermented than the drinks of the adults, it does support that the Cora utilized the maguey as a source of the native wine that was closely associated with ritual events. The *tepachi* of the Cora was unquestionably a more fermented form of pulque, the sweet wine of the agave. Once again, it is important to notice that *tepachi* was associated with Cora ceremony.

The Huichol

The Huichol inhabit the rugged sierra east of the Cora (Thomas and Swanton 1911:22). There seems to be some relationship between the Huichol and the Guachichiles, Lumholtz (1902:47–8) presents a good description of the Huichol deer sacrifice. He states that the dancing continued for two nights, then halted. The third night was spent eating and drinking, the beverage being a native brandy. He continues to describe this activity:

> Most of the elderly men were so overcome with native liquor and want of sleep that they could hardly walk from the temple to assist at the race but ... no detail of the ceremony was lost ... The intemperance of the older people in no wise affected the behavior of the young set. The latter did not see anything indecorous in the condition of the principal men, who had fully complied with their duties to the gods, but they themselves were perfectly sober. The privilege of imitating the gods and getting intoxicated extended apparently only to the elders (Lumholtz 1902:47–8).

The Huichol celebrated their ceremonials with intoxicating drinks, but as Lumholtz so keenly observed, only the elder people were allowed to be intemperate in their use. This, once again, sounds like the Nahua/Mesoamerican pattern referred to throughout this study.

The Otomi, Zacatecos, and Guachichiles

The Zacatecos had a very similar pattern of subsistence to that of the other groups discussed so far. They lived on sweet nuts, tuna, honey, maize and melons. Amador (1943:24) states that it was a custom among the Zacatecos to celebrate alliances with other tribes. To do this, they would elect one of their own members, contain him for twenty-four hours without food, and intoxicate him with several strong drinks. In this ceremony of alliance, at which time there was a great deal of bloodletting, peyote was also used as an intoxicating tea. Amador (1943:31) also mentions that the Chichimecas, a term frequently applied to the Guachichiles and Zacatecos, "were given to robbery and to intoxication."

Alegre (1956:417) refers to the "Chichimecs" of the villages of San Marcos and San Luis de la Paz, in the state of Guanajuato. In the latter village he wrote of the women making wine from the fruit of the tuna cactus which, when drunk, caused a loss of feeling. He then described the process used in making this wine:

The way of manufacturing it is to remove the shell from this fruit, filter the juice in some straw sieves, and put it on the fire or in the sun, where, within an hour, it ferments rapidly. As a kind of wine it is not very strong, drunkenness does not last long, and they return to drink again. This is one of the major obstacles for the propagation of the gospel (Alegre 1956:417).

In his general discussion of the "Chichimecs," Alegre mentions "some Pames and Otomis." At San Marcos, Alegre accounts for an old custom of the "Chichimecas" of that locality. He speaks of the "time of the tuna," and how it was a "terrible temptation" for the Indians. They would leave their huts abandoned and go live in the mountains in uninterrupted intoxication. Only a few, at the time of Alegre's writing, still went without permission of the priest. The mission efforts evidently had a great effect on the extent of the old custom and the majority did seek the consent of the priest. They went to the mountains, escorted by the "better" Christian Indians, returning to the village to sleep off their intoxication (Alegre 1956:447).

Speaking of the Otomi Indians of Tepotzotlán, Alegre (1956:447) tells us that they also were given to much intoxication and "idolatry." It is worthy noting that he included inebriation and idolatry together, where we once again get a hint as to the relationship between intoxication and ceremony, the obvious meaning behind Alegre's use of the word "idolatry."

From this brief distributional analysis, drawn chiefly from early historical accounts, we can see that the use of intoxicants north of the Mesoamerican line into the Greater Southwest is of great antiquity. While the details are woefully lacking, the information is sufficiently suggestive to allow us to trace the distribution of this important agricultural complex, extending northward from Jalisco to what is now southern Arizona. We see not only similarities of the sources for beers and wines but we also note that in almost all cases, intoxication is closely woven into agricultural ceremonies of the different peoples.

Whether we can say that this complex is a diffusion of a Mesoamerican practice, or rather, that it came into being before the rise of the more complex civilization is still open to further scholarship. It seems feasible to me to hypothesize that the extraction of liquids from the fruits of wild plants and fermenting them for intoxicating effects precedes the development of agricultural civilization and that the fermenting processes observed in wild plant collecting were later employed in fermenting the domestic grains. The ceremonial aspect of the complex, however—that is, the use of the intoxicants in agricultural community rituals—is undoubtedly a much later development than the use of the intoxicants. The utilization of wild plant beverages in agricultural, rain-producing magical rituals seems to be a synthesis of the older hunting-gathering complex with that of the later Mesoamerican agricultural society. The juxtaposition of agricultural life upon the older Desert Culture tradition may have occurred as Mesoamerican influences spread northward and were variously adopted by a large portion of Aztec-Tanoan speaking societies. This is borne out in the numerous examples of cactus fruit wine or agave pulque being related by many Uto-Aztecan tribes to fertility of maize and man.

The fact that such plants as maguey, tuna, sahuaro, mesquite, etc. were common throughout this Greater Southwest area is one good reason for accepting at least part of the hypothesis, but the presence of the plants in the landscape does not by itself account for the particular cultural use of wine in agricultural rituals. The fact that these tribes had contacts with each other over time is a more important dimension of the hypothesis. And most important of all, the whole complex must be seen as Mesoamerican in origin but with a strong substratum of culture derived from the Desert Culture. The variations that we can observe in the historical accounts may partly be attributed to the lack of accurate and unbiased reporting by the Spanish Chroniclers and partly by the fact that each local tribe or group would tend to localize the trait to fit the local patterns of culture. So while we must take note of variations as well as similarities, the wide distribution of the use of native alcoholic beverages for ceremonial life seems to give much of the Greater Southwest a certain identity and coherence in culture.

We began this survey by looking first at the Mesoamerican pattern as exemplified by the Nahua of the Aztec domain in the Valley of Mexico. We then jumped far northward to look at the Pimans, who probably represented the northernmost extension of the ceremonial drinking complex. Then we worked our way southward again, discussing tribes that were just on the northwest margins of the Valley of Mexico—those that were most likely the first to come under Mesoamerican influence.

DISTRIBUTION OF THE
AGRICULTURAL-CEREMONIAL COMPLEX

If the agricultural-ceremonial complex has a fairly uniform distribution northwestward as far as the Pimans, how far north and east did this complex spread? Is there any evidence of a breaking-off point, where this trait-complex no longer extended? There is some controversy as to whether the agricultural pueblos of the United States Southwest had ritual intoxication associated with their rainmaking ceremonies. Delving into this question is important in our assessment of drinking patterns as we observe them in the case studies making up most of this book.

Northeastern Mexico and Texas Southwest Tribes

There is little or no indication that the native peoples of Coahuila, Nuevo León, and Tamaulipas used intoxicating beverages, derived from wild plants, in increase or fertility ceremonies. There is indication that other forms of mind-expanding or dionysian agents were available and utilized. Salvidar (1943:11, 19) mentions how the Indians of Tamaulipas, those who lived along the river banks, had access to such plants as mesquite, zapate, wild fruits, nopal, and tuna but in referring to their ceremonial or ritual activities, speaks of how they "intoxicated" themselves by breathing the fumes of peyote. The peyote was so important to them that they made pilgrimages to Coahuila for it. Hence, it is peyote that appears as the important substance of ritual in this area.

Pérez de Ribas (1944c:248) very briefly mentions the Laguneros, who celebrated their fiestas or ceremonies with drunkenness by using peyote, which was also used in moderation for medicinal purposes. He described it as producing "diabolical imaginations" and "fantasy." This "drunkenness" was induced by chewing the buttons or breathing the fumes of burning peyote and was an important part of ceremonial behavior. It seems that peyote was such an established theme among the Laguneros, Coahuiltecans, and Tamaulipecos that there was little need or desire to utilize the wines and beers as did the tribes to the south and west of them. It is perhaps a weak assumption but it may be a correlate of the relative underdevelopment or lack of agriculture in this area that the beverages were not used in ritual. There is some evidence that the wines might have been used in social life but it seems to be peyote that has important ceremonial usage. I am suggesting that the Indians of the so-called "cultural sink"[2] (Nuevo León, Coahuila, northern

---

[2] Newcomb (1969:21) rejects the term "cultural sink" as a ridiculous and unfair label to describe a people who lived so effectively in such a rugged terrain. He prefers the term "relict region," implying an isolated backwash of unchanging, simple cultures (Newcomb 1969:32). This is certainly an adequate descriptive term but in the body of this chapter I shall stick to the use of "cultural sink" to describe the area, only because it seems to have a wider usage and is, hence, more descriptive and definitive for my purposes.

Tamaulipas, and eastern Chihuahua) bypassed the agricultural-ceremonial complex, including the usage of native beers or wines in ceremonies. With limited or no agriculture, it is not likely that the synthesis of native wines with agricultural rituals could occur. On the other hand, the social usage of the beverages may have continued.

The Coahuiltecans of Texas and northeastern Mexico seem to have made an intoxicating drink from the leaves of the agave. The beverage was mixed with the red bean of the mountain laurel (Newcomb 1969:41). But in the religious ceremonies or *mitotes,* where supernatural forces were tapped to bring rain and a bountiful supply of prickly pears, Coahuiltecans used peyote, not wine, to heighten perception and invite ecstasy (Newcomb 1969:53–4). The same could be said for the Karankawas of the Texas coast (Newcomb 1969:79, 115). It could probably hold for the Jumanos and Lipan Apaches as well. While alcohol seems to be known, there is no record of its use in the most significant rituals, many of which also have to do with rain but not for agriculture, obviously.

Beals (1932) finds evidences of intoxicating alcoholic drinks among the Tamaulipecos and Laguneros and traces them on his map for the distribution of liquors. Mesquite and other fruit-bearing plants were known to them but it appears that peyote, not alcoholic liquor, was most important in ritual.

It is my suggestion, then, that the tribes of the "cultural sink" or "relict region" constitute a northeastern parameter for the dispersal of the agricultural-ceremonial complex and the use of alcoholic drinks. It is this fact that makes the earlier suggestion of a northeastward dispersal from Casas Grandes up the Río Grande to the Pueblos as the easternmost possible extension of the complex. So we must turn to the Athapascans along the "Apache Corridor" that penetrates the agricultural area from the north and east; the Pueblos along the Río Grande, which allowed a northeastern spread of Mesoamerican traits; the Western Pueblos, to whom some traits may have spread from the River Pueblos; and the Yumans, those river agriculturalists who belong to a somewhat different complex of culture traits but who did have some relations with the Pimans.

Pueblos, Athapascans, and Yumans

This venture into the evidence for ceremonial drinking among tribes at the eastern and northern limits of the Greater Southwest can only be a superficial one. Bandelier and Hewett (1937:211) suggest that the roving bands in northern and central Chihuahua had knowledge of the

River Pueblos because they were able to communicate to Spaniards about the people who lived along the river. The Conchos, Pazaguates, Tobosos or Jobosos, and the semi-sedentary Jumanos were all contacted during the Chamuscado and Espejo journey from the Santa Barbara mines in southern Chihuahua in 1581–1582. The Chamuscado party travelled 31 days, contacting naked or poorly clad Indians or "Chichimecs" who wandered about the barren landscape eating roots and the fruit of the tuna. They then went a period of 19 days without any human contacts until they happened upon some sedentary people, possibly Jumanos, along the Río Grande south of Big Bend country. The party's northerly and easterly movements stopped at that place, whereupon they turned northward along the Río Grande following a guide to the southernmost of the River Pueblos, the Piros group. Continuing northward, they passed through the Southern Tiwa and Tewa complexes, first eastward to Pecos, then back to the west where they touched the area of the Keresan Pueblos moving west to Zuni, bypassing Acoma, but learning of the Moqui (Hopi) Pueblos (Bandelier and Hewett 1937:217–18).

This rather arduous journey over vast and sparsely populated lands provides us a good example of the impact of the "sink" or "relict" region that separated the Río Grande Pueblos from the Uto-Aztecan farming tribes of northwest Mexico. The hunting-gathering and limited-or-no-agriculture tribes in the "sink" seemed to serve as an area of demarcation, yet as was mentioned a bit earlier, the same area may have been within the route whereby those Mesoamerican traits made their way into the Pueblo area.

The first Pueblos to be contacted by the Spaniards' expedition of 1581–1582 were those of the Piros-Tiwa speaking clusters. Bandelier and Hewett (1937:233–6) regard the accounts of Piros and other Pueblo customs by Antonio de Espejo quite reliable in spite of the latter's notoriously bad demography. The Piros description is the most complete but Bandelier thinks that its description should generally apply to all of the other Pueblos the party visited as well. In Espejo's description,

> the painting of the houses and whatever the use for dancing, their music and the rest, they have like the Mexicans. They drink *pinole*, which is toasted maize dilluted in water, and no intoxicating beverage is known among them (Bandelier and Hewett 1937:235).

Hewett, in discussing the more recent ethnology of the Pueblos, mentions the most constant of all southwest ceremonials are those having to do with rain and growth ceremonies or harvesting and consecration of food products (Bandelier and Hewett 1937:47). In only one of his descriptions, that of the Green Corn Dance, does he refer to drinking in ritual context. Of course it is well known that the secrets of the ceremonial chambers have been, in large part, closed to outside observers so we should not expect that most reports of ceremonies will be complete on all fronts. In the main, ethnographers have had to rely on informants' words about ceremonials in the chambers, and there seems to be a general disavowal of intoxicants and drunkenness in rituals. In any case, the Green Corn Dance discussed by Hewett seems to have a form of ritual drinking. At one point in the ceremony messengers are sent to the west to bring word of the location of the Apache and Navajo and to the east to bring word of the whereabouts of the Comanche. Next, runners from the north and south bring liquids, the character of which is not provided by Hewett, that all of the Koshare dancers take for purification before departing, symbolically, to fight their enemies (Bandelier and Hewett 1937:50). There is no mention of the liquids being intoxicants. In discussing Sandia Pueblo, the community whose culture has been most disturbed by Spanish, Mexican, and Anglo influences, Hewett noted that drunkenness seems to have corrupted the old growth ceremonies of the Sandia people unlike anywhere else.

Parsons (1936:96) likewise did not refer to the use of intoxicants in any of the important ceremonies about which she could get information. At the One Spring Time ceremony performed by several kiva societies, she mentions the participants going to the mountains to spend the night, after which they got up in the morning to bathe in the creek and wash their hair. As part of the morning ritual, medicines of pulverized herbs were mixed with water and drunk from a gourd, with the remainder being tied up in leaves and buried. It seems to suggest a possible purification role for the "liquid" mentioned by Hewett above. There is no evidence that alcoholic intoxicants were used in agricultural ceremonies.

There is only one suggestion of the ritual usage of an intoxicating wine or beverage among the River Pueblos that I have been able to find. In San Juan Pueblo, Ortiz (1969:99–100, 114) refers to the "bringing-the-buds-to-life" ceremony, where village rule is transferred from the winter moiety to the summer moiety. It actually initiates the agricultural cycle and the "works" related to that cycle. In this simple ceremony, two female *Sehshu* serve a sweet drink of fermented grain to society members.

The Zuni, at the time of Stevenson's visits, were certainly acquainted with white man's whisky; the whisky was brought in by gallon kegs by a Carlisle-trained Laguna who was peddling for a German. In 1879 whisky was rarely used but by the turn of the century it was being peddled at the most important Shalako ceremonial. The Zuni, while they did drink it socially with friends, were actively involved in trading it with the Navajos who came in large numbers to look in on the public portions of the Shalako. Among the Zuni observed drinking, the younger men were more involved and extensive in their drinking than the older men. This may be indicative of the relative recency of this pattern at Zuni. While it was "disgusting in the extreme" to Matilda Stevenson, she was quick to point out that no whisky was ever served in the ceremonial chamber (Stevenson 1904:253).

The Zuni were familiar with a number of drinks that they claimed were not intoxicating. One beverage was made from sprouted corn. Another drink, *ta'kuna'kiawe* or "bread water," was made from pop corn. This was used as a daily beverage as well as in the ceremonies and fasts of the rain priests (Stevenson 1904:369, 1915:76). A plant from the mustard family was used to make a tea called *ila'ko'lokta,* which was drunk by only the male members of the Galaxy Fraternity in the ceremonial chambers "to loosen their tongues that they may talk like fools and drunken men" (Stevenson 1915:99). During voluntary initiation of young men into *ko'tikili,* a great deal of buffoonery in dance took place, where dancers drank urine and then simulated intoxication (Stevenson 1904:107). At the ceremonial *Hle wekwe* dance the participants drank "bread water," red medicine, and portions of whisky brought in by an old woman. Singing and dancing continued at this ceremonial until the morning star appeared (Stevenson 1904:478). In none of the examples above are agricultural increase rites involved; the apparent goal of taking the drinks seems to be that of cleansing or purification or, in the case of the *ko'tikili,* ribaldry. The use of intoxicants for ceremonials, particularly the increase ceremonies, does not appear to be a feature of Zuni ritual. In some ceremonial activity there is some suggestion that drinks were employed but, with the one exception of the *Hle wekwe* above, the drinks are of dubious intoxicating quality and seem to be denied this quality by the Zuni. In the instances where drinking is reported, they are indicative of either recent origin or confined to situations of conviviality and sociality and not for use in the sacred chambers.

The Zuni do appear to have known of intoxicating beverages. Cushing (1920:635–6) implies that their grandfathers, in earlier distant travels, once knew the use of mescal wine and were aware of how to make it but that recent Zuni had abandoned its production. Once in a while they were known to purchase mescal that was prepared by neighboring tribes such as the Western Apache, Havasupai, and Walapai.

By 1949, much drunkenness was reported at the Zuni Shalako, being common among both men and women (Smith and Roberts 1954:58–9). During their field studies of 1942–1948, Leighton and Adair (1963:883) also noted extensive intoxication at Zuni but an informant, referring to the old days, said that the people did not drink until some of them went away to school and learned the white ways. The basic characteristics of Zuni drinking are that 1) they had knowledge of and utilized native beverages such as mescal wine, learned from their neighbors, but these wines were used only on social occasions and not integral to important agricultural and other increase ceremonies; 2) they adopted many patterns of social drinking with other tribes that came to their villages, and later, accepted the white man's distilled liquors for similar usage at large public gatherings, with the incidence increasing in more recent years; and 3) they used non-intoxicating beverages of several types, including use at ceremonies, which were most used for purification. It could be that the avid denial that alcohol is used in the ceremonial chambers is testimony that it has penetrated the ritual in more recent days. I would argue that ritual intoxication was not an integral feature of Zuni ceremonialism in spite of evidences that social drinking has had greater currency at Zuni for a considerable period of time. In this respect, they seem somewhat different than the River Pueblos, at least until more recent times.

The Hopi seem to have a distinctive pattern of non-drinking, even for social purposes, although Titiev (1972:108, 117, 185) cites several instances of intoxication and prolonged drunkenness among some Hopi, which cause great concern to most Hopi villagers. But Hopi seem to emphasize that it is the white man's custom and that those who went away to school or to military service are the ones who brought the problem in. In spite of public statements that the drunkenness observed elsewhere on the Mesas would not be allowed at Oraibi and that offenders would be driven out or forbidden to dance as *katcina,* some of the heaviest drinkers were close friends of the Bear Clan chief, recognized leader of the village. All of this illustrates to Titiev that the matter of drunkenness is so new to them that they still do not have any established way of dealing with it socially. The Hopi claim to be traditional teetotallers who did not have *honakkuyi* or "crazy water" until the whites introduced it to them. Like other Pueblo peoples, the Hopi strongly assert that drunkards are never allowed to participate in the rituals, and it seems quite clear that drinking, even ceremonially, has never been a part of Pueblo ritual (Titiev 1972:328–9).

The Western Apache were familiar with intoxicants. Infrequent excursions by small numbers of them to the low country to the south were undertaken to obtain mescal, mesquite, or sahuaro cactus fruit. These were usually the undertakings of small groups. In wild food harvests nearer their home territories, the camps were much larger and more people were together in the related activities. It was the spring and summer periods when the large public ceremonies took place. In June there were ceremonies for protection against snakes and lightning; in July and on through August there were special lightning dances to bring the rains (Goodwin 1942:159–60). The mescal sprouts were the first signs of the new harvesting seasons; these were collected and prepared in April. In May, local groups moved back to their farms and planted. At this time, elderly men who were specialized in the agricultural rituals relating to preparations of ditches and first ceremonial plantings played significant roles but there is no record of drinking ceremonies. In fact, sahuaro fruit collecting was not a very important activity and for the same reason that collecting mescal was not important—it was too far away. The collecting of acorns in July and mesquite beans in August were more important as were the collecting activities for piñon nuts and juniper berries in November, after which the emphasis was upon hunting (Goodwin 1942:156–7).

The Western Apache evidently carried on trading expeditions among the Hopi of Oraibi and also seem to have had intermittently friendly relations with the Zuni, at least since the end of the eighteenth century, also for trading purposes. The Keres and River Pueblos had little or no contact with the Western Apache (Goodwin 1942:74, 76, 82). *Tułpai,* the brew made from corn sprouts, came to the Western Apache from the Chiricahua Apache, so the Western Apache themselves say. The Chiricahua acquired the practice from the Mexicans (Goodwin 1942:85). White Mountain bands had contacts with the Opata, but these relations were usually hostile as they were with the Papago, Pima, and Mexican Spanish. Forays into Mexico were probably not the sources for their knowledge of preparing intoxicants from corn. It is more likely that the practice diffused northward via contacts of adjacent tribes where it finally came to the Western Apache directly from the Chiricahua. It was during the larger gatherings or when there was occasion to visit back and forth when visitors came to camp from far off, that feeding and social drinking of *tułpai* became important mediators in social relations. Once again, there appears to be no pattern of ceremonial drinking related to their limited agricultural activity even though there are ritual concerns during the planting and harvesting season.

Turning to the River Yumans, we note that people such as the Maricopa did not use the flowers or stalks of the mescal for making intoxicants nor did they make beer from corn sprouts as did the Western Apache (Spier 1933:58). The Maricopa and Kaveltcadom, along with perhaps a few Halchidoma, joined in a number of villages in the vicinity of Gila Bend south and west of Phoenix and at the junction of the Gila and Salt Rivers. Some of the Halchidoma seem to have had recent contacts further south when they fled from the Lower Colorado area to Sonora about 1825. In any case, a number of these Yuman tribes had much in common with each other. They had close relations with the Pimas to the east and south of them and the Papagos to the south. Some Maricopa joined with the Pima and borrowed significantly from them (Spier 1933:1–4, 124).

Most of the tribes of the Lower Colorado River area did comparatively little planting but the Maricopa had summer fields along the Gila River bottoms. But their chief interests were in wild plants and their products, primarily the mesquite (Spier 1933:58). Mesquite beans, sahuaro fruit, and other fruit, stems, and leaves of wild plants were far more important in the diet than maize. The screw bean and straight bean from varieties of the mesquite were the staple foods, being gathered in early July and extending into August. It is interesting to note that mesquite juice, derived from this staple food, was not fermented (Spier 1933:52). A number of other wild seeds were used for both flour and drinks that were thought to be especially soothing for those engaging in the rabbit hunts. Berries that were gathered in May were boiled, strained, mashed, and made into sweet drinks, e.g. the mistletoe that grew parasitically on the mesquite.

Mescal, from the agave, was not much eaten since it did not grow in their locality in sufficient amounts. It was brought from Papago country by men who went on expeditions for it. The heads were baked to be eaten without mashing and the mescal was soaked in water and chewed on or made into a sweet liquor (Spier 1933:55–6). Sahuaro fruit collecting was an important seasonal activity but not so much for its foodstuff as for its importance in public social gatherings. Gathering the sahuaro fruit was forbidden until it was ripe, sometime in mid-June. It would then be boiled and set in perhaps as many as 100 large clay pots in the community meeting house where it would ferment. It was stored while hot and kept warm by a small fire that was kept going until the wine was ready, usually in a couple of days. The pots were owned by particular families and, when the wine was ready, were carried home. Friends were then invited to come from neighboring communities as well as from tribes that were sometimes at hostile relations with them. The camps of visitors were set up outside the host villages until messengers were sent out to invite named guests in. The men invited would bring three or four friends. The host would send his wife out with a cup of wine to extend to the friend or guest; this would continue until the visitor was drunk, then the host drank, after which drinks were then extended to the friends of the guest. They would then be an invitation to dance, a dance called *xatca* after the name of the wine. When drunkenness progressed, the participants sang of war. Frequently the drinking parties were occasional enemies but the drinking together apparently allied them, while intoxicated, to go on a joint raid to an enemy location (Spier 1933:57–8).

CONCLUSIONS

In this brief survey of the Greater Southwest, a number of variant patterns with regard to aboriginal usage of native intoxicants seem reasonably clear: There are regions where 1) a wide variety of intoxicants, including alcohol, were known and widely used; 2) a variety of intoxicants were likely known but not widely adopted into the ceremonial core of the culture, and 3) intoxicants were known but culturally rejected. Given the extensive distribution of a number of cultural traits throughout the area, it is highly unlikely that any region could be in total ignorance of intoxicants.

There were finer variations on the extent and character of usage in different regions, even where knowledge of intoxicants was pervasive. There were tribes with hunting-gathering pasts that in early historic times were well established in sedentary farming. These groups utilized both the fruits of wild plants and cultivated plants in the production of alcoholic beverages, which were prescribed primarily for usage in ceremonies related to plant productivity and social status identification. This ritual pattern obtained among riverine farmers as well as among those dry-field farmers who still depended to a significant extent on the older hunting-gathering way of life.

The Uto-Aztecan tribes from the Pimans in the north to the Valley of Mexico and southward made extensive use of intoxicants derived from both wild and domestic plants. Further, they utilized the intoxicants as integral parts of their increase ceremonies and other sacred events. In other words, intoxication itself was defined as a sacred and godly state, essential to a healthy community that depended on rain for its very survival.

The tribes to the east and north, in the relict region of arid northern

Mexico and southern Texas and New Mexico, had knowledge of mescal wines and, perhaps, other plant beverages but a number of these tribes employed peyote in their ceremonials of increase. The difference between these peoples and those mentioned above seems to be, however, not in the use of an intoxicating agent in ceremony but in the absence of agricultural ceremony among these latter nomadic peoples. The sparsely scattered tribes in this region show a more irregular distribution of particular substances used. Their northwestern limits constituted the easternmost margin for the diffusion of Mesoamerican patterns of culture.

The River Pueblos, the Zuni, and the Hopi shared the prevalent Mesoamerican pattern of sedentary agriculture and sacred ceremonials devoted to community well-being, but intoxication in the context of such rituals was consciously rejected. Social drinking did become established·in some Pueblo communities but it did not get integrated into the ritual core of culture upon which community integrity depended. In fact, it was marginal to the essential core values and was consciously rejected from that core, as evidenced particularly in the Hopi case.

The Athapascans, who lived in proximity to Pimans and the Pueblos or made forays into Mexico, seem to have adopted processes for producing intoxicants from both wild and domestic plants, such as mescal and corn, respectively, but there is no evidence that they worked them into any ceremonial complex, even where agriculture was marginally adopted. Navajos and Apaches seem, rather, to have employed intoxicants primarily to engage and intensify social relations at occasional meetings of band or local groups. While summer was a time for larger group gathering for both planting and ceremony, there is no evidence of alcohol being used primarily to facilitate the increase of plants.

The Yumans, who had knowledge of a mildly intoxicating wine derived from the sahuaro cactus fruit, seem not to have made much use of either the mescal or maize as sources of intoxicating drinks. When they got together for their summer socializing, cactus wine, derived from the Pimans as were other elements of their culture, seems to have been used to cement social relations among adjacent groups that were actually or potentially hostile toward each other. This pattern is more similar to the Athapascans. Friendships established between individuals of different communities or groups were extended to mutual friends of the partners. When drinking was involved in ceremonial dancing, war and raiding were the primary themes, not agricultural increase. Drinking seems to function to establish social alliances and to prepare for war-like states of mind.

With this background, we can now take a more intensive look at contemporary patterns and styles of drinking among some select Southwest peoples who represent some of this historical variation that we have been tracing.

The Papago represent a people with historical roots in the agricultural-ritual-intoxication pattern, the typical Mesoamerican form. The Taos Pueblo people represent a people tied to a tradition based largely on the Mesoamerican-agricultural-ritual pattern but without the intoxication element. The Navajo and Apache represent people with hunting and foraging pasts lacking many of the basic Mesoamerican patterns, especially the agricultural-ceremonial complex involving the use of intoxicants, but adopting intoxicants for social or more secular purposes. The Navajo had more extensive social contacts with the Pueblo people while the Western Apache had more contacts, even if generally hostile, with the Piman peoples. I would suspect that this might find some expression in the extent to which intoxication might be involved in ceremony. I think it does in some of the uses of intoxicants by Apaches during their summer ceremonial period, such as the rite of preparing the ditches and to control the lightning and rain, even though alcoholic beverages do not seem to be integral parts of the ceremonies. As Topper later points out in Part Two of this book, older Navajos do seem to justify drinking in ceremonial activity, certainly not a Pueblo attitude. But the drinking seems only an adjunct to the social gathering, not vital to the outcome of the ceremony itself.

In the studies in Part Two, these historic traditions should be kept in mind when reading the patterns of contemporary alcohol usage. Papago drinking, while having a multiplicity of social contexts in which it does take place, must still be viewed in terms of the central role drinking and intoxication played in the agricultural-ritual setting. Taos drinking, while also expressed in social settings, particularly outside of the pueblo, must still be viewed in terms of the central pueblo ethos of community solidarity, enhanced by ritual solidarity and affiliation not indigenously dependent upon intoxication. Navajos, who adapted to many aspects of Pueblo culture, seem not to have incorporated intoxication into their health-giving rituals but do seem to have widely adopted alcohol as a social lubricant. Lastly, the Western Apaches, like the Navajos, use alcohol, native-derived and commercial, to build social bonds between families and groups and have, perhaps very marginally, made drinking an adjunct to summer collective ritual activity.

REFERENCES CITED

Alegre, F. J., S. J.
1956   *Historia de la Provincia de la Compañía de Jesús de Nueva Es-
        paña,* Tomo I. Books 1–3 (1566–1596). New Edition by E. Burrus
        and F. Zubillaga. Rome: Institutum Historicum.
Amador, E.
1943   *Bosquejo Histórico de Zecatecas (Hasta el Año de 1810),* Tomo
        Primero, Zacatecas: Talleres Tipográficos "Pedroza" ags.
Anderson, R. K.
1946   A Study of the Nutritional Status and Food Habits of Otomi Indians
        in the Mezquital Valley of Mexico. *American Journal of Public
        Health* **36**:883–903.
Bancroft, H. H.
1882   *The Native Races,* Vol 1: *Wild Tribes.* San Francisco: A. L. Ban-
        croft and Co.
Bandelier, A. F. and E. L. Hewett
1937   *Indians of the Rio Grande Valley.* Albuquerque: University of New
        Mexico Press.
Beals, R.
1932   *The Comparative Ethnology of Northern Mexico Before 1730.*
        Ibero Americana No. 2. Berkeley: University of California Press.
1933   *The Acaxee: A Mountain Tribe of Durango and Sinaloa.* Berkeley:
        University of California Press.
1943   *The Aboriginal Culture of the Cahita Indians.* Ibero Americana No.
        19. Berkeley: University of California Press.
Castetter, E. and W. Bell
1942   *Pima and Papago Indian Agriculture.* Albuquerque: University of
        New Mexico Press.
Cushing, F. H.
1920   *Zuni Breadstuffs.* Indian Notes and Monographs, Museum of the
        American Indian, Vol. 8. New York: Heye Foundation.
Departamento del Trabajo
1936   *La Raza Tarahumara.* Mexico: Departamento del Trabajo.
Documentos
1857   *Documentos Para la Historia de Mexico,* Cuarta Serie Tomo III.
        Mexico: Vicente García Torres.
Driver, H.
1969   *Indians of North America.* Chicago: University of Chicago.
Goncalves de Lima, O.
1956   *El Maguey y el Pulque en los Códices Mexicanos.* Buenos Aires:
        Fondo Cultura Económica Mexico.
Goodwin, G.
1942   *The Social Organization of the Western Apache.* Chicago: Univer-
        sity of Chicago Press.
Haury, E. (ed.)
1954   *American Anthropologist* **56.** Special Southwest Issue.
Kennedy, J. G.
1963   Tesguino Complex: The Role of Beer in Tarahumara Culture.
        American Anthropologist **65**:620–40.

Kirchhoff, P.
  1954   Gatherers and Farmers in the Greater Southwest: A Problem in
           Classification. *American Anthropologist* **56**:529–50. Special
           Southwest Issue. Emil Haury, ed.

Leighton, D. and J. Adair
  1963   *People of the Middle Place*. New Haven: Human Relations Area
           Files.

Lumholtz, C.
  1902   *Unknown Mexico*. New York: Charles Scribner's Sons.

Manje, J. M.
  1954   *Unknown Arizona and Sonora, 1693–1721*. English translation of
           Part III by Harry J. Karnes and Associates. Tucson: Arizona
           Silhouettes.

Newcomb, W. W.
  1969   *The Indians of Texas*. Austin: University of Texas.

Ortiz, A.
  1969   *The Tewa World*. Chicago: University of Chicago Press.

Parsons, E. C.
  1936   *Taos Pueblo*. General Series in Anthropology, Number 2.
           Menasha: George Banta.

Pérez de Ribas, A.
  1944a   *Historia de los Triunfos de Nuestra Santa Fe Entre Gentes las Mas
           Bárbaras y Fieras del Nuevo Orbe,* Tomo I. Mexico: Editorial
           Layac.
  1944b   *Historia de los Triunfos de Nuestra Santa Fe Entre Gentes las Mas
           Bárbaras y Fieras del Nuevo Orbe,* Tomo II. Mexico: Editorial
           Layac.
  1944c   *Historia de los Triunfos de Nuestra Santa Fe Entre Gentes las Mas
           Bárbaras y Fieras del Nuevo Orbe,* Tomo III. Mexico: Editorial
           Layac.

Rea. V.
  1943   *Apuntes Sobre la Vida de Los Tarahumaras*. Mexico: Biblioteca
           Aportación Histórica.

Sahagún, Fr. B.
  1957   *General History of the Things of New Spain,* Florentine Codex
           Book 3. Translated by A. O. Anderson and C. E. Dibble. School of
           American Research and the University of Utah, Monograph No.
           14, Part IV. Santa Fe: School of American Research.

Salvidar, G.
  1943   *Los Indios de Tamaulipas*. Instituto Panamericano de Geografía e
           Historia, No. 70. Mexico: Instituto Panamericano.

Smith, W. and J. Roberts
  1954   *Zuni Law: A Field of Values*. Papers of the Peabody Museum, Vol.
           43. Cambridge: Harvard University Press.

Spicer, E. H.
  1962   *Cycles of Conquest: The Impact of Spain, Mexico, and the United
           States on the Indians of the Southwest, 1533–1960*. Tucson: Univer-
           sity of Arizona Press.

Spier, L.
  1933   *Yuman Tribes of the Gila River.* Chicago: University of Chicago Press.
Stevenson, M. C.
  1904   *The Zuni Indians.* Annual Report of the Bureau of American Ethnology, Vol. 23. Washington: Government Printing Office.
  1915   *Ethnobotany of the Zuni Indians.* Annual Report of the Bureau of American Ethnology, Vol. 30. Washington: Government Printing Office.
Swadesh, M.
  1964   Linguistic Overview. In *Prehistoric Man in the New World.* J. Jennings and E. Norbeck, eds, pp. 527–56. Chicago: University of Chicago Press.
Tello, Fr. A.
  1891   *Libro Segundo de la Crónica Miscelanea.* Guadalajara: Esquina de la Maestranza y Loreto.
Thomas, C. and Swanton, J. R.
  1911   *Indian Languages of Mexico and Central America and Their Geographical Distribution.* Bureau of American Ethnology, Bulletin No. 44. Washington: U.S. Government Printing Office.
Titiev, M.
  1972   *The Hopi Indians of Old Oraibi.* Ann Arbor: University of Michigan Press.
Underhill, R.
  1954   Intercultural Relations in the Greater Southwest. *American Anthropologist* **56**:645–62. Special Southwest Issue. E. Haury, ed.
  1969   *Papago Indian Religion.* New York: AMS Press.
Vaillant, G.
  1962   *The Aztecs of Mexico.* New York: Doubleday.
Voeglin, C. and F. Voeglin
  1966   *Map of North American Indian Languages.* Washington, D.C.: American Ethnological Society.
Waddell, J. O.
  1976   The Place of the Cactus Wine Ritual in the Papago Indian Ecosystem. In *The Realm of the Extra Human: Ideas and Actions.* A. Bharati, ed. The Hague: Mouton.
Waters, F.
  1972   *The Book of the Hopi.* New York: The Viking Press.
Willey, G.
  1966   *An Introduction to American Archaeology: North and Middle America.* Englewood Cliffs: Prentice Hall.
Wolf, E.
  1959   *Sons of the Shaking Earth.* Chicago: University of Chicago Press.

PART TWO

Drinking Patterns
in Four Southwest
Native American Societies:
Contemporary Assessments
By Non-Native
Anthropologists

Introduction

In the previous section, the focus was on the variations of cultural pattern in the use of intoxicating beverages in the aboriginal Greater Southwest. In Part Two we are interested in variations in contemporary patterns of alcohol use. Each of the tribal cultures included as case studies has far more internal variation than the specific study has time or space to elaborate. Instead, each study focuses on a major theme while attempting to capture the essence of the drinking situation as it is perceived by representatives of the culture in question. Each anthropologist serves as a mediator of the native perspectives and provides a final assessment with his own opinions about the significance of such perspectives in building meaningful linkages with rehabilitative or educational programs. In addition, each of the contributors touches upon a few particular aspects of contact history relevant to the understanding of each current situation.

Waddell attempts to link current Papago drinking with a number of persisting values in Papago culture. Many of these are social in nature while others are related to basic values articulated in ritual and in concepts of spiritual power. The urban setting is particularly important in evaluating the various modes of Papago drinking, not only because it is possible to see how traditional values are articulated in the complexity of the urban scene but how new modes of social accommodation are facilitated by social drinking.

Brown, focusing on a very difficult-to-get-at aspect of Taos Pueblo life, looks at the incidence of drinking as it affects community harmony, a highly valued component of Pueblo ideal culture. While the field research upon which the study is based took place several years earlier than the research in the other three studies, the lack of any other study on Pueblo drinking makes it valuable here. Brown has provided us important insights "from the inside," so to speak. The ethos of community solidarity is undoubtedly still strong, even as the threat of disruption from uncontrolled or indiscriminant drinking increases.

Topper is primarily interested in the generational differences in the categorization of drinking styles as well as actual behavior. His central concern is with adolescent or youthful males, but many insights of Navajo drinking across the generations and sexes are provided as well.

Lastly, Everett draws our attention to the important question of how a people, in their own terms, draw the line as to what is appropriate drinking and what forms of drinking are serious "trouble."

All four of the native societies represented use drinking as means of establishing social and cultural identities, as Waddell points out. And all four are concerned with what is or is not good for the essential social unit, be it family or community, as Brown contends. Further, all four societies show differential perceptions and patterns of behavior along age and sex lines, just as they all have culturally relevant means for defining the proper and improper, as Topper and Everett illustrate. The significant point is that we must see drinking behavior in culturally meaningful contexts as well as induced by certain structural conditions.

The case studies are presented in the sequence suggested in Part One: namely, a society with the full Mesoamerican agricultural-ritual-intoxication pattern; a society with an agricultural-ritual pattern but without the integration of intoxication into that complex; a society with a non-agricultural-ritual pattern but one that accommodated a wide variety of social usages of alcohol outside the context of ritual; and a society with a non-agricultural ritual pattern and extensive social usages of alcohol, with perhaps marginal association with the ceremonial calendar.

near present-day Phoenix, the Santa Cruz River near present-day Tucson, and a number of river valleys in Mexico where they could work, for produce, in the fields of closely related Piman populations in those locations.

The Papago were marginally but substantially affected by early Spanish efforts to missionize the natives of the Sonoran Province. While Spanish colonial administration was relatively insignificant for Papagos, they did find certain mission establishments and presidios, such as those at San Xavier and the pueblo of Tucson, attractive to them; hence, the Papagos have had a long-standing orientation to the Tucson vicinity. This relaxed, superficial exposure to mission life and Spanish-Mexican socioeconomics persisted into the early American period beginning about 1846 (see Dobyns 1976). The early Spanish-Mexican settlement and the subsequent American occupation of the Tucson vicinity served as a nexus for Papago activity and provided a base for a persistent Papago community as well as a temporary visiting location for those who maintained themselves in the Papago country to the west.

Besides serving as farm or ranch hands for Mexican or American farmers and ranchers, Papagos also served as soldiers and guides for military efforts to protect the settlement in Tucson from Apaches, the *ob* or enemies of the Papago. The alliances brought guns, knives, cloth, seed, tools, and "agricultural" demonstration to many Papagos, who also established themselves economically to the settlers by selling wood, garden products, and other items to inhabitants of the Tucson area. By the latter part of the 19th century, government efforts in aiding Papagos near Tucson and at San Xavier were well underway, though it was not until 1917 that official government regulation materialized for Papagos living in the vast area west of Tucson.

The old Mexican pueblo was eventually transformed into a cosmopolitan urban place as Tucson became a territorial center of goods and services. The Mexican pueblo (with its cantinas), the rural frontier town (with its bars and saloons), and the cosmopolitan hub (with its wholesale and retail beverage industries) all converged, with their different styles, into a model for drinking activities. Papagos, in their seasonal journeys to the Spanish missions and towns, in their commercial dealings with Mexicans and, eventually, in their temporary attachments to American commercial centers, military establishments, and farming and ranching interests, have undoubtedly been occasional users of a great variety of commercial or locally produced alcoholic beverages. From these many kinds of contacts, there were opportunities for observing and modeling after several different drinking styles. The earliest beverages were the corn liquor and corn beers common among native and Mexican populations in Sonora. It is likely that commercial Spanish brandies were occasionally used by Papagos on visits to Mexican towns where they might have been available. Tequila as well as Mexican beers had a rather extensive history of usage, as evidenced by the current heavy commercial traffic at the Mexico-Reservation border between Papagos and Mexican merchants. The beverages, after Papagos obtained them from their sources, were consumed in those social quarters that Papagos came to occupy, usually detached from Mexican or American social settings. In short, these beverages have long been used in social settings occupied by Papagos. In such contexts, Papago social controls have always been operative.

In spite of mid-19th century reports of the absence of alcohol abuse among Papagos observed west of Tucson, it is too much to assume either their total abstention or an absence of intoxication. But it is likely that as long as Papago integrative controls in their natural communities were intact, intoxication reached its community-wide importance only during the annual rain-making ritual or other large-scale feast days. It was during "time out" periods in the towns and cities where an observer, during the late 19th and early 20th centuries, might find the incidence of intoxication much higher.

Significant turning points in Papago alcohol usage were the influx of veterans returning home after World War II or urban workers returning home after the war industries declined. A further important pivotal point was the increasing population living on an economically depleted reservation resource base, pushing more and more Papagos into greater dependency on marginal economic outlets in the cities, commercial farms, or mines.

Over a period of more than three hundred years of culture contact with Spaniards, Mexicans, and Americans, many changes have occurred in the Papago political economy and style of life. Yet it is apparent throughout these periods of change that changes have occurred through a persisting cultural system, with many of its features still intact. It is the major purpose of this case study to demonstrate how alcohol has served to maintain or articulate some of these important sociocultural values in the behavior of contemporary Papagos in and from Tucson.

PERSISTING PAPAGO CULTURAL ORIENTATIONS

James (1961:721) contends that wherever aboriginal personality configurations persist into modern times without any corresponding cultural causation, they must be seen as functions of new cultural conditions that are not the same as their primitive antecedents. Further, as Hallowell notes (1945:199–200; 1952:106), people, being the striving organisms that they are, continually adapt and readapt to new situations by utilizing existing cultural ways of behaving. New habit patterns are called for and new ways of thinking must be assumed. There is no reason, however, for suggesting that the new habits themselves have to significantly alter the core of the cultural personality. Devereux (1969:59) has demonstrated in a classic way the manner in which areal and tribal cultural patterns have persisted in the psychology of a contemporary Plains Indian (see also Vogt, 1961, for a similar demonstration for the Navajo). I would like to show in this chapter that contemporary cultural attributes having antecedents in earlier Papago culture are employed for adapting to new social situations.

There are a number of empirical indicators of this cultural persistence in current Papago habit patterns. Drinking experiences and their cultural correlates will be demonstrated as adaptive measures for meeting newly emerging cultural conditions as well as maintaining some familiar, conventional conditions. I now want to isolate a few of these specific Papago culture patterns, suggesting that they may reflect a more general southwestern areal pattern as well.

There are many elements of current behavior which Papagos refer to as *O'odham himdag*, Papago ways of doing things or customs. That these customary ways of doing things might be fusions of aboriginal and European-derived practices is of little moment; what is significant is that *himdag* varies considerably between *O'odham* and *Miligahn* (whites or Americans). These distinctive styles may be recognized to merge along many fronts in contemporary situations but in many other important domains of *himdag* or custom, the *O'odham* and *Miligahn* ways of life are distinctively different. In areas of meaningful work or daily activity, occupational styles, social obligations and courtesies, recreational and entertainment or amusement interests, economic motivations, conceptions of sex-role behavior, group activities, norms for appropriate or inappropriate behavior, use of time, etc., Papagos can account for many ways that they differ so much from whites.

My field investigations with Papagos suggest that they perceive themselves to drink in ways different from whites. This difference seems to be in the conceptual sense, that is, *himdag* establishes certain expected parameters within which drinking occurs. Although drinking outwardly appears much the same for all drinkers, regardless of background, it is *O'odham himdag* or Papago custom which makes the drinking different. The way Papagos conceptualize alcoholic beverages is in itself different, in spite of any possible similarity in the physiological effects they produce.

To drink, *ih'e*, can be used in reference to taking any liquid refreshment. To thirst for a drink, *i'imk*, expresses the normal body need for liquid satiation. It is therefore not surprising that thirsting or craving persistently for an alcoholic drink to satisfy a demand of the body should also derive from the same root word; hence, the closest Papago conception of an "alcoholic," *s-i'imkam*, is one who craves alcoholic drink, just as the human body that needs water craves it. There does seem to be a Papago conceptual equivalent to the notion of addiction. The *s-i'imkam*, alcoholic drunkard, however, is not necessarily the same kind of drinker as the *naumki*, the drunkard who gets drunk because he wants to or because it is expected of him, the one who sets out to get intoxicated, or *naumk*.

Many of the beverages that Papagos have been acquainted with and used for a long time are interesting in another respect besides their capacity to produce *s-naumk* or intoxication. The native sahuaro cactus wine, *nawait* (used in rain-making rituals), Spanish- or Mexican-derived beer, *sil-wihsa* (cerveza), unsweetened liquors such as Mexican-derived tequila and corn whiskey, *wihnui* (vino), while leading to intoxication, do not fit into that category of substances that promotes the growth of *bihtagi ha'ichu* or "dirty substance." Only the sweet wines of commercial distribution, the Tokay, Thunderbird, Cream Sherry, etc. that are the most recent and widely used beverages among Papagos produce *bihtagi ha'ichu*. These are the cheapest, the sweetest, and the most popular beverages consumed by heavy drinkers or *s-i'imkam*, and they are the drinks most often associated with bodily malaise (Bahr et al. 1974:85). Its signs are the mucous or slime emitted from the oral orifices, commonly seen in drunks. The dirty substance can be thrown out by inducing vomiting, thus cleaning out the system temporarily. If it gets really complicating, a medicine man or *mahkai* may be sought out to facilitate the cleansing.

Drinking alcoholic beverages has been a long standing part of *O'odham himdag* in a variety of social contexts. It is not necessarily inappropriate to become *naumk* or intoxicated, even frequently, if the social situation calls for it. If one becomes a *s-i'imkam* or a craver of alcohol and it too often contradicts *himdag* by bringing harm to other socially important people, it could be seen as a serious problem. There are some who have become drunkards in the latter sense and they are apt to be the ones who have socially removed themselves from daily work or *chikpan himdag*, customary work habits. But even for the one who is *s-i'imkam,* an alcoholic person, there are ways to articulate important social values, even if in limited social contexts, as we shall see. Let us look at some important features that characterize Papago *himdag* or custom.

O'ODHAM HIMDAG

Many ethnographers of Papago culture have described Papago social life as being primarily familistic (Underhill 1939, 1946; Joseph, Spicer, and Chesky 1949; Williams 1956; Fontana 1960; Waddell 1969). It is in the family and its extensions where material and human resources are reciprocally shared. A political unit larger than the kinship community and related sister communities is still, in large part, external to Papago experience. A number of Papagos and their families have been either "tribalized" or "Anglicized." That is, there are those who have been opportunistic enough to find a place in the federally subsidized tribal bureaucracy or who have assumed lifestyles not too different from other Americans. In spite of this trend, the family and kinship communities are still significant social environments of everyday life in which *himdag* is perpetuated or regenerated.

The basic economic interdependency required of extended families and kin settlements discouraged individual ostentation through excessive acquisition of material goods and nonconforming personal behavior. Egalitarian economic and social relations are *O'odham himdag.* It is through mutual obligation that Papagos maintain social ties. This is important in understanding Papago drinking experience.

Papago adults deal with their children in ways that will facilitate the learning of *himdag,* or proper behavior for living in an anticipated adult world. There are cognitive models for ideal adult behavior and these are communicated in various ways to children. To assume, from the apparent permissiveness of Papago parents, that Papagos are not conscious of the kinds of adults they want to be or that they want their children to be, is grossly naive. What Papago men consider as important or appropriate behavior, however, is not the same as that which middle-class American men consider essential (Bahr 1964:11–13; Waddell 1969:148–50). Adult Papago drinking experience should be expected to express important aspects of the adult personality and the adult performance for which the Papago family has been preparing its young.

High mobility is another basic feature of *himdag* that has characterized Papago social life for several centuries (Spicer 1962:139). The ecological realities of living in a desert environment, where no single locality can be totally self-sufficient economically, have prompted this pattern. Drinking has come to assume an important role in establishing social ties when individuals are far removed from their local communities of kinsmen and familiar surroundings.

Another important expression of *himdag* has to do with a person's achievement of individuality. Underhill (1946:17) stresses the significance of individualized achievement of power, an essentially democratic idea where every Papago has a right to seek a source of spirit-strength. The cultural encouragement to privately seek out awesome, ego-enhancing strength or *gewkdag*, however, often prompts a certain amount of personal apprehension and interpersonal tension because there is also that dimension of *himdag* that discourages aggressive individuality (Williams 1956:160–2). The Papago ethos fosters interpersonal suspicion of others at the same time that it encourages an egalitarian ethic. A group system of social control through calendrical ceremonies and family and community gatherings works to off-set an inordinate amount of idiosyncratic self-expression.

The aboriginal ethos that encouraged quests for personal guardian power is by no means fully operative in Papago society today. But interpersonal suspicions of the private powers of others are just as real an aspect of the Papago ethos as is the egalitarian aspect. Both of these features of past Papago society have persisted in contemporary Papago social life. Papago drinking situations reveal that beneath the surface of the sociability that characterizes a group of individuals drinking together, there is a strong undercurrent of interpersonal anxiety about the individual powers of others in the group. By participating in corporate drinking, an individual personally achieves individual power (drunkenness) while simultaneously magnifying his social credit (Waddell 1975).

Himdag distinguishes the kinds of behavior expected of men and those expected of women. The periodic power that women have during their menstrual cycles render them *s-ta ehbidma* (dangerous) to men. Many activities that are customary for women are incompatible with what men do (Underhill 1946:253). While traditional practices related to the segregating of women in *huhulga kihki* (menstrual houses) during their monthly cycles are not as widely observed as in earlier times, Papago men do exhibit frequent anxieties about the strange powers of women. Cross-sex jokes and gossip frequently reflect sex antagonisms that are apt to occur between the sexes (Williams 1956:110–11). Male drinking allows maximum opportunity for seeing some of the ways these cross-sex tensions manifest themselves.

Unpredictable shortages of rain and food in a hot and arid land stimulated the cultural occurrence of communal rain-making rituals and festive gatherings revolving around food and drink exchanges (Underhill 1946:41; Wallace 1966:111; Cohen 1961:341). The *himdag* of frequent intercommunity feasting and major annual calendrical ceremony, the *nawait* or wine feast, indicate anxieties about food and rain shared by larger aggregate groupings. In bringing large numbers of concerned people together, social bonds are also cemented (Turner 1969:4). Predispositions for sharing food and drink are related to culturally induced anxieties about food (Cohen 1961:312ff) and Papago communal festive activities abound in enumerable food exchanges. This predisposition for sharing is also abundantly evident in the convivial drinking that is a trademark of almost any kind of social gathering.

In this section I have chosen to mention only a few aspects of *himdag* that could be expected to be expressed in Papago drinking experiences. We shall return to them later. There is no intention of proposing the persistence of some untainted aboriginal cultural syndrome. But this case hopes to demonstrate that through the course of time, cultural modes of behaving viably operating in past social conditions have been adaptively reworked to accommodate to new social conditions. These persisting orientations have allowed for the acquisition of new habit systems that seem more workable in the current world, while not making it necessary to significantly alter the basic Papago cultural personality.

PAPAGO DRINKERS IN TUCSON

While the basic social reality for a number of Papagos is still the extended family ranchería settlement surrounded by more distant communities of kinsmen, for many it is often only a sentimental location where few people may actually reside. This sentimental tie supplements the strong kinship social ethos of Papago society in making drinking locations in non-Indian areas significant for forming, cementing, and sometimes reviving social bonds. In every town or city surrounding the reservation there are strategic congregating centers where Papagos gather to engage in social drinking. The Tucson urban area is one such location.

The research from which this chapter derives its data was focused on Papago drinking behavior in Tucson and is therefore biased in that direction. As in any population, there is much greater variation in Papago drinking behavior and attitudes about drinking than may be evident in this study. Because I was primarily interacting with drinkers, much of the field strategy was directed to locations where drinking

Papagos assembled, socialized, and shared drinks. Nonetheless, these public congregating places attract a wide variety of Papagos from the reservations as well as from the Tucson Indian community. Table 2.1 and Figure 2.1 portray a larger social parameter in terms of which the more opportunistic selective sample of drinkers' perceptions reported in this chapter can be interpreted. In selecting individuals for more intensive interviewing (N=25), randomness was not employed but I did attempt to represent as much variation in drinking styles and attitudes as time and field circumstances allowed. Hence, I wanted to include individuals of different age range, educational experience, occupational background, military experience, residential history, religious beliefs, drinking experience, etc. Two important and unfortunate exclusions are a female perspective and the perspective of a Papago monolingual.

Arrest records also became useful for identifying social facts related to drinking behavior among a much larger sample of Papagos (N=258). Information such as locations of arrest, drinking associates, reported residence, occupational and marital information, attitudes of police toward drinkers, descriptions of unusual behavior, times of day and week arrested, money or other possessions on the person, etc. was continuously collected throughout the seven-month fieldwork period.

Extended field observations also revealed that public drinking could be categorized into seven basic locational contexts: 1) behind specific public buildings and in alleys; 2) in and around a finite number of bars and dance halls; 3) in a select number of public parks; 4) in well-known abandoned buildings; 5) in certain public buildings in obvious view; 6) in yards of private non-Indian employers' homes; and 7) in yards of private Papago homes where Papagos frequently congregated for open-air drinking in view of passersby.

Most of the Papago drinking observed was of a publicly noticeable character but certainly could not cover all possible specific contexts, especially those taking place in the privacy of homes.

Since Papagos are a small minority in a large city, they concentrate in very specific locations where they can constitute a localized majority, thus becoming obvious in their drinking together even when other non-Papagos are present or nearby. Papagos do drink with other Indians, Mexicans, blacks and Anglos on occasion, particularly in certain recognized areas, but my observations convinced me that much of their drinking largely involves each other. There are areas where other Indian groups are apt to do their drinking and where Papagos will usually not go. Sometimes other non-Indians will drink in and around where Papagos are drinking, but not often do they drink with Papagos, at least

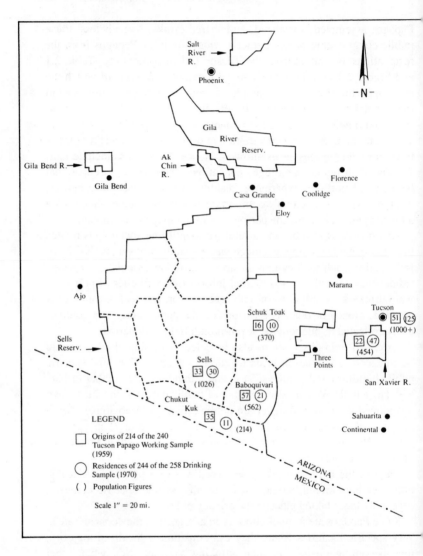

*Figure 2.1 Papago orientations to the Tucson urban area, showing
the districts of origin of two different Papago samples*

TABLE 2.1   Maximum Papago Population Oriented to Tucson and
the Actual Number of Papago Individuals Arrested
for Drinking Offenses in Tucson, January through
June, 1970.

Residence	Papagos	Papagos 20 yrs or Older	% Papagos 20 or Older	No. Arrested
Sells Reservation*	2,172*	1,150*	6	72*
San Xavier Reservation	454	230	20	47
Tucson and South Tucson	1,000	520	24	125
	3,626	1,900	13	244†

*Includes only the districts of Baboquivari, Chukut Kuk, Schuk Toak, and Sells, where most of the Tucson-oriented Papagos originate or claim residences (Kelly 1963:56–9; Waddell 1969:24).
†Fourteen Papagos appearing on the arrest records claimed residences in other towns, rural areas, or reservation districts.

from my observations. Of all the non-Papagos, other Indians, especially those from distant locations, are most apt to go and drink where Papagos are known to be drinking, whether or not they choose to drink with Papagos.

A second factor that accounts for the distinctiveness of Papago drinking is not so much a part of the ecology of drinking but rather a part of what could be called the sentiment of drinking. Here I refer to some of the reasons Papagos give for why they drink what they do, where they drink, and with whom they choose to drink. It is in the domain of Papago sentiments that I will seek to identify specific cultural behaviors that underlie their attitudes about drinking. Contexts for drinking are sought out because of the cognitive and emotive satisfactions which they offer. Papagos know precisely where to go when they arrive in town to find a friend and to assure a drink; the two quests are frequently synonymous. A third pursuit, to do some work and make a little money, is also intricately tied up with finding friends and sharing drinks.

In what better manner could a man make it clear to himself and to others that he is Indian, is Papago? These are not just places in a city, they are emotional spaces, where people gather, talk, eat, sleep, get arrested, reassemble, etc. Through the whole process the Papagos are not only defining themselves to each other, they are inviting definition by other non-Indians in whose overwhelming midst they find themselves. Employers, police, judges, jailers and guards, tavern keepers, businessmen, and passersby all play a part in this circuit to help Papagos and other Indians define themselves. There are, of course, Papagos who, even after years of drinking, are defining themselves in new terms; they are molding social selves apart from these locations of convivial drinking, although this is often a very painful and frequently discouraging process.

For a large number of Papagos in Tucson, however, social identity is maintained in these social locations. Alternative identities, especially those imposed from the outside, are frequently ineffective because in trying to promote sobriety and moderation, they seem to destroy the power of social bond that develops in these intensely social settings. This, of course, is not totally unique to Papago drinkers, for other chronic drinkers also have similar problems of social identity and seek out social contexts to help alleviate them. In this respect, similar social behaviors can be found among other Indian peoples of the Southwest in their particular areas of concentration. Therefore, Papagos may manifest a broader areal pattern that has much in common with other Southwest Indians such as the Navajo, the Pueblo, the Yaqui, and the Apache. At the same time, more careful attention to the particular ways that Papagos prefer to do things can help to illuminate their specific behaviors. This can best be illustrated by seeing what a few Papago drinkers have to say about their drinking experiences.

KINSHIP SOLIDARITY AND RESPONSIBILITY

Family and kinship ties are extremely important in Papago social life. A Papago need not be constantly nor directly in contact with any of his kinsmen in order for their claims upon him to be felt. The family-centered character of his early childhood and later maturational years convinces a Papago of his obligations to his relatives and their obligations to him. Even the chronic Papago drinkers who have broken all physical connections with their fathers' village households or residence units are never without the ties of kinship. Most of these individuals claim a number of relatives among their drinking associates to be in the class *ni wehnag,* that is, "my sibling." The sons of siblings, who in many instances grew up together, ate in the same kitchen, and were constant companions in their fathers' neighboring households, often are close drinking friends in adult life. Drinking groups frequently consist of *wepnag,* "siblings," that cross generations.

Papagos who drink together in Tucson frequently refer to each other as "brothers," using the English term. They made it clear that, in many instances, "cousins" would be the more appropriate term in English. Corroboration with available Papago family genealogies and queries directed to the informants confirmed the wide range of kinship connections that can be traced among drinking compatriots.

It is true, of course, that several were frequently without close kinsmen at hand when drinking was most urgent. In such situations, the term *nawoj,* "friend," frequently is extended to another person and has the same power of relationship as "brother." Individuals attached to drinking groups are frequently each other's constant companions and they seek each other out especially when they are away from their kin communities on the reservation or away from their spouses and children in town. Since drink is the all-important mediator of both relationship and friendship, it is the avenue through which drinking Papagos test avowed friendships and relationships with others, whether non-related Papagos or even non-Papagos and non-Indians.

The sentiment of kinship is so prevalent that its bond unites the living and the dead. In dreams, visions, hallucinatory experiences, or memory recollections, deceased relatives or drinking friends are frequent characters. V,[2] a 53-year-old man from a village close to the Mexican border, illustrates this theme, which I found quite common.

> I had been drinking for over two months and then stopped. That's when I heard people singing out there in the desert. I looked around, thinking maybe there were some guys out there who had some drinks. But there wasn't anybody around. I got up and went around the house, then went back in and lay down again. Then the singing would start again. There were Indian people singing out there and I would go out again. I wanted to see if maybe they had a drink over there. But I couldn't see anyone. I heard them singing the old drinking songs. The old people were telling me to learn those songs.

V's recollection involves a spiritual element. The experience involved deceased kinsmen, the old ones, singing traditional drinking songs and inviting him to do the same.

J, a 45-year-old man from a village just east of Sells, describes an experience that I found to be very similar to the early experiences of several other informants.

---

[2]Letters are used in this chapter to assure anonymity.

Yes, my father was a drinking man but I did not drink at that time. I just watched him to see what he was drinking. Everytime he went someplace, I would follow him. I just wanted to see where he was going. He went to see some old men, his friends. They would all start drinking. My older brother is the one that started giving me that Tequila. It made me drunk pretty fast. Some of these old men told about drinking. They told me it was all right if I wanted to take a drink. One time I was sitting with them and my brother told them to give me a drink. So I took a little swallow. He poured a little into a tin cup and I drank it. I drank about three cups and I could feel it hitting me. It made me drunk.

F, a 52-year-old man now living in Tucson, recalls a similar early experience.

My father was like me. He liked the wine. But he never did bother anybody. He would just go out, sit down, and start singing Indian songs. Whenever he had a chance he would sit down and start singing Indian songs or talk to himself or to his friends, especially on weekends. They would get together and have a big party. They used to come out around our house, too. They'd just drink socially among themselves. They'd get drunk and pass out or just walk off and go someplace else. They never had any fights.

T, a 28-year-old from Sells hanging around Tucson when I became acquainted with him, mentions an occasion when drinking took on a different kind of family significance at the death of his mother.

We went down there to my grandpop's place. He gave us a big old bottle of booze, man. He told us to take it with us. I didn't want to look at my mother's body. I was feeling real bad but I didn't want to let it out. Finally I took that whisky, then I just started crying and crying. I couldn't stop.

Many situations like these were openly shared with me throughout the fieldwork. The few incidents reported here show different contexts involving kin relations. V heard the singing voices of deceased relatives. The experience could be explained in terms of delirium tremens resulting from a period of abstinence but the mode of expression is rich in Papago symbolism. F and J recalled the drinking models that fathers, siblings, and parents' siblings provided during frequent social gathering for leisurely drinking, talking, and singing. T's experience centers on the manner in which drinking is used to buffer a mood or give expression to feelings at a time of personal loss.

Williams (1956:174) points out that Papago boys "are very proud of their fathers and constantly seek to copy their manner of speech, walk and action." It is clear that Papago child-rearing practices depend in large part upon the imitative responses of the young to adult role-models and many young people over many years have seen drinking as a regular part of adult social behavior, in spite of the feelings of an abstinent mother or a relative that converted to Christian sobriety. The strong familistic, kin-oriented character of social life has served to reinforce the significance of social drinking in Papago adult society. This is not a deviant pattern for many Papagos. To consider it such would be the same as acknowledging the deviant quality of their familistic experiences. Such is not the case. Definitions of deviance appear only as it becomes necessary for them to redefine themselves in terms of new reference group norms. To have a *nawoj* or *wehnag* with whom to seal friendship and sociality is congruous with much that they learned as they were growing up among kinsmen.

EQUALITY AND CONFORMITY

Today, there are individual Papagos and Papago families that have acquired greater wealth, more powerful political positions, and greater achievement incentive for things of non-Papago origin just as in aboriginal times certain individuals had greater success in seeking individual power. Nonetheless, a very prevalent and intense value for social and economic egalitarian living still exists. It is verbally expressed in denouncements of ostentatious individual displays of wealth and behaviorally expressed in reciprocal drinking, where status differences and monetary surpluses are liquidated through the medium of drinking associations. Daily social contacts on Tucson streets constantly exhibit the manner in which Papagos, who happen to have either a surplus of cash or a supply of liquor, are intimidated by *naipiju*—"friends" or "brothers"—to share of their surpluses. These social pressures attributed to others could very well be defense mechanisms rationalizing excessive drinking, but they also operate simultaneously to level wealth and status differences, thus creating a clientele of social and economic equals. In the drinking circle, any noticeable advantages of wealth or social position formerly held by individuals are reduced to the common denominators of proven friend or "brother"—all economically poor but socially rich and sometimes very drunk! It is this constant seeking out of others and transforming them into social equals that makes the experiences of drinking and drunkenness self-perpetuating and so socially obvious to non-Indians.

M, a Papago of 53 from San Xavier, expresses it this way:

> I know one guy. I ran into him and he asked me if I wanted a drink.
> He just gave me a shot from his pint. He's like that. Anytime he gets
> a bottle, when he sees me he will offer some to me; or if he wants a
> drink, he asks me if I got anything. I like to stay with my kind of
> people. If we both had the money, we'd get a bottle and share. I can't
> refuse it if a fellow offers me a drink.

T, a more outgoing, aggressive young man, describes the intensity of
the social pressures to drink:

> I was doing good down there at Sells until I brought a friend over
> there to the house to stay with me. He told me to go with him to get
> just one drink. We spent three bucks there at Sells for a fifth. He
> pawned his radio and got two more fifths. We drank all that up. If
> friends have money—God! Pat 'em on the back and you have it
> made. If I have a dollar, other guys know that I am good for
> a dollar.

One young Papago man of 36, A, from a village in the eastern part of
the Sells reservation, had moved to South Tucson about three years
prior to my study. At the urging of his wife, A was trying to keep sober
and to keep steadily employed. He had been to a *mahkai* (medicine
man) on the reservation a few years before to seek help in getting wine
out of his system and to help him stay sober. He seemed to have an
exceptional amount of incentive to curtail his excessive drinking and
seemed to know where the barriers to his sobriety were likely to be. He
told me he did not like to go out on the cotton chopping bus because all
of the workers would start spending their recently earned money to buy
drinks and they would all end up drinking together.

The following episode relates the kind of pressure with which A
frequently had to deal.

> Some guys came by and told me that I could drink with them. They
> bought the wine, then we drank it all up and I bought the wine. We
> went to the park and went into the restroom and drank one pint in
> there. Then we left the park and went to the streets to drink. Those
> guys told me that if I didn't drink anything, I was trying to show off
> that I was smarter than they were. They would say I was trying to be
> a priest. That's what they called me. They also called me queer—
> *uwikwuad*. I told them that if they thought that, maybe I would have
> all their bottle. One guy told me to go ahead and made a bet that I
> couldn't drink it all. This one guy bet me $20 and this other guy bet
> me $10. So I said I could do it. I just picked up the bottle and drank
> up. So I won the bet but I also started drinking again.

There are, without question, many different personal reasons why Papago individuals drink, just as there are for any people. While there are undeniably physiological explanations, the social dimension also provides a very real explanation, as L describes.

Me, I'm a drinking man, a drinking Indian. There are always friends who go around with a bottle. They'll give me the drinks. Like yesterday, I was getting on the bus to go to work. My friend came up and called me off the bus. I walked over to him and he asked me if I needed a drink. I told him I did and asked him if he had anything. We walked over to the alley and drank a whole pint up. And I told him I was supposed to go to work but he asked me not to go to work. All the time there's always somebody around. It's hard to refuse a drink when others call you names like *oks*. That means queer [actually the Papago word for adult woman]. They call us all kinds of names.

R, a 45-year-old man, expresses his view of the strong social pressures operating among drinking friends.

Indians usually congregate together when they have a bottle. For some reason or other they usually are willing to share with a person, especially if they notice he is in need of a drink. We find a common bond friendship. They'll be offended if another refuses to take a drink with them. It usually starts among friends. I hate to offend them so I start to drink.

I was talking with B, V, and L on one occasion when B, well supported with alcohol, related how he responds to the pressure of others.

Suppose the three of us had a bottle but I don't want to drink. V is going to call me a sissy. I try to walk away but he's going to follow me. He will call me a sissy if I don't take a drink or he will call me a preacher and everything. Well, I'm going to take a drink if I'm going to be happy, right?

J tells us how his very best friends treat him.

They are kind and buy me drinks. They see me walking around in different places and ask me if I want a drink. Some guys get mad if you say no. They say they're not going to be your friend anymore and give you any more drinks. They will even try to put the bottle in your mouth and make you drink, so you just say o.k. and take their drink.

These intimidating pressures appear to provide both the rules for initiating drinking encounters and adequate rationalizations for why one gives in to another's pressures.

Being surrounded by numerous drinking models and social pressures over so many years is sufficient reason why so many Papagos seem to be habituated or physiologically addicted to alcohol. Many of these models have been provided within their own families and among kinsmen as noted earlier. In addition, there are numerous festive occasions for group drinking, including the aboriginal wine feast for rainmaking, feast days for saints, and other special occasions, where drinking and drunkenness are the expected mode. Likewise, the ways Papagos were introduced to drinking and the ways they have had to carry out their drinking under stringent rules of prohibition are also important in understanding the intensity of drinking.

When the egalitarian, kin-oriented ethos is challenged by new experiences and new personal expectations, new personal problems develop which undoubtedly help to foster and reinforce drinking behavior. The frustrations experienced in trying to adjust to new or different statuses and roles in family life, in village activity, and economic ventures are examples of this.

Not to be forgotten are the enumerable personal tragedies that drinking has visited upon so many of these people. Among the few Papagos who are mentioned in this chapter, M's father, while drinking with a friend east of their reservation home, rolled into a campfire and burned to death. T, while drunk, drove over his brother-in-law, killing him, but had no recollection of the event. A was a juvenile, living with his family at a farm north of Tucson, when, in a drunken condition, he killed an uncle while driving a truck. Personal traumatic events involving some form of drunken behavior are common in the interview material. The psychological effects of these tragedies must have some relationship to habitual drinking in at least some instances.

In spite of these varying explanations for drinking, I have chosen to emphasize the social functions of drinking behavior. Social bonds are established to produce social equals and to promote and maintain equal economic status. In this way drinking serves the purpose of perpetuating important Papago values of economic equality and unostentatious, highly conforming personal behavior. Put another way, the many reasons and motives behind individual drinking are articulated in an intensely social setting where these values can be best realized. Individuals do not have to be totally comfortable and happy in such settings, but they must find meaning and value in their social and personal striving. They require social definitions as to who they are and what they should be; and social drinking continues to serve this purpose in a goodly sector of Papago society.

ACTIVITY AND LIFESTYLE

The ecological settings in which economic and social activities take place help to shape historical cultural styles that come to characterize a people. The major Papago ethnographies (Underhill 1939, 1946; Joseph, Spicer, and Chesky 1949; Williams 1956; Fontana 1960; Mark 1960; Jones 1962; Kelly 1963; Bahr 1964; Waddell 1969) emphasize the most significant of these economic realities. With the very recent intrusion of the metropolitan political economy (Jorgensen 1971) of the United States into Papago country, significant changes in lifestyle or habit patterns began to intrude upon older habit patterns and lifestyles.

The farming and cattle herding way of life supplemented by some hunting and gathering has been a continuing economic pattern for Papagos that persisted in their kinship communities and even on temporary sojourns to other areas, to farm or herd for Mexicans, for Anglos, or for other Indians. While some quite early in the 20th century were becoming more permanent city dwellers, most Papagos who encamped in the vicinity of growing towns or cities did not abandon their "rural" outlook. Cities and towns have been centers for obtaining certain goods and services, as well as places to market certain produce, such as wood and cheese. Even today, while Tucson is a sprawling urban complex, South Tucson Pueblo, a mile-square incorporated town within the heart of the city, contains a number of very "rural" neighborhoods. A step off the main streets to the historical Papago neighborhood reveals adobe houses, interspersed with cactus and desert shrubs, dirt roads and alleys, stockyards, etc. This rural frontier character is a sharp contrast to the bustle of the main thoroughfare.

While the Papagos involved in this study find certain features of the city more desirable than remaining in a lagging rural labor market or an underdeveloped reservation community, there is little about most of them that reflects urban styles characteristic of middle-class Americans or even lower class urban ghetto dwellers. By and large these are not men of the professions, the white collar, or even of the blue collar or hard-hat. An increasing number have experienced higher educational or vocational training and have had some opportunities in tribal work forces or urban industries. But the cowboy and farmer image is most noticeable. Their ways are rural and non-city.

There are, of course, Papagos who have thrown off the visible cowboy identity and who don the working man's garb or the casual clothing available in welfare stores or low-cost discount stores. But cowboy hats and shirts, Levi's, and boots are all commonly seen attire in the Papago drinking circuit, worn by both reservation visitors and "town" Indians.

The casual farming labor or the day labor available in gardening and landscaping allow for a social and economic margin in which many of these men can maintain this essentially rural lifestyle. While the monetary credits are minimal, the social credits are maximized through drinking cliques that assemble in a number of selected locations. This "margin" can also be successfully occupied in other cities such as Phoenix or such towns as Casa Grande, Gila Bend, or even more distant urbanized settings. It is a margin that is amenable to a floating population of reservation Indians or economically unstable town-oriented Papagos. It is a margin of social security where Papagos coming from their reservation communities can join town Papagos in a style of social behavior and activities more congruent with their expectations.

Certainly these people use the city drinking circuit to drink unencumbered by the exorbitant bootleg prices on the reservation and to escape some of the social censure that operates in their tribal court and justice system. Yet a lifestyle can be articulated in the drinking margin of the city that is very similar to what can be found on the reservation. They are able to maintain social relationship with kin and kind and can have extended periods of relaxed social leisure, accompanied by intermittent money-making activity in casual farm or gardening jobs. This urban margin perpetuates a style that does not coerce individuals to usurp the noncompetitive, unaggressive, relaxed, and unostentatious manner so characteristic of the Papago ethos. Further, it emphasizes the responsibility a Papago has to the group and how his own wishes must be subordinated to the group. A Papago's social consciousness and his awareness that he should not put his behavior at a conspicuous, nonconforming level has been a part of his emerging social personality throughout his gradual attainment of adulthood (Joseph, Spicer, and Chesky 1949:140ff). This Papago disposition to be sensitive to public opinion and to acquiesce to the group by cordial and conforming behavior is well maintained in the margin of the drinking circuit.

It is not accurate to maintain that chronic drunkenness and its social and psychological correlates are a part of Papago culture. Nevertheless, the drinking circuit in the city does provide a means to favorably articulate the group consciousness, of which Papagos reared in Papago society are keenly aware. Many of the activities that characterize the socioeconomics of the middle class and that are considered important measures of successful social adjustment are very antithetical to the Papago ethos. Hence, of the limited options available in the urban setting, the drinking margin does allow for the articulation of the intense group loyalty that characterizes Papago social personality. The drinking itself may take on extreme proportions, even in excess of that found in the normal routines of reservation life perhaps, but the traditional style of social life is nonetheless expressed through it.

Papagos manifest this lifestyle in their behavior more than in the way they are able to verbalize about it. It is expressed in their preferences for farming or stock raising activities, even when lands are no longer actively farmed or when family stock has been liquidated. It comes through strongly in preference for dress style, such as jeans, cowboy hats, boots, and western shirts. At informal social festivities or in urban bars catering to largely Indian throngs, casual socializing and festive spirit are cemented with liberal exchanges of drink and food.

It may well be that relegation to menial jobs in the white man's market is a product of a lack of preparation to compete in that world; but I also think that some preferences for so-called unskilled tasks reflect an ethos in which individuals value the animate world over the mechanized world, and see themselves as capable custodians over it. To like to work with plants and animals, to value the potency of social obligations and responsibilities toward others also operate to retard achievement in a things-oriented world.

Money is of value, not because it helps to acquire more things for personal consumption but because it is a way to get food and drink with which to seal the meaningfulness of social bond. Money is social power, not material power. Papagos are sharers, not hoarders. This is a product of cultural lifestyle, not a sign of underachievement motive or retarded acculturation. L's narrative of his experiences in California portrays something of the lifestyle that I have found in many other cases.

> I got off over there in L.A. I still had money in my pocket and I was walking to the restaurant to eat something. A white man came up to me and gave me $2 so I had enough to go in there and eat something. That afternoon I walked to downtown Los Angeles. When I got in town, I saw some Indians going around. I knew most of them. They hang around at 17th and Main Street out there in Los Angeles. I finally found my brother over there. We went in the alley and he took out a bottle and handed it to me. I drank it and he then asked me if I was hungry. I told him I was so he took me to a restaurant to get something to eat. We went to some place on Main Street where they sell chicken bones for 7^e. He bought about 15 chicken bones and we took them to the alley to eat before some other friends could see us. In the meantime we were also drinking. As soon as we finished the bottle and finished our eats, my brother suggested that we go after another bottle. So he went back to his hotel room and got some more money and went to get another bottle. We then went upstairs to his

room. We were there about four hours, drinking and eating. About 8 o'clock in the evening we went back to the Ritz Bar where the Indians hang around. Well, we drank in there but at 10 o'clock I lost track of my brother. He went some place. But I still had a little change in my pocket. I left the bar and walked around. I couldn't see anything. There weren't any Indians on the streets so I went to the hotel and slept in an alley there. I didn't even have a blanket.

During this particular sojourn in California, L decided to go north to do farm labor near Modesto, California, where he ran into another Papago that he knew from back home. After working with this Papago friend for two days, the two of them then made their way south to near Fresno and ran into another Papago friend while doing farm labor there. After leaving the fields they went drinking, then went back to their camp. This pattern continued for several weeks until L returned to his village at Topawa and then to Tucson.

Whether in California, on the reservation, or in Tucson, the same style of life is apparent. It is typical of many of the informants. L describes an event involving himself and two other very close friends. It demonstrates the magnitude of the social bond that is created out of their common life style.

I was with D and G. We just got out of Danny's Hideaway Bar when the police saw the pint that I had. I had bought pickles and hot dogs and had just given them to my friends. We needed something to eat, too. One policeman walked to me and asked me what I had in the paper bag. I told him it was my food. The police looked in the bag and took out the pint. He pulled out the pint and D asked him what he was going to do with it. It hadn't been opened yet. D told him we were going to go home to drink it but the policeman told us he was going to drink it himself. I said to him that he was a policeman and not supposed to drink that liquor. It was ours; we bought it with our own money. But the policeman walked to the street, then opened that pint and poured it into the street. Then he walked to us again and told us to go home and not ever come back to that bar again. Well, I gave D and G some pickles and we stood there eating after that policeman left. Then we walked over to the Shamrock Bar across the street to listen to some good western music. Finally we saw that Kadjan's Liquors was open. We walked over there and bought another pint, then we walked over there where that trailer used to park. We sat down and drank our pints right there. I also bought some sardines and some chili so we sat there and ate and drank.

V provides a historic context for Papago activity in the South Tucson Pueblo where the above event took place.

There are so many Papago people living around there. That is why they have to drink out there, see, among their friends. That's the problem, right there. They want to be drinking among their friends. It was an old Papago village before the town was there, as I say, so they have to drink around there.

Not all Papago informants talked as extensively about the meaning that these social experiences have for them but once I got acquainted with them, it became clearer that the kinds of experiences L talks about are commonly experienced in many places. To see people sharing drinks and food, to see them spending hours talking in bars or out of the way places while the bottle is constantly passed, convinces me that this way is a shared style of life. It is not free of interpersonal discord and rivalry; it is not without frustration and despair; but it is valued and capable of providing happy and memorable moments. It is sought out not because it is the best of all possible worlds but because it is a world they know and one in which they can feel comfortable. They know how to behave in this social universe and it does have meaning for them. It is a cultural style with antecedent foundations in prior generations. Although the quantity of alcohol consumption has increased in more recent years, and their drinking has become increasingly more obvious to outsiders with different values, these individuals live in a viable social world and manage it much better than we are prone to credit them.

MOBILITY

The necessity and the choice to move about widely, near and far from their usual habitat, has been characteristic of Papagos, probably from prehistoric times. As Underhill notes (1939:201), the Papago were a people environmentally forced into a low subsistence level. But when their former system, held together by family ties and community cooperativeness, was affected by generations of contacts with Spanish, Mexican, and eventually Anglo-American influence, which were all largely rural until well into the 20th century, they found it expedient to engage in temporary migration, either as families, or as individuals. Southern Papagos found the farms and ranches of Mexico a useful source, and small encampments of Papagos could be found for temporary periods around some of these ranches and small towns. Eastern Papagos have, for many generations, been oriented temporarily to the farms and ranches around the Tucson vicinity and a number of small Papago settlements have been adjacent to the Tucson pueblo since it was first inhabited by Spaniards and later Mexicans. The old village, referred to above by V, was the remainder of one such settlement, right where South Tucson now is (Tooker 1952). The economic aspects of these temporary movements of Papagos to Tucson are discussed in a prior study (Waddell 1969).

Papagos of the north were more inclined to move toward the Gila River to work for Pimas and, later, for white farmers and ranchers in the area around Phoenix. A number of small towns have grown up in this area revolving around farming and ranching and many Papagos from the central and northern districts of the reservation still follow patterns of movement toward those communities (Waddell 1969:22). (See Figure 2.1.) With the development of mining, especially in the western portion of the reservation at Ajo, many more Papagos have been oriented in that direction since the first part of the century, especially 1917 to present.

While the Second World War and the development of industries to sustain the war brought on the first large orientation of Papagos to distant places, earlier development of railroads in the southwest found many Papago men following their construction at the turn of the century. Informants also have conveyed to me that they had relatives who had worked and lived in California for a number of years prior to World War II. Hence, while Underhill is correct in stating that most of their wanderings were confined to their hot desert environment in shifting villages, depending upon season and circumstances, Papagos have not been unfamiliar with periodic and rather extensive movement away from their usual settlements when their economic needs so dictated. Only the heyday of Apache marauding (1750–1870) tended to prompt Papago communities to consolidate and restrict their distant movements. Certainly, whenever possible, they preferred to remain in their familiar desert environment where small kin-centered rancherías were the prevailing mode. But history seems to suggest that such a way of life has seldom been totally self-sustaining without contacts with outlying peoples.

Certainly, within the time spans of most of the people involved in this study, periodic movement to other areas has been commonly experienced, both during childhood and adulthood. Farm labor, both around the reservation and in other southwestern states, has been within the recent memory and experience of most. Mine labor has also been tried by most of the men, most usually in Ajo. Railroad work, some temporary reservation labor, combined with occasional attempts at landscaping and gardening in Tucson or other towns, are similarly reported by a large number (Waddell 1969). More recently, a considerable number have been available for fire-fighting.

In collecting occupational histories carefully, it is impressive to note how so many of these occupational patterns cohere in a single individual's career. Besides being economically necessary, this mobile work pattern also is a part of a valued style of life of which drinking, as a social bonding mechanism, is so vital an activity. Some idea of this can be seen in statements made by Papagos elsewhere in this chapter. An example of one of T's recent adventures should suffice to illustrate this mobility. It narrates elements common to many other personal histories that were gathered during the field work.

> Last Tuesday night we got on a good drunk. So I told my buddy we ought to hop a freight and take off to Los Angeles. He agreed, so we walked down to the freight yard and asked the brakeman where we could hop on. I didn't sober up until we got to a hut down there close to Yuma. We jumped off the freight and went downtown to walk around. First we went to the mission downtown and slept off our hangovers for a while. Afterwards, we met some Indian guys and went down to skid row. But my buddy said we shouldn't drink right there where the cops run around. We had gotten all cleaned up down there at the mission so we were too noticeable. When we were ready to leave the area, we would then put on our dirty clothes again to wear on the freight.

Instead of proceeding on to Los Angeles as they had planned, T and his buddy headed back to Phoenix.

> We went down to the park on 16th and Washington and sat down with some other Indian guys. Those guys asked us if we were sick, which is a way to ask us if we needed a drink. We told them that we were sick so we drank with a whole bunch of Indian guys there. The whole nation was there ... Pimas and Papagos.

T, on this occasion, was not really seriously considering going to these places to find ways of making money by the usual casual labor. He just wanted to be on the roam and the story illustrates how group drinking consolidates a number of Indians from a variety of places who happen to be in the area for a variety of purposes, including efforts to make a little money. T himself has been to many places in California, to Chicago (not on relocation), and to a number of farm towns surrounding the reservation, all with sincere intentions to work. In his many accounts, circumstances similar to the above are invariably recounted. Drinking, even in those circumstances where obtaining work was the object, usually occurs and at times, without intention, interferes with the work activity.

Papago adults, generally, have had very mobile careers, largely dictated by the need to gain an economic livelihood in a world of limited economic opportunities. Not all of them are plagued with perpetual

drinking on the streets, but very few have found it either easy or necessary to avoid these congregating places. They, in fact, seek them out,
often with every intention to go to work but, as often occurs, the social
pressures and the desire to exchange drinks tends to dampen economic
intentions. After sobering up, they may go to work or return home,
wherever it is, or go to some other location to find other work. It must
be kept in mind that many of these occupational locations have been
known for a long time, even in their fathers' generations, and at these
locations there are well-known places to congregate and to drink. The
patterns of movement are a part of the style and they have been in
operation for a long time. If there is word of where work might be
found, the lead will be picked up in one of these congregating places.

QUESTS FOR INDIVIDUAL POWER

Levy and Kunitz (1971:97) suggest that their studies among Navajos
and Hopis indicate that explanation of social pathologies as they relate
to alcoholism can be seen in terms of the persisting elements of aboriginal culture rather than the anomic influence of social disorganization brought about by modern conditions. In this section, I would like to
look at an important aspect of the Papago culture as it has been described and see how it might relate to the high incidence of drinking
among present-day Papagos.

Underhill (1946:17) mentions that the system of group control revolving around communal calendric ceremonies and the democratic notion
that personal power was a highly individual quest were distinctive
Papago avenues to the supernatural. The former stresses the necessity
of subduing individual wishes in favor of the social and economic
concerns of the whole community. This system of group consciousness
is best expressed through public ceremony (Waddell 1976, 1979).
The latter stresses the necessity of seeking one's own source of power
for individual achievement. It is a system of self-fulfillment that is best
expressed through private experience. These systems encourage both a
strong commitment to persuasion by corporate opinion and a commitment to one's own private experience, and therefore a suspicion of
another's private source of power. The interplay of these quite different
sources of power operates in the drinking situation. The social group
insists upon the conformity of its members. The suspicion and apprehension of others in the group who may try to use their powers of
persuasion to coerce one to drink against one's better judgment create a
potential source of spontaneous aggression.

There is much in drinking that is convivial and socially rewarding in achieving drunkenness together; but being drunk also conveys to individuals very unique and private experiences that could readily be seen as variations of vision or guardian-spirit quests, encounters with private sources of supernatural power. The guardian-spirit quest and shamanic individualism are, of course, far more awesome than a mere "drunk" but I am inclined to agree with Levy and Kunitz (1971:110) that in the state of individual intoxication, there is an analog to the experience.

A number of Papago informants discussed their feelings regarding the attainment of drunkenness and I am impressed that to attain a state of intoxication is a highly desired pursuit in many instances, not just a way to escape from problems. Some Papagos seek to get high to increase their social power or their individual achievement of a state of mind that allows them to express themselves more openly and effectively with each other. Without it, they are socially and individually powerless and helpless, highly suspicious of their own abilities to relate to others, and highly uncertain about what powers others hold over them. It is when the usually very reserved, placid, and peaceful Papago is braced with a source of individual power, alcohol, that he is able to open up and express himself with confidence, even to the point of risking verbal and maybe even physical abuse or, perhaps, inflicting it. A few examples from the Papago themselves might illustrate this better.

On one occasion T, his wife, and her brother were stopped by the Tribal Chief of Police, whom T's family knew personally, on their way to Sells from Tucson. Notice the interpersonal hostilities expressed in his account of this incident.

So the Chief of Police asked what I had in the bag behind the driver's seat. He told me he wanted to check it out but I told him he couldn't. So he just opened the door and told my wife's brother to get out. The Chief took the damn bag and ripped it open. All the sandwiches fell out on the ground. I told him he was a dirty rat and warned him that one of these days when he was off duty, I would get him. We did, too. When Christmas came around he tried to buy drinks for everybody but nobody wanted to drink with him.

Well anyway, this time when he stopped us going to that dance at Sells he warned me not to do any bootlegging there or else he would really slap it to me. I told him he couldn't do that to me because he wasn't the judge. So he told me to get the hell out of there. This one buddy of mine is a cop too, but he said nothing because he knows that I'd get on him later too if he tried to take me in. There are a lot of them over there, real good guys; they just tell you to drink your bottle and go home. But this Chief will pour that bottle out right in front of you and make you sweat it out.

I doubt whether any of this verbal exchange could have happened the way it did without ample drinking on T's part. The incident illustrates not only the fact that interpersonal resentment and suspicion do exist and occasionally flare up in verbal and physical encounters. It also points up how the very person who is required by tribal law to take action against the drinking violations of others will, on other occasions, use alcohol gifts to buy back the support, friendship, and goodwill of those that he has had to act against. And there is no better way to put another down than to refuse the drinks he offers.

T mentions another similar incident in which an important tribal official asked for a ride from the reservation to Tucson:

> Old E told me when we were stopped at Three Points that he would buy me some gas and also asked me if I wanted some drinks and cigarettes, too. I told him yes so I went into the store and asked for some cigarettes. E was standing there and said to put a six pack of Coors on his credit card. He also had a pint of whisky and put that on the damn credit card. I told myself that that guy really knows how to do it. So pretty soon I started thinking that we're really the ones who are paying him—God! And he's using our gas, too. E also gave me some money. He used his credit card, got some cash, and paid me off. He gave me $11, just for bringing him to Tucson from Sells. You know, that place is crooked at Sells. The whole deal is run by a family.

One can sense the resentment T has for the privileged position of members of this "family." The behavior of the tribal official is predictable; he tries to purchase T's friendship with drink and money, hoping to soften the resentment that he certainly must know T has toward him because of his better position.

L and another friend of his were trying to get a ride to L's sister's house in the south part of Tucson where they hoped to get a bite to eat. They ran into a person from the reservation and asked him how much he would charge them to take them to L's sister's place. This person, unknown to them, said he would take them for $5. L said to his friend: "This man, I think he is a rich man, that's why he charges us so much. He is dressed like a cowboy so he must have a lot of cattle back home." So L and his friend, not having the money nor wanting to pay it if they did, stayed at the Spanish Well Bar to drink up their pint of wine instead.

There is considerable resentment expressed toward other Papagos who not only have more but who refuse to share and, instead, try to make money off their poorer fellows. When another person fails to share, whether food, drinks, or whatever one has, personal suspicion of the stingy person is intensified. Sharing drinks with another is one way to tell that person that he is not suspect and it is a way of telling one's self that "since my drinks are received, I am not suspect." Even in convivial social binge drinking, there is a considerable amount of latent suspicion of others' motives, and drinking together allows members of the group to feel socially more powerful in each others' presence. Verbal altercations frequently take place in such situations and people, sometimes through jesting, give and take displays of ego threatening or defending. Sometimes, even among friends, physical displays of hostility can occur but most often it stays at the verbal level, where personal grievances are aired with words.

B expresses how his own family of orientation has been affected by suspicion, rivalry, and differential handling of wealth and drink. He comes from a family of considerable reputation in the modern tribal political economy. Regarding other members of his family, B says:

> They'll take a drink, but not like me. When I hit a bottle, I keep on going. I am the black sheep of the family. Just the other day I saw one of my half-brothers; he's bigger than I am. He started talking about what we own. We were talking about the house that I was offered $1000 for. He actually told me that I didn't own anything out there at Sells because I would rather own the bottle. Finally, he pushed me, knocked me over. In a way, I don't blame him but at the same time my father willed that house to me, nobody else; except maybe my sister. My sister actually doesn't have anything to do with it. I'm supposed to be the breadwinner but you know, I'm too good hearted. I gave the house to her actually. Suppose I was to get that money from the house? It would go for a bottle, see. There I go again, yeh.

Here B judges himself in relationship to his other siblings and sees himself a loser, being cut out of the family estate even though he feels a right to it. Yet his siblings do not seem to trust his ability to manage it because of his constant association with his drinking friends. The drinking group is actually, in this case, a buffer against the ill respect that he feels his family has toward him. In it he finds supportive behavior where he cannot find it among immediate relatives.

To outsiders, Papagos seem timid and reserved in their social relations and contacts when they are sober, at least those appear so who are least acculturated to Anglo habit patterns. As Joseph (Joseph, Spicer, and Chesky 1949:198) concludes from her study of Papago personality formation in children, there is a tendency to shut themselves off from the outside world. It is not totally the type of withdrawal where one escapes to a fantasy world; it "resembles more closely the psychological state of a seer or medium and seems to be related to that peculiar fusion of reality with supernatural and magical concepts, which is an important part of Papago life and child training. It seems to operate as a ready and almost automatic control in occasions of stress and conflict" (Joseph, Spicer, and Chesky 1949:198).

Papago culture seems to have provided few institutionalized alternatives for handling interpersonal tensions. When the latter occur, as they must in all human groups, Papagos seem to resort to suppression of outward expression of these tensions. Given the strong values of allegiance to group cohesion through cooperative work and sharing, responding to the wishes of seniors and fearing the supernatural, Papagos either mask their feelings when agitated by others or shut themselves off from the painful interpersonal situation. It is in this context that individualized power through attainment of a supernatural spirit functioned in Papago society traditionally, to fortify the self against a potentially harmful world. And it is in this same context that I think drunkenness has come to assume such importance. It is both a way of withdrawing from one's usually sober and reserved self and at the same time a way of gaining more social power, either to express oneself better in the presence of friends or to defend oneself when verbally or physically attacked by a hostile source. It is a persisting feature of the Papago ethos.

Some of these tensions regarding other persons and the role of the supernatural or magical component underlying them are very evident in some of the delirium tremens, dream, and other hallucinatory experiences several men have shared with me. Some are educated enough to sense, or at least state, that it is their mind playing tricks on them due to their heavy drinking; others speak about them with more awe, as if they were actual experiences involving visitations by deceased relatives or supernatural strengths.

CROSS-SEX TENSIONS

Papagos have been described as well adjusted to their ideal of family unity, where husband and wife loyalty seems to be quietly assumed (Joseph, Spicer, and Chesky 1949:210). Joseph's part of the study indicates that very little about male-female relationships existing between boys and girls could be ascertained through their testing. In this section, I would like to present evidence for what I think to be the presence of a rather strong cross-sex antagonism. It should not be forgotten that Papagos, like many other Indian tribes, strongly feared menstruating women. They were seen as having harmful power, thus to be avoided lest harm and danger befall the men if contaminated.

Joseph (Joseph, Spicer, and Chesky 1949:201), Underhill (1939:50), and Williams (1956:174) assess that boys from ages 5 to 12 tend to identify with their fathers and associate their pleasant emotions with him rather than the mother, and that girls tend to identify with their mothers. With such strong sex-role identification one might expect to find latent cross-sex tensions and suspicions. I, too, have been generally impressed with the degree of husband and wife regard for family unity in some of my associations with a few families. At the same time several informants talked at length on how many of their problems stemmed from their inability to get along with women. It may be more prevalent only for those who have developed such pervasive drinking habits and total involvement in drinking cliques that their hostilities were intensified beyond repair. But I think it is more extensive than this, at least latently.

B speaks out most strongly about his negative feelings toward women. He refers to women as the source of man's problem, calling it a crossfire. He has been through a marriage and a number of liaisons and speaks of the constant conflict that he and his women experienced. M, who now drifts about the city since he and his wife split up, speaks of his wife as being the cause of his drinking since she was a heavy drinker herself. My own impression of his situation is that his wife actually tried to bridle his excessive drinking and her sons told him to not come around any more.

In a number of the cases where men have had some success in staying away from the drinking groups and prolonging their sobriety, women were playing a rather strong supportive role. This is similar to conclusions reached by Graves (1971:303). Such situations are not, however, without their oppressive quality since women sometimes play rather stern roles in controlling their husbands' activities.

The male as father is the main source of authority in the Papago family and the wife, through her constant hard work around the home, defers to her husband in all matters, staying inconspicuously and modestly in the background as she performs her family duties (Williams 1956:99). Further, as Underhill (1939:55–6) mentions, while there is much in Papago life that stresses equality of the spouses, sex is always important in regulating behavior since men and women work and play in sex-limited groups. Where these traditional, mutually supportive sex roles are maintained and the family still functions largely in terms of these patterns, it is likely that traditional social controls of age, public opinion, and mild male authority will not allow open expression of any cross-sex hostilities inherent in the relationships. It would seem, however, that when women assume authoritative and assertive roles over their households either due to greater education, greater adoption of middle-class female roles, or a greater access to economic stability through domestic jobs, etc., inter-sex conflicts are more apt to be manifest. When these roles change and partners happen to marry "opposites" from the traditional expectations, a number of interesting things occur.

First, because of the greater ability to make decisions affecting the family and because of their ability to make the money through more steady work, women may well contribute to their husband's self-depreciation as a father and mild authoritative decision maker, precisely because the men are unable to make the decisions or the money. This would inevitably lead to breakup of marriages and the tendency of the men to find their reference group norms in cliques who share somewhat the same status. The drinking group provides support wherein men can, through drink and camaraderie, bolster their deflated egos.

Second, if such relationships obtain where women occupy more viable positions than men in the family situation, some men might seek to retain their attachments to such women because they provide some economic stability and also some strong persuasive influence over their drinking behavior, threatening to cut off the relationship if the man slips too much. This situation has, in some of the cases, helped to control the amount and extent of binge drinking that some men do. This type of relationship is of interest because it does not involve traditional male-female relationships but actually a kind of reversal. The relationship, however, can be functional from the standpoint of providing a margin wherein men, who are trying to assume a more stable economic and social position via a regular and reliable occupational pattern, can be sheltered from their drinking group by yielding to female control. It may operate in several ways.

The initial marriage may take place between a more dominating woman and a dependent man, with the female providing the main force in the relationship and actually trying to control her husband's behavior. It may go on for some time with the man vacillating between the pressures of his wife and family and the pressures of his drinking cliques. It appears as if the outcome, that is, the style of life that the man eventually chooses, depends upon which of the two types of supportive behavior turns out to be the most effective in providing the man with an acceptable definition of himself. If the man eventually selects exclusively for the supportive drinking group and abandons his ties to

spouse and family, I would suggest that the man will have more negative remarks to make about women since there would have been a rather
prolonged period in their relationship in which her demands were
strenuously competing with the expectations of drinking cliques.

I have known many men and families over several years where this
has been going on. In a few instances, the supportive family relationships seem to have won out over the drinking group but the process has
not been easy for the men who have this choice. In fact, it is difficult to
predict how long the stabilized relationship will last. Some men report
extended periods of sobriety and faithful performance of occupational
tasks only to find themselves once again engulfed in the obligations of
the drinking group. During the intermittent periods of occasional sobriety, there is good evidence that women were playing strong, relatively
stabilizing influences in their husbands' lives, even if their relationships
were fraught with antagonisms.

The strength of the drinking group is especially devastating to the
male's family responsibilities because, I think, of the greater impact
that changing sex roles have had upon men. Papago women have always exercised strong, if modest, influence as managers of the home
and children. What has changed is that they have had longer periods of
successful adjustment as wage earners in the homes of whites or in
service jobs and have, at the same time, learned more directly some of
the features characteristic of white middle-class homes. Thus, women
have become the economic supporters of homes through their regular
incomes or management of welfare monies, thus depriving men of
important economic and decision-making functions in the family. In
addition, the social drinking scene has helped to perpetuate behavior
patterns that are not conducive to any economic pattern other than
menial day labor; and the money gained is more apt to be spent to
sustain a man's relationship to his supportive drinking group rather than
to his wife and family.

A is a good example of one who is presently influenced by both a
strong wife and the persuasions of drinking friends. When I was best
acquainted with him, he was doing some binge drinking on the streets of
Tucson with his old friends; but his wife, who was working regularly,
was trying to keep him from going out and drinking. A also had some
fairly dependable work at various homes, where he did landscaping. As
he puts it:

> Sometimes I don't drink wine unless I have a hangover. I just go
> straight to work. Other times I just feel like getting drunk. Sometimes
> when me and my wife are arguing, I just feel like going out to drink,

just to forget it. When I get back home, she's talking nice to me again, so it's just fine between us. Right now I am drinking a lot. She gets to feel bad about it so she sometimes drinks too but not to get drunk. She just drinks to forget about what I've been doing, and then when I come home, she's pretty nice to me again.

His most recent binge he describes this way:

Sometimes I go out and drink with my friends because they know me and we're friends. So I start drinking with them, but I don't feel like drinking too much. But when my mother died, I started drinking heavy again. Then I didn't drink for a year and six months. Not long ago I started drinking again and I kept on drinking. Sometimes I drink for a week. But right now I just kind of do what people do, you know. So I have been thinking, I'm going to stop again. So I told my wife I was going to stop again and she said that would be nice because if I could stop drinking, I might not end up dead like so many of my friends.

While A joins the drinking group now and then, he also speaks judgmentally about it.

There are some guys who just like to enjoy it and stay on it. They just keep drinking and don't think about their homes or their jobs. A lot of those guys from Sells are like that. They hang around town and just sleep anywhere, like I told you the other day, sleeping in those empty houses. Whenever they see a little money in their pockets, they go around town with the money and get a fifth or a pint. That's all they want to do.

Although A was doing some drinking, I did not see him around the drinking areas as frequently as some other men. I think his wife was having a strong stabilizing influence on his thinking although he did sense the strong pressures of his friends whenever he would walk along the streets.

T, on the other hand, had been separated from his wife for at least three years. She was working steadily at San Xavier and had their three children. T said he occasionally saw the children around town but his wife refused to see him. T, at the time of my study, was operating within the drinking crowd exclusively. He was very sensitive about incompatibilities with his wife:

Well, the reason why I drink a lot, too, is because of my old lady. You know, I would tell her I was really going to try. I thought maybe she would take me back if I got a good steady job and stopped drinking. She used to hide my bottles where I couldn't find them very good. That's when we broke up right then. She used to try to get my checks, so I told her that was it. God, one time I was drunk. I still had some money but she took my check away from me. She told me she wouldn't give it to me unless I gave her half of it. I took it from her and told her I would cash it. I stuck it in my pocket and I told her I would see her later. I jumped out of the car and she went to call the police on me. When they came I told them she was lying. I said I was going to cash it for her. But the cop told me he would go with me to cash it and see to it that I gave her some money.

Much of the "cross-fire" between the sexes seems to be a result of the changing sex roles and the subservience of economically less stable men to more stable females. This is clearly not an expression of ab-original culture. However, my contention here is that the Papago male-female patterns of a more traditional type are still very visible to the people concerned; that is, they have living models of the traditional family and sex roles before them, both on and off the reservation. These models still clearly exist in the minds of most of the people, in spite of the changing character of life on the reservation and off. It is still an important feature of Papago life that men have important positions of authority, important roles in decision making, and meaningful and im-portant activity roles that are to be complemented by a woman who cooks, raises children, and watches after the needs of the household. But there are now more individuals who find it increasingly difficult to conform to the traditional model of appropriate male and female family roles, and therein lies the conflict.

One of the strong indicators of sex distinction was the super-natural power that women, through their menstrual cycles, could exer-cise on men. On one occasion I was talking with L about women and we happened to get on the taboo topic of menstrual segregation of women. L started to comment that "white people don't really under-stand what that means. Indian people send them over ... no, I don't think I'm going to say anything about that because there are a lot of things about what you ask me that are dangerous for us Indians."

In the current situation where traditional sex-role models are cogni-tively perceived but where no social sanctions are able to operate to reinforce them, new situations of sexual distrust and antagonism are intensified and the old pattern of fear of women's powers has no tra-ditional male role to accommodate it and no social mechanism to regu-late it. A careful study of male-female marital relationships, drawn from a stratified sample of cases, would throw considerable light on this topic. I would hypothesize that there have always been sexual antagonisms potentially possible in human relationships but that the regulation and repression of these antagonisms vary considerably from society to society. It was institutionalized in the Papago menstrual taboos and expressed in the rituals relating thereto.

With the passing of these traditional patterns or with their coming into conflict with newly emerging patterns, the ritual controls are reduced and the new patterns intensify the conflict. I would impressionistically guess that when Papago men drink together, they could be expressing, perhaps unconsciously at times, animosities toward the women in their lives. If they succeed in marriage, it is because either traditional patterns tend to eventually reestablish themselves or the new non-Papago middle-class patterns prove to be adaptable to new circumstances. In any case, the resolution of sex-role conflicts is very much related to the regulation of the drinking pattern. Drinking can be employed as a device to antagonize a spouse just as threatening to withhold economic support can be used to antagonize a spouse who drinks too much.

FOOD AND DRINK ANXIETY

Related also to the understanding of the social dimensions of Papago drinking behavior are other considerations at a psychological level. Underhill (1946:17–8) argues that both communal ceremonies such as the rainmaking wine ritual *nawait* and individual power-seeking ceremonies are oriented to one final end, the acquisition of rain, which means food. Thus, Papago life expresses extreme concerns about food and its potential scarcity. Using Cohen's (1961:314ff) typology of local group organization, the Papagos can be described traditionally as having maximum community solidarity, where there is physical and social proximity of localized kinsmen with predominantly sedentary patterns. Persistent corporate kin groups have not been characteristic of Papago social structure since physical mobility and changes in community membership have occasionally been necessary under the circumstances of desert life. Following Cohen (1961:318) further, Papagos can also be considered as a sharing society—that is, they indulge their children and each other on every occasion that food, drink, and other commodities happen to be available. These recurrent and repetitive exchanges of food and drink have long been characteristic of Papago life.

Obviously, the maximum solidarity of the aboriginal pattern has changed and the prevailing pattern for a growing number of Papagos is a community structure which maintains occasional solidarity and mutual assistance when its members are together, but which splits apart on numerous occasions. Then, too, some Papago families have become the "nonnucleated" type of community, where isolated and highly migratory nuclear families are separated from other family units for prolonged periods of time. Money, rather than recurrent sharing of food and resources or mutual assistance of families in times of need, is increasingly important for such nuclear family units. Some Papago families have become highly individualized, where accumulation of wealth is an end in itself, without recourse to sharing among related kinsmen. Social and physical distance from other kinsmen are maximized and social obligations toward them are minimized.

The community types with maximum solidarity are most apt to manifest a fear of impoverishment and recurrent sharing is the best way to maximize the functioning of the unit in times of scarcity. Sharing, then, must be based not only upon the reality of nutrient impoverishment but also upon a fear of social impoverishment; that is, fear of being cut off from one's sustaining community.

The fear of social impoverishment has already been discussed in the sections concerning the significance of sharing drinks among social equals and how, when one does not drink or refuses to take drink extended by another, he is clearly saying that he does not consider himself the other's friend and equal. The importance of social gatherings and feastings where food and drink are abundantly exchanged has also been discussed.

What needs emphasizing is the extent to which Papagos appear to express anxieties about a shortage of food. I found that food and hunger were constant concerns in drinking circles. Some of the men told me that drinking helps to keep them from feeling the gnawing pangs of hunger which they frequently feel when there is no one to prepare food or few resources with which to buy it. I asked L why he considered himself a drinking man and why he drank as much as he did. His response is interesting:

Well, I'll tell you. I'm a drinking man. I'm a drinking Indian, all the time. Like if I was in town right now, I could get a bottle to drink. There's always a friend going around who has a bottle, to help. We are the true Americans. That's why we drink. When I have no money and I see my friends around town, they give me a drink. Pretty soon I'm going to get hungry and all my friends will be gone. If I have no money and I'm sitting on the bench someplace, I start to thinking about how I am going to eat or drink. You can get drunk pretty easy if you don't eat anything.

L, like several of the informants, freely talked about food, when there was none, its lack of satiable quality when there was, or the kinds of food preferred. In a few of the statements presented above, food can be seen as part of the narrative, as in L's recounting of his experiences in California. More frequently the men complained about the food that they got in jail, primarily because it was not greasy enough or hot enough (in the chili hot sense), yet these meals, no matter what they consisted of, were perhaps the only regular meals the men were eating. I think many men use drinking as a way to get in jail, which is a way of getting some food. On the other hand, so much drinking has been going on that it is likely that little food is being consumed because the steady diet of alcohol depresses the appetite and because the limited monies are used to pool for drinks rather than for foods.

There is also something of significance related to male and female roles that might be of importance in discussing the matter of food. One important aspect of the male-female relationship is the measure of a wife's usefulness in cooking for her husband. When these men, whatever the reasons behind it, parted ways with their wives, they also parted company with important sources of food preparation. I used a series of five drawings to encourage open discussion about hypothetical situations portrayed in the pictures. One picture card had a man lying on a bed and a woman standing at a table with her back to the viewer. Many of my sample saw this woman as preparing food or making lunch for the man to carry to work. The picture was not intended to bait this response. Still, it is of interest to note this commonly perceived activity of the female figure. It must be kept in mind that many Papago ethnographers have reported the indulgent manner in which parents deal with children and their gustatory demands. I think it is the economic source of strength relating to food provision that keeps some Papago men attached to their controlling wives in spite of the tension it creates when the drinking friends are also putting on the pressure. They seriously consider the possibility of the threat of withdrawal of food when they break company with a wife. All that is left once this happens is the food and drink exchanges that take place in the drinking circles or the food that they periodically get in jail. Drinking becomes the primary means of oral indulgence and they freely indulge each other in liquid reciprocities.

Since early childhood they have seen the feelings of others expressed toward them through food and drink, both in the intimacy of the nuclear family, the extended family patrilocal household and at community feasts and gatherings. In the same manner, they have expressed their attachments to their kinsmen by returning goods when they became old enough to assume the patterns of adults. This, as Joseph, Spicer, and Chesky (1949:110) and Williams (1956:166) note, may be as early as five years old. The patterns of sharing food, cooperative labor, and other family resources since early childhood sets the stage for the reciprocal indulgence that so abundantly prevails in adult drinking circles.

The relationship between an unpredictable economy, community solidarity, and the presence of recurring food exchanges (Cohen 1961:321) clearly obtains in the case of the Papago. The familistic, cooperative, egalitarian nature of the Papago ethos, nourished by a prolonged mothering indulgence of children, is the basis of the emotional predispositions for recurrent sharing in adult life. Wherever one has kinsmen, although his resources may be limited, one can always expect sharing. In fact, one's needs can be met only by securing these needs through mutual interaction with others (Cohen 1961:325). The social structure organizing and integrating Papago social life maximizes the expression of reciprocal obligations. Likewise, the social structure of the drinking situation allows for the expression of these basic motivations especially in the face of their disappearance in the changing Papago society of today.

Since sharing food and drink has been the primary means for expressing social values in Papago society, and since these resources are to be assured in the context of maximally solidified groups, Papagos experience great anxiety when outside the reciprocating network; that is, outside of the groups where food and/or drinks are exchanged freely. Unfortunately, alcohol is addictive and when it is heavily consumed, it tends to deprive indulgers of basic nourishment. Social nourishment takes place at the expense of physical nourishment because of both the addictive quality of alcohol and the social significance of alcohol in the circles where it circulates.

In reality, it might be asked whether the reciprocities of drinks do actually maximize the sense of trust in another person for, as Cohen (1961:331–2) notes, the predisposition to give or share also makes possible the expectation that others will give. When one sees the extent to which individuals intimidate and coerce each other to drink, it seems to have little to do with willing giving and receiving, in the sense of charitability in our society. Charitable giving is a transaction between social unequals. Recurrent exchange among social equals does not involve "willingness" at all. It is just something that is supposed to take place.

Food and drink exchanges are messages of trust. Failure either to extend or to receive that extended by another is a public announcement of distrust. When T and his friends refused the drinks offered by the Indian policeman who had earlier exercised his tribal authority to arrest them, they conveyed their mistrust of him. He had lost social credit. When A or L or any of the other men decline drinks offered, no matter what the intimidation, they are not exercising good moral judgment: they are saying to those who offer, "I don't trust you."

When Papagos use verbal intimidation to get each other to drink, it should not be viewed as vindictive intimidation with the intent to tempt another to do "evil." These are quite standardized forms of expression and heavily laden with intended humor and good-natured frivolity. The men, by and large, actually enjoy drinking even if they do not always enjoy the physical or social and economic aftereffects. The intimidations are efforts to build up and maintain proper social relations through a conventional token of trust in Papago society, namely food or drink. On the other hand, extensive drinking must, under any circumstances, incline individuals to seriously consider whether heavy drinking is really an adequate answer to human problems. I think these Papago drinkers are anxiously aware that their excessive drinking is not a totally viable coping device.

Outside of tribal herding and family farming or extended family migratory farming there have been few if any new occupational roles for men which allow for the combination of meaningful male work activity, and which provide situations wherein recurrent sharing can be socially maximized. A few stereotyped menial labor jobs have served to articulate these values but what little money might be earned is pumped back into drinking situations in order to rekindle social-trust relationships that would otherwise disappear, leaving one all alone to face the uncompromising world. Papagos seem to have a strong need to maintain a mode of social relatedness, a need originating in the sharing contexts of their families of orientation. On the other hand they have lost many of their strong ties with these essential units of relatedness, their patrilocal households. Food and drink are oral tokens that can still communicate the importance of social relatedness that is derived from early primary group experiences. Having in many cases lost physical attachment to family units, they have sought out a viable social group in which these predispositions for sharing trust can now best be articulated. It would be hard to propose to these men a more viable alternative. Certainly the best intentions of our modern society have not yet produced an alternative that is capable of creating as meaningful a social bond and interpersonal trust as can be found among one's drinking peers.

PAPAGO DRINKING BEHAVIOR AND "ALCOHOLISM": A REHABILITATIVE DILEMMA

I found a number of Papagos who seem to have some understanding of the folk taxon "alcoholic." I refer to it as a folk taxon because the concept of alcoholic is not clearly defined, either medically or socially (Roueche 1960:110; Kessel and Walton 1965:15; Plant 1967:39; McCarthey 1964). It has something to do with a condition that a specific individual is in, as measured by certain physiological need dependencies for alcohol that his system supposedly has. We are told that there are certain signs for the onset of alcoholism, that condition which alcoholics have. The condition is diffuse, however; it seems to be pervasive throughout both the body and the psyche. It is extremely influenced also by the response of the "alcoholic," the one who has the pervasive condition of "alcoholism," to a social universe involving human interactions and to a cultural domain of values, symbols, and things. Hence, what is seen as problem or as pathology not only relates to what individuals perceive about the functioning of their bodies, but what kinds of social norms regulate behavior and what kinds of particular cultural symbols are cognitively operative (Spradley 1970; Wiseman 1970).

Considering these complexes of variables, it should become clear why I refer to the terms "alcoholic" and "alcoholism" as folk taxa. The terms define states of psychosocial being, physiological responses, and normative conditions of behavior only from the perspective of a single cultural orientation. It may be the most correct assessment of any that exist, although this has not been satisfactorily demonstrated. Clearly, there is a lack of either medical or social psychological preciseness of definition or characterization of the condition. It takes on the character of an "ism," which may refer to either identifiable physiological reactions, the body, or may refer to psychosocial peculiarities, the mind. Clearly, the body-mind dichotomy inherent in our own world view is part of the problem.

Given the advanced state of biochemistry, physiology, and physiological psychology, it may be possible to record and describe the body's response to alcohol with some degree of precision, where some notion of physiological pathology is an acceptable explanation. In some areas of symptomology, there seems to be little trouble identifying physiological symptoms that could point to pathology. Definitions of social pathology, however, are very much related to normative dimensions of social life; and these are culture-specific. Hence, the sociocultural norms operating in one society are frequently employed to judge the social behavior of others and to define its tolerable limits.

It is when social definitions are applied to alcohol-related behavior that psychosocial conditions are assessed as within normal range or pathological. It does not seem to be the volume of alcohol consumed or the condition of drunkenness per se that defines alcoholic or alcoholism. It may be more definable if certain physiological conditions, i.e., alcoholic cirrhosis, blackouts, or withdrawal symptoms such as shakes, hallucinations, vomiting and the like are manifest. But one is also frequently termed alcoholic if he neglects family responsibility, fails to stay on a job, dresses slovenly, goes to jail a lot, or hangs around on skid row. These are normative dimensions that, while obvious behavior extremes to people who do not have them, are discerned by certain select outsiders who call the pervasive combination of all of these things "alcoholism," a severe condition that some work ardently and devotedly to remedy. From the point of view, then, that the condition as defined is so diffuse and nonspecific and because so few actually contribute to its definition, I must still consider it a folk taxon—a folk category peculiar to a limited social segment. In fact, there are several folk taxa, depending upon whether the definition comes from one of a variety of medicophysical points of view, psychosocial points of view, or as vague constructs employed by an uninformed general public. If so few, even in middle-class Anglo society, can bring both knowledge and norms to bear down on the nature of the problem it may be a bit restrictive to build tribal rehabilitation programs on so fuzzy a definition.

I began by stating that I think a number of Papagos I came to know were beginning to perceive themselves as alcoholics. They were learning the language of their benefactors—policemen, judges, ministers, Alcoholics Anonymous personnel, "recovered" Indians, doctors, and other institutional personnel. I am sure that those who are beginning to accept the definitions of their conditions that their more authoritative benefactors provide cannot hope for precise definitions if their benefactors are also conceptually ambiguous. In short, there is the possibility of even greater cognitive confusion resulting from the ambiguities fostered by competing folk taxa.

A few now, I think, are able to judge themselves conceptually in terms of the "alcoholic" taxon, but there are many more lacking education, facility with English, and adequate socialization into significant aspects of the white normative culture who cannot hope to perceive for themselves what, to even the most educated and most socialized of our own culture, is difficult to understand and elucidate. Our intracultural confusion, compounded with the problem of cross-cultural communication, makes it extremely difficult to accept fully the idea that Papago men are "alcoholics," plagued by the condition of "alcoholism" as it is presently defined. It is not to deny the existence of a problem.

I think several of the Papagos on Indian skid row and congregating in various locations are distressed men, as all men on occasion must be. They certainly can account for personal tragedies arising out of uncontrolled drinking. They report and are diagnosed as having many of the common physiological signs of "alcoholism." And they are, many of them, disengaged from meaningful primary groups such as families and households and they do miss a lot of work as a result of their frequent binge drinking. I think what is missed in all of our judgments is an appreciation for the intensity of the meaningful social life that is expressed in their drinking behavior. I am not yet convinced that a majority of Papago drinkers bring the same negative judgments about drinking and drunkenness upon their own behavior as do those who look in from the outside. They do not denounce it as an evil in the same sense as our particular moral foundations have apparently done in our culture. In the sense that drinking and drunkenness contribute to the viability of social group relations, no matter how narrowly defined, it is hard to label the resulting behavior as pathological. Meaningful relationships are confirmed by drinking; individuals define their self worth by drinking; they communicate the desire for trust in each other by sharing drinks; and they even seem to enjoy being happily drunk with friends. If they are distressed by certain outcomes of their drinking behavior, it is not because of the drinking or the drink but because of other causes external to themselves. Hence, drink and drinking do not have the same negative connotations and are not likely to produce guilt as we think of it.

Lest it be construed that I support a status quo disregard for the problem, I would like to stress that there is a social problem involved that does call for resolution. What should be considered are Papago cultural definitions of what is appropriate drinking behavior and what is not. *O'odham himdag* must have something to say about the misuse of drink and improper behavior but I do not think Papago *himdag* has ever been seriously considered by rehabilitative programs. There are probably several Papago models, only a few of which have been presented here. The usual model of rehabilitation guiding our cultural orientation is a combination of punitive action (incarceration), wise counsel and advice from knowledgeable institutional practitioners, some moral instruction rising out of Christian (frequently Protestant) ethics, some physiological treatment and a dose of AA philosophy, most usually in English. Sometimes these various cognitive and physiological administrations miraculously work independently or together to provide a Papago individual with a new orientation and a new lifestyle. But the significant thing is that seldom if ever are meaningful Papago cognitive considerations or *himdag* taken into account in remedial programs, probably because nobody really knows what these are or else they have judged them as contradictory to workable programs of action. I would like to propose that if Papagos do find meaning in their reciprocities of drink and find a viable social existence in the drinking circuit, there must be something from this situation that could positively be appropriated and worked into culturally meaningful rehabilitative strategies.

REFERENCES CITED

Bahr, D.
    1964   Santa Rosa, Arizona. MS in files of the Bureau of Ethnic Research, University of Arizona, Tucson.
Bahr, D. M., J. Gregorio, D. I. Lopez, and A. Alvarez
    1974   *Piman Shamanism and Staying Sickness (Ká:cim Mumkidag).* Tucson: University of Arizona Press.
Cohen, Y.
    1961   Food and Its Vicissitudes: A Cross-Cultural Study of Sharing and Nonsharing. In *Social Structure and Personality: A Case Book,* Y. Cohen, ed. New York: Holt, Rinehart and Winston.
Devereux, G.
    1969   *Reality and Dream.* New York: Natural History Press.
Dobyns, H.
    1976   *Spanish Colonial Tucson: A Demographic History.* Tucson: The University of Arizona Press.
Fontana, B.
    1960   Assimilative Change: A Papago Case Study. Unpublished Doctoral Dissertation, University of Arizona, Tucson.
Graves, T.
    1971   Drinking and Drunkenness among Urban Indians. In *The American Indian in Urban Society,* J. Waddell and M. Watson, eds. Boston: Little, Brown and Company.

Hallowell, A. I.
  1945   Sociopsychological Aspects of Acculturation. In *The Science of Man in the World Crisis*, R. Linton, ed. New York: Columbia University Press.
  1952   Ojibwa Personality and Acculturation. In *Acculturation in the Americas*, S. Tax, ed. Chicago: University of Chicago Press.
James, B.
  1961   Socio-Psychological Dimensions of Ojibwa Acculturation. *American Anthropologist* **63**:721–46.
Jones, D.
  1962   Human Ecology of the Papago Indians. Unpublished Master's Thesis, University of Arizona, Tucson.
Jorgensen, J.
  1971   Indians and the Metropolis. In *The American Indian in Urban Society*, J. Waddell and M. Watson, eds. Boston: Little, Brown and Company.
Joseph, A., R. Spicer, and J. Chesky
  1949   *The Desert People: A Study of the Papago Indians of Southern Arizona*. Chicago: University of Chicago Press.
Kelly, W.
  1963   *The Papago Indians of Arizona: A Population and Economic Study*. Tucson: Bureau of Ethnic Research, University of Arizona.
Kessel, N. and H. Walton
  1965   *Alcoholism*. Baltimore: Penguin Books.
Levy, J. E. and S. J. Kunitz
  1971   Indian Reservations, Anomie, and Social Pathologies. *Southwestern Journal of Anthropology* **27**:97–128.
McCarthey, R. G. (editor)
  1964   *Alcohol Education for Classroom and Community*. New York: McGraw-Hill.
Mark, A.
  1960   Description of and Variables Relating to Ecological Change in the History of the Papago Indian Population. Unpublished Master's Thesis, University of Arizona.
Plant, T.
  1967   Alcohol Problems: *A Report to the Nation by the Cooperative Commission on the Study of Alcoholism*. New York: Oxford.
Roueche, B.
  1960   *Alcohol: Its History, Folklore, and Effect on the Human Body*. New York: Grove Press.
Spicer, E.
  1962   *Cycles of Conquest: The Impact of Spain, Mexico, and the United States on the Indians of the Southwest, 1533–1960*. Tucson: University of Arizona Press.
Spradley, J.
  1970   *You Owe Yourself a Drunk: An Ethnography of Urban Nomads*. Boston: Little, Brown and Co.

82   *Contemporary Drinking Patterns*

Tooker, E.
    1952   Papagos in Tucson: An Introduction to Their History, Community
            Life, and Acculturation. Unpublished Master's Thesis, University
            of Arizona.
Turner, V.
    1969   Forms of Symbolic Action: Introduction. In Forms of Symbolic
            Action. *Proceedings of the American Ethnological Society,* R.
            Spencer, ed. Seattle: University of Washington Press.
Underhill, R.
    1939   *Social Organization of the Papago Indians.* New York: Columbia
            University Press.
    1946   *Papago Indian Religion.* New York: Columbia University Press.
Vogt, E.
    1961   Navaho. In *Perspectives on American Indian Culture Change,* E.
            H. Spicer, ed. Chicago: University of Chicago Press.
Waddell, J.
    1969   *Papago Indians at Work.* Tucson: University of Arizona Press.
    1975   For Individual Power and Social Credit: The Use of Alcohol
            Among Tucson Papagos. *Human Organization* **34**:9–15.
    1976   The Place of the Cactus Wine Ritual in the Papago Indian Ecosys-
            tem. In *Realm of the Extra Human: Ideas and Actions,* A. Bharati,
            ed. The Hague: Mouton.
    1979   Alcoholic Intoxication as a Component of the Papago System of
            Experiential Reality. *Journal of Ultimate Reality and Meaning* **2**,
            no. 1:4–15, 69–73.
Wallace, A. F. C.
    1966   *Religion: An Anthropological View.* New York: Random House.
Williams, T.
    1956   Socialization in a Papago Indian Village. Unpublished Doctoral
            Dissertation, Syracuse University.
Wiseman, J.
    1970   *Stations of the Lost.* Englewood Cliffs: Prentice-Hall.

3

Drinking as an Indicator of Community Disharmony: The People of Taos Pueblo

Donald N. Brown

Heavy drinking has become a major concern among many groups of North American Indians. The Pueblo Indians, however, are often mentioned as having the least such problem because of the nature of their social structure and the relative stability of their culture since contact with Europeans (Dozier 1966:80). Statistics on criminal activity among the Pueblos, however, indicate that alcohol use is a major problem (Stewart 1964:63), and comments by leaders from various pueblos indicate their concern about it (Smith 1966).

This study deals with alcohol use at Taos Pueblo, the northern-most Rio Grande Indian Pueblo.[1] Taos Pueblo is located sixty-five miles

Donald N. Brown, Associate Professor of Anthropology, joined the faculty at Oklahoma State University, Stillwater in 1971. He is involved in research on contemporary Native American communities and federal programs as they influence those communities. Developing training programs for staff members of tribal programs occupies a considerable portion of his activity.

[1]Field research on alcohol use at Taos Pueblo was initiated during the summer of 1962 with a grant from the National Institute of Mental Health administered by the University of Kansas. Further field research was conducted in 1964, 1967, and 1968 under the sponsorship of the Comins Fund of the University of Arizona, the Doris Duke Fund of the University of Arizona, and the University Research Council of Vanderbilt University. The cooperation of several officers of Taos Pueblo, local law enforcement officials, and the assistance of many interested residents of the pueblo made the research possible.

north of Santa Fe and three miles from the Spanish-Anglo community of Don Fernandez de Taos (see Figure 3.1). Although Taos is probably the best-known Indian community in the southwest as far as tourists are concerned, it is one of the least known through anthropological investigation. The traditional kiva organization remains active, and the Taos dialect of the Tiwa language is still spoken in the homes. Electric lights and running water are still banned by the Pueblo Council from the large house blocks which form the traditional Pueblo. The population growth of Taos Pueblo during the last century has been phenomenal. In 1864 the population was 361; in 1968 the enrolled population was 1470, a 400% increase.

THE HISTORY OF THE PROBLEM

Apparently there were no alcoholic beverages available to the Indians at Taos Pueblo before the arrival of Europeans. There is no evidence among the prehistoric Rio Grande Pueblos of any form of fermented beverage, such as the corn-based beverage found among the Tarahumara in northern Mexico (Bennett and Zingg 1935:54–7) or the cactus-based beverage of the Papago living in southern Arizona (Underhill 1946:41–67).

With the arrival of the Spanish in the 16th century and the settlement of New Mexico during the following two centuries, wine and brandy, or *aguardiente,* were introduced into the area. Among the Pueblos wine was used in the service of the church, with about 10 liters listed as needed at the Taos Mission in 1776 (Adams and Chavez 1956:109). The only Indian Pueblo mentioned as manufacturing wine in the 18th century was Isleta, some 130 miles southwest of Taos (Adams and Chavez 1956:207). *Aguardiente* was produced in many of the Spanish settlements of New Mexico. There is a strong possibility that *aguardiente* was traded at the annual Taos fairs during the late 18th century, since the trade of this beverage was widely practiced, even officially encouraged, among the Comanche and Apache Indians who traded at these fairs (Worcester 1951:46–7, 72).

With the arrival of Anglo-Americans in northern New Mexico during the early decades of the 19th century, a new form of alcohol was introduced—whiskey. The first whiskey distillery in New Mexico was established in the winter of 1824–1825 by four Anglo-Americans in a canyon near Taos (Gregg 1954:262, 636–7). By the middle of the 19th century "Taos Whiskey" or "Taos Lightning" was becoming a well-known beverage among western travelers, and was widely used in the Indian trade (Garrard 1938:246).

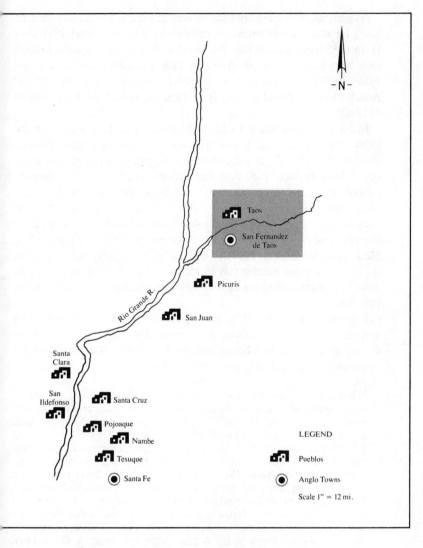

Figure 3.1   Map of present-day northern Rio Grande Pueblos of New Mexico, including Taos and San Fernandez de Taos

As early as 1850 there are indications that the Pueblo Indians north of Santa Fe were having problems with heavy drinking (Abel 1915:154–5). In 1852 Indians from Taos Pueblo as well as visiting Apache Indians were mentioned as being drunk in Don Fernandez de Taos (Abel 1916:230, 231). Again in 1881 reference is made to both Pueblo and Apache Indians drinking heavily in Don Fernandez de Taos (Bloom 1937:43).

In the published report of her field research at Taos Pueblo in the 1920s Parsons mentions heavy drinking by a few Taos men (Parsons 1936:48, 50, 72, 92). She also contrasts the future of peyote and whiskey at Taos Pueblo: "And then there is whiskey; that will win out over peyote, from present indications, for those who want both Americanization and stimulation" (Parsons 1936:120). According to both Taos Indian informants and Anglo-American residents of the area, up to the 1930s heavy drinking was not a serious problem at Taos Pueblo. Men drank, and drank heavily, but not as frequently, not as publicly, nor in as great numbers as in recent years. In 1934, according to Taos informants, drinking at a ceremonial became a problem for the first time.

Following World War II the problem of heavy drinking became more serious. Men returning from military service began to drink more freely, and a few women began to drink. One Anglo-American resident noted the increase in heavy drinking as follows:

> When we first came here about 30 years ago there wasn't any drinking to speak of among the Indians. Sure, J got drunk and was known as the Pueblo drunk, but the Council took care of him. They just took his pay checks away so he couldn't buy any. We were just amazed when we returned in 1945. We were out at the Christmas Eve celebration and there were several men drunk. They were using real ammunition in their guns. We were afraid. A lot of these young men were returning from the Army, but not all the soldiers had returned. Nowadays I am always finding drunks staggering into the courtyard here or under the lilac bushes. The bad thing now is that the young women are also drinking and getting drunk. And drinkers seem to be getting younger every year. A few years ago none of the women drank.

An Indian point of view of the recent history of heavy drinking was expressed by an older Taos man when asked, "How many people drank when you were a young man, say in 1920?"

> It was not too bad in those days. Just the older men drank, not the young people. The old men who drank liquors in the old days said

they drank only good liquor, not the cheap stuff like today. The worst thing about this is that back in 1934, we didn't know anything about liquor at religious activities. We heard that some people may have had some. One man brought some to Blue Lake that year. After the Second World War, it got much worse because it was then that young men started. They would hurt each other when they drank. In the army they were free to drink and when they came back home they said that since they had been helping Uncle Sam, they could drink all they wanted. They would go for a night in town, boys and girls, too. They learned to drink from each other; they didn't learn this in the pueblo. They learned in town. Indians didn't make liquor, just the white man. But now, even the small kids try to take to drinking. When Eisenhower passed the rule that Indians could go into a bar,[2] Taos Indian councilmen didn't approve of what he did. They called a meeting and decided that our pueblo didn't want any liquors on Indian land. This rule was posted on the wall, saying that liquors could not be brought into the village. But since Eisenhower opened it up, it has just gotten worse. Soon women also began to take it. Before that just one woman was known as a heavy drinker.

With the repeal in 1953 of the federal law prohibiting the sale of alcoholic beverages to Indians, public drinking became more common among both men and women. At a meeting held in 1953, following the repeal of the prohibition law, the Taos Pueblo Council ruled that no alcoholic beverages were to be brought onto pueblo land. Most Taos Indians feel that since 1953 heavy drinking has become an even more serious problem. Whether or not the percentage of problem drinkers has increased since 1953, they believe public drunkenness has increased.

THE RELATION OF HEAVY DRINKING
TO CRIMINAL ACTIVITY

Taos County arrest records[3] of Indians from Taos Pueblo, covering a period from January 1957 to August 1965, reveal that 1365 arrests or 90% of the total arrests of Taos Indians were for drunkenness. This is about twice the 1963 percentage for total arrests of whites for liquor-law violations, driving while intoxicated, and drunkenness (Hoover 1965:111). It is also about 20% higher than the national average for all

---

[2]The reference to Eisenhower concerns the signing of Public Law 277 (67 *Stat.* 586) in 1953 which repealed prohibition on the sale of alcoholic beverages to Indians.

[3]The Sheriff of Taos County and his staff assisted in the collection of available arrest records from their own office, the New Mexico State Police, and the Town of Taos Police.

Indians in the United States (Hoover 1965:111). These arrests involved
158 individuals, of whom 49 were arrested only once. Four women are
included in the 158: two of them were arrested once and the other two
were each arrested twice. Twenty individuals, each with 20 or more
arrests, account for 54% of the total arrests for drunkenness. These 20
frequent offenders range in age from 31 to 67 years, with the average
age being 47.5 years. Ten of these individuals accumulated a total of
496 arrests, or 36% of the total. The two most frequent offenders were
arrested a total of 153 times, or 11% of the total arrests for drunkenness.

The total number of arrests per year for drunkenness for the eight
years beginning in 1957 ranges from 67 arrests in 1958 to 317 arrests in
1963. The number of offenders ranges from 42 in 1958 to 86 in 1963.
There is a tendency for both the total number of arrests and the number
of individuals involved to increase through time. The number of arrests
per individual with more than one arrest also appears to be increasing.
In 1957 the average number of arrests per multiple offender was 3.48;
this dropped to 2.71 in 1960, but rose again to a high of 5.28 in 1963.
Residents of Taos Pueblo believe there is a correlation between available money and number of arrests. They account for the increase in
1963 by referring to an increase in income that year, primarily from
forest-fire fighting activities by the Taos Pueblo fire-fighting team and
community projects, which paid an hourly wage.

A seasonal pattern also appears within the arrest records. The lowest
number of arrests for drunkenness occurs in the months of January and
August, the highest number in April and October, with July and December also peak periods. This fluctuation may be related to ceremonial
activity within the pueblo. The annual "quiet period" in which all
forms of activity are subdued occurs in December and January and
preparations for the annual Blue Lake retreat late in August begin early
in the month.

Criminal activity other than drunkenness is also related to alcohol
use. According to law enforcement officials, Taos Indians involved in
such activities as thefts or fighting are invariably "under the influence
of alcohol," although this may not appear on official records.

THE RELATION OF HEAVY DRINKING
TO HEALTH PROBLEMS

To determine the relation of heavy drinking to health problems at Taos
Pueblo, the files of the Taos Indian Health Center were reviewed during
the summer of 1962. These files contained medical histories for the

period from 1957 to 1962.[4] There were 168 entries for 79 individuals which related directly to heavy drinking by the patient. Eight of these 79 individuals were women. These entries include: numerous lacerations, contusions, and fractures resulting from falls, fights, and automobile accidents while drinking; one case of seizure following an episode of heavy drinking; one case of cirrhosis; eight cases of delirium tremens; one case of acute alcoholic poisoning resulting in death; three attempted suicides following drinking episodes; and two suicides following drinking episodes.

As well as the 79 individuals whose entries indicate they are heavy drinkers, 15 other individuals, all women, appear in the clinic files with problems related to the heavy drinking of a relative. These entries include: four assaults by husbands on wives; one assault by a brother; three attempted suicides following arguments with husbands who had been drinking; and numerous anxiety reactions resulting from arguments with intoxicated husbands or worry related to their husbands' heavy drinking. A total of 94 individuals, then, may be considered to have some form of medical problem related to the problem of heavy drinking within the pueblo.

THE EXTENT OF HEAVY DRINKING WITHIN THE ENTIRE POPULATION

In an attempt to determine the extent to which the problem of heavy drinking is socially recognized within Taos Pueblo, a census listing all adult residents of Taos Pueblo was reviewed in 1962 with a married couple at Taos Pueblo. Both informants were middle-aged and had lived in the Pueblo their entire lives. The man had served in various official positions within the civil government, including the office of sheriff. Of the 698 individuals over 16 years of age listed on the census, these informants were able to identify 340. The difficulty in identification resulted from the use of Spanish-Anglo names on the census, while traditional Tiwa names are still used within the pueblo. When several individuals with similar or the same Spanish-Anglo name appeared, the informants found it almost impossible to identify the individuals. From the individuals identified, 25 women, or 21% of those identified, and 159 men, or 72% of those identified, were considered to be drinkers.

---

[4]The staff of the Taos Indian Health Center assisted in the review of the medical records maintained within their facility.

Combining the arrest records (1957–1965), the clinic files (1957–1962), and census information (1962), 229 men and 31 women can be identified as drinkers. Each of these individuals was scored on the basis of number of arrests, number of clinic entries, and recognition by others as a heavy drinker. Each arrest and each clinic entry was counted as one point. Identification as a drinker on the census review also counted as one point. Arbitrarily, individuals with three points or more were classified as problem drinkers. Those with nine points or more were considered to have an acute drinking problem. On this basis, of the 229 men identified as drinkers, 103 or 45% may be considered to have problems with heavy drinking. Of these problem drinkers 57 appear to have acute drinking problems. The problem drinkers range in age from 20 to 72. Those having an acute problem are primarily within the 40 to 69 age group. This age group forms 54% of the adult male population at Taos, but includes 77% of those having acute problems. The focus of the problem appears to lie with the 40 to 49 age group which forms only 15% of the population, but includes 40% of the drinkers with acute problems. The problem drinkers are about equally divided between married and unmarried men.

Only six of the 31 women listed as drinkers appear to have problems from heavy drinking. This is only 2.1% of the adult female population of Taos. These six women range in age from 41 to 55 years, the average age being 48 years.[5]

INDIVIDUAL DRINKING BEHAVIORS

The spectrum of drinking behaviors from non-drinkers to acute heavy drinkers is indicated in the following brief case studies of six Taos men.

Number 1. A is about seventy years old, is married, and has several children and many grandchildren. He is well known within the pueblo and outside the village. He has traveled to many parts of the United States, appeared in several movies, and his photograph has been published in national magazines. In spite of his contact with the outside

---

[5]This contradicts the observation made by Siegel in the 1950s: "In regard to the net role satisfaction of women it is instructive to note that no reports of drinking among women have been brought to the attention of any outside observer at Taos Pueblo" (Siegel and Beals 1960:416). Data collected for this study indicate that several women have long histories of heavy drinking. The full extent of drinking among women at Taos Pueblo is probably impossible to determine at this time because of the general attitude that the "good" woman does not drink.

world, A has remained very conservative in his attitude toward the pueblo—continuing to take an active part in both the pueblo government and the traditional religious activities. He also participates in peyote meetings at Taos.

Today he is a nondrinker. The reason he gives for his total abstinence is a promise that he made to his mother. As a young man he and another young man were drinking. He doesn't remember coming home one night, but when he awoke the next morning he found himself in his own house. He asked his mother if he had been drunk. She answered, "yes," and asked him to stop drinking. "I still remember saying to my mother, 'I promise, Mother.'" He is proud today that he doesn't drink and believes that he has raised his family not to drink. He doesn't condemn drinking as such, only the behavior and problems that result from heavy drinking. His explanation for the effect of alcohol on the human body follows:

When a drinking man takes liquor, the alcohol goes to the brain. Like anything you eat, alcohol goes all over the body. The brain gets the alcohol and people change in the way they think. The brain is the only place we do our thinking; everything we understand in the brain. Alcohol also goes through the belly. First, you taste it in the throat, then it goes to the stomach, then it goes all over the body and makes a person weak. Some take just enough alcohol to understand better but if they take too much they cannot understand. Alcohol affects eyesight so a person cannot see. That's why people drive off the road when they have had too much.

Number 2. B is about the same age as A, is married, and has one daughter who is now married. He is also well known in the pueblo and has traveled throughout the United States. He continues to be active in ceremonial activities, and is said to be the only individual who knows some of the ceremonial songs. He has been employed for several years by the Indian Health Service.

Today he is a nondrinker, having stopped several years ago. "I didn't get anything out of it. It didn't make me feel good or anything. I would just come home and lay down." He believes that he lost many friends when he stopped drinking. "They used to come around all the time, but now no one comes around." Another reason he gives for not drinking is the possibility of losing his government employment if he continued to drink. He especially resents those men who receive welfare yet continue to drink. "They should buy things they need—food, and clothing, and all."

Number 3. C was born in 1905, is married, and has a married daughter and three grandchildren. As a young man he traveled widely and received more education than most adults at Taos Pueblo. He has been active with the Pueblo Boy Scout troop, the 4-H club, and was an instructor in the BIA (Bureau of Indian Affairs) day school. He has a summer home high on the side of Taos Mountain, about six miles from the pueblo. During the summer months, he, his wife, and his daughter's family spend most of their time at this "ranch," planting and irrigating some 15 acres of alfalfa and caring for about a dozen horses. By Taos Pueblo standards he is a wealthy man.

He might be classified as a social drinker in the usual Anglo-American sense of the term. He and his wife like to attend Anglo-sponsored dances in Don Fernandez de Taos where he frequently buys drinks for his Anglo friends. He is able to consume large quantities of alcohol without noticeable alteration of his behavior. The best summary of his drinking behavior is a statement made by another Taos man about C: "He takes a drink; never gets into trouble."

Number 4. D was born in the 1930s, is married, and has three young daughters. He has found it difficult to find steady employment in the Taos area and is out of work much of the time. He is rarely involved in ceremonial activities. Recently he spent two summers working in Colorado.

At the pueblo he is frequently involved in heavy drinking episodes. While drunk he has been involved in several fights with "Mexicans" in which he has suffered a broken nose and numerous cuts. His father and brothers are also heavy drinkers. While he was working in Colorado, his employer reports, D "gave him no trouble" during both summers he was employed and apparently drank little if at all. On his return to Taos for the winter months D resumed his heavy drinking—drinking for several days then stopping for several days. His wife, who does not drink, reports that on a number of occasions he would be gone several days without providing wood or money for food for his family. On his return he would be abusive to his wife. Now when he is on a drinking spree, his wife usually takes the children to her parents' home and remains there until he returns.

Number 5. E was born in the 1920s, is married, and has four children. He and his wife both work when employment is available. Recently they both were employed in Don Fernandez de Taos where he maintained a large yard and his wife worked in housecleaning. At other times his wife has been employed by Anglos in Don Fernandez de Taos at a small factory. E's wife has found employment easier in the Taos area than he has. On numerous occasions he has had the responsibility of caring for their children at the pueblo while his wife is employed in Don Fernandez de Taos. E has been ill several times with "liver trouble" for rather lengthy periods of time, being hospitalized in the 1960s for chronic pancreatitis. He rarely participates in ceremonials and wears his hair cut short.

Both he and his wife drink and occasionally are found together in bars in Don Fernandez de Taos. On several occasions he has been injured when drunk from fighting with "Mexicans." When drinking he may also fight with his wife and father-in-law. The following was stated by one of E's relatives:

> When he is drinking and doesn't give her any, she gets mad and starts to fight. When he comes home drunk, she and her father start fighting with him and arguing with him. Then they go to the officers and tell them he started it.

On one occasion when he had been drinking he received a scalp laceration when hit on the head with a cane by his father-in-law. According to the physician at the Health Center, his "liver trouble" may be largely related to his heavy drinking.

Number 6. F was born in the 1920s and never married. He lived with his elderly parents and during the summer months did some farming for them. He cut his hair and dressed entirely in the Anglo fashion. He occasionally participated as a singer in the non-ceremonial dances, such as the 4th of July war dances. F had several brothers, three of whom "get mean when they drink."

A neighbor of F described him as follows:

> He is always drunk, and when he is drunk he fights with all of his family. His brothers seem to be good, but he sure drinks a lot. He even fights with his mother. I don't think he is much of a worker. He doesn't even know how to drive a wagon. He is always drunk. I don't remember seeing him when he wasn't drunk.

His maternal uncle tells of being called to stop fighting between F and his family on several occasions, but once was asked not to harm any of the boys. "Since then I don't pay any attention when they come and ask for help."

In the summer of 1965 F was found dead in an alley in Don Fernandez de Taos. Apparently he had fallen while intoxicated and hit his head.

PATTERNS OF HEAVY DRINKING

There is no single pattern of heavy drinking at Taos Pueblo, but several patterns that appear to be based on the degree to which the individual has been influenced by the Anglo-American culture, the sex and age of the individual, and the setting in which the individual finds himself.

Two "traditional" patterns might be termed social heavy drinking and drinking with "drinking partners." The historical references suggest that the early heavy drinking took place at social gatherings in which both Taos and Apache men participated. Today social heavy drinking occurs on picnics, at family celebrations such as marriages, and on feast days. Drinking in this pattern usually continues until everyone is intoxicated or the supply of alcohol is exhausted. Most of the women drinkers follow this pattern, and it appears to be most characteristic of the older age groups of men.

The second "traditional" pattern is that of "drinking partners" or "drinking friends" (*chu' puyena* in the Taos language) in which two or three men will be identified as drinking together frequently. Drinking in this pattern may occur at any time and frequently lasts for several days at a time. After a period of time which may last several days or weeks during which they refrain from heavy drinking, another episode of extended heavy drinking can be expected. This pattern is most characteristic of the middle-aged and younger men.

The third pattern is individual heavy drinking. This pattern is relatively rare at Taos and the individuals who participate in this pattern may be considered as cultural deviants. It usually occurs among middle-aged men who have been strongly influenced by Anglo-American culture. A few women also participate within this pattern. These individuals tend to drink away from the pueblo, and when intoxicated may approach tourists and other strangers on the streets of Don Fernandez de Taos and attempt to carry on a conversation. Such conversations usually include descriptions of military service or other experiences with the Anglo-American world and end with comments about their difficulties within the pueblo. "The old men just don't understand our problems" is a statement frequently made. It appears that these individuals are attempting to identify with the Anglo-American world when they are intoxicated, yet they are unable to break away from the pueblo world.

A fourth pattern, Anglo social drinking, should also be mentioned. This occurs at Anglo-American sponsored events that include Indian guests. On such occasions, when alcoholic beverages are provided, heavy drinking may occur. Several individuals, both men and women, were mentioned during the census review as seen drinking only at such parties and nowhere else.

A characteristic common to all patterns is the ability of the heavy drinker to abstain from drinking when he is needed at the pueblo for ceremonial participation or has strong family responsibilities. Another common characteristic is the choice of alcoholic beverage. Sweet wines and beer are used heavily, while distilled beverages are rarely used. According to Taos informants, this choice is a matter of both personal preference and economics. They like the taste of the sweet wines and beer, and distilled beverages just cost too much.

The Taos terminology related to drinking reflects the relatively recent introduction of heavy drinking as an activity. The Taos term for a heavy drinker is *chuna* ("drinker") from the verb stem *chu* ("to drink"). The same verb would be used to refer to drinking any liquid. Two Taos words refer to both whiskey and wine. The compound *po chapu* ("water bad") is said to be "used by the old people" while *chu po* ("drinker's water") is a more recent form. Beer, which "came in lately," is generally referred to by the English loanword.

EXPLANATIONS FOR HEAVY DRINKING

Residents of Taos Pueblo suggest four explanations for the extent of heavy drinking that occurs outside the traditional context of social heavy drinking. These four explanations are: boredom, marital troubles, "something in the wine," and genetic intolerance.

Boredom is the explanation most frequently given for heavy drinking among young men. A middle-aged Taos man expressed this idea as follows:

A young man comes home and can't find work. There just isn't any work around here for him to do. He just sits around his house doing nothing. A friend comes by and says, "Let's get a drink. I have some money. I'll buy." So off they go and get drunk. He's just bored sitting around doing nothing, so he starts drinking.

A second explanation relates heavy drinking to marital troubles at the pueblo. One young married Taos man responded as follows to the question, "Why does a man drink?"

A man may drink when he is not in control of his family, for instance, when the woman is older than the husband. A man needs to be older to feel superior. P is an example. His wife is older and is always telling him what to do. M is another example. They both drink a lot.

A third explanation is "something in the wine." The following remarks were made by a Taos woman concerning her husband:

> He sometimes gets real drunk. He gets real mean. Sometimes he drinks for a week or so. When he gets started, he just can't stop. I think there is something in the wine which makes a man keep on drinking, something like dope that makes a man just keep on drinking once he takes just a little bit.

An elderly Taos man suggested a similar cause:

> The wine is doped up more with chemicals. They are turning people into winos. The wine gets in the system and they can't give it up. They are out of commission mentally. It's the kind of wine that they get on the market.

The fourth explanation, which might be termed "genetic intolerance," appears to have originated within the Anglo community and is now occasionally used by residents of Taos Pueblo. A long-time Anglo resident of Don Fernandez de Taos commented:

> I think there is something about the Indians, something in their genes or blood that makes them more sensitive to alcohol. Even the Indians that are invited to parties can't seem to drink. White people may get drunk or sick when they first drink, but they build themselves up to the point of immunity—or they know how much they can hold. Indians seem to get drunk on very little. They may buy a pint of wine and get as high as a kite. Or even a couple cans of beer gets them high. T (a middle-aged Taos man) used to drink some when he was invited to parties. After one drink he was talking like mad. Two drinks and he was drunk. Now he knows he can't drink, so he just holds a glass when he is at a party.

Taos Pueblo residents often express this idea as: "Indian people just can't drink like white people."

ATTEMPTS TO CONTROL HEAVY DRINKING

The older residents of Taos Pueblo believe that as well as an increase in the number of participants in heavy drinking during the last twenty years there has been a significant change in behaviors related with heavy drinking. An elderly Taos woman described her brother's drinking behavior during the 1920s as an example of the earlier behavior associated with heavy drinking.

My oldest brother was a heavy drinker. He would bring bottles home. We never touched those bottles. My other brothers didn't touch them either. He was never mean; he was always quiet when he drank.

Number 3 described above was referred to by several Taos residents as drinking in the earlier pattern. "He takes a drink; never gets into trouble."

In recent years problems related to heavy drinking have become more obvious to Pueblo residents. Fighting among family members, misuse of family resources, and injuries resulting from beating while drunk or automobile accidents are now frequent events. An example of fighting within the family concerns a middle-aged Taos man who has been a heavy drinker for a number of years, as an informant recounted:

One day when he was drunk he fought with his wife. He chased her in the corn field and hit her. He sat on her and hit her with his fists. She yelled for help. He was sitting on her and hitting her right in the middle of the corn field. A man heard her yelling and told the officers and they stopped him. Another time he beat up his mother-in-law. She is a big woman, but he sat on her and hit her. He was drunk and had been fighting with his wife, and her mother came to help her. They rolled around on the floor, and he sat on her and hit her. His wife had gone to her mother-in-law for help. That woman isn't much good. She wouldn't help. His mother-in-law was yelling for help, and he even yelled for somebody to come help her. It sure was funny, him yelling for someone to help her.

Behavior such as that described above is referred to as *koyohana* ("not knowing") or "acting crazy" in English.

Misuse of family resources has become a serious problem for several families in which the husband is a heavy drinker. One young Taos woman reported that her husband drank frequently and was abusive to her and their children when he was drunk. Part of the money for drinking came directly from their "assistance check" and part he obtained by purchasing such things as cigarettes on the family's credit bill at the store and then reselling them. She had threatened "to leave him if he didn't stop drinking," but he continued to drink.

In recent years a number of residents of Taos Pueblo have been seriously injured, or killed, from beatings received while they were drunk. Most of these beatings are reported to have been carried out by "Mexicans," yet several young Taos men have also been involved in beating and robbing men who were drunk. Several individuals, including teenagers, have died from injuries received in automobile accidents following heavy drinking.

In response to the many problems related to heavy drinking following the repeal of the federal law prohibiting the sale of alcoholic beverages to Indians, the Taos Pueblo Council attempted to control the use of alcohol within the pueblo by passing a resolution prohibiting possession or the use of alcoholic beverages on pueblo land. Individuals who have alcoholic beverages in their possession, who are found to be drinking on pueblo land, or who are reported to the council as drunk can be arrested, confined in the pueblo jail, and fined. With alcohol readily available only three miles away in Don Fernandez de Taos prohibition has become almost impossible to enforce. The failure of the council's resolution is noted in the remarks of a former pueblo sheriff.

> We put the drunks into the jail here at the pueblo. After a day or two they are brought before several council members who lecture them about drinking. The drunks usually say that they will not get drunk again, but I know they will be back in jail in three or four days. Those liars.

As well as the ready availability of alcohol, the council's resolution has failed because a number of the councilmen also participate in heavy drinking. A baseball game between the Taos Pueblo team and a visiting team from San Juan Pueblo was disrupted repeatedly by a councilman who was finally led away from the playing field. He called "bad things" at the Taos team and ran onto the field. After the game one of the Taos players commented:

> He wasn't drunk, but he had been drinking. They all say he used to be a good pitcher when he was a young man. We all respect him. He's a member of the council. The War Chief said after the game that we have a right to make anyone leave who interferes with the game. After the game was over my dad went over and punched him in the mouth.

Another Taos resident recalled talking with a councilman who was drunk.

> I said that he should be in the council meeting. I told him he was an officer and shouldn't be drinking, and he said, "Why should I worry. Men higher than me are drinking."

The attitude of the pueblo governor, who is elected annually by the council, toward heavy drinking apparently influences the amount of heavy drinking among the men. One pueblo resident noted:

> There seems to be less drinking this year than for the last three or four years. This governor is hard on the drinkers.

CONCLUSION AND GUIDELINES

In recent years heavy drinking at Taos Pueblo has created a dilemma within the Taos cultural system. Drinking by either women or children generally is considered "not good," while drinking by men is a culturally acceptable behavior. Heavy drinking by men, however, frequently leads to unacceptable behaviors. The Taos cultural system emphasizes cooperation within the community, respect for elders, and maintenance of harmony with others and the universe. Behaviors contradictory to these basic Taos values are associated with heavy drinking. Men become uncooperative and aggressive. They speak in a disrespectful manner to their elders. They create disharmony within their households and within the community. The dilemma is seen even within the Taos Pueblo Council, the heart of the community. Although the council has prohibited alcohol use at the pueblo in order to prevent these unacceptable behaviors, a number of councilmen continue to participate in heavy drinking activities.

Rather than consistently enforcing prohibition through the officers of the pueblo, the council has relied on outside law enforcement officers to control heavy drinking. Even within the pueblo, arrests for drunkenness are usually made by Bureau of Indian Affairs officers rather than the pueblo sheriff. This reliance on outside institutions reflects two attitudes held by many residents of the pueblo. The council should maintain harmony within the pueblo, and arrests by pueblo officers could lead to disharmony among the residents. It is believed that arrests by outside officers will not create this problem. The second attitude is that heavy drinking is related directly to the "white world." This attitude was expressed by a councilman as follows: "It was the white man that brought liquor here, not the other way around." Since the non-Indian introduced the problem, he is held responsible for its solution.

Since the mid-1950s heavy drinking is causing more serious problems at Taos Pueblo. An increasing number of women and children are participating in heavy drinking, and more men appear to be having problems related to drinking. Heavy drinking is no longer a concern of a few families only, but is now recognized as a problem facing the entire community. The pueblo cannot rely on the outside world for a solution. It must seek a solution within the pueblo.

Based on this analysis of drinking patterns and attitudes toward heavy drinking at Taos Pueblo, a set of guidelines can be developed for a program aimed at controlling heavy drinking by residents of Taos Pueblo and treating individuals who have developed problems as the result of heavy drinking.

A. Controlling heavy drinking:

1. Any program for controlling heavy drinking must be developed within the community and directed by individuals who are aware of the Taos drinking patterns. Outside resources, such as funding and specialists, may be needed, but direction for such a program must come from within the pueblo and have the support of the residents of the pueblo.

2. Generally speaking, prohibition is an inadequate approach to the control of alcohol at Taos Pueblo because of the location of the community. Prohibition may be possible at specific events, such as ceremonials, but the availability of alcoholic beverages in the surrounding communities precludes prohibition as an adequate solution.

3. Attempts must be made to provide alternatives to heavy drinking for the residents of the pueblo. The introduction of the Peyote religion in the early decades of the 20th century provided an alternative for a number of young men at that time. In recent years some participants in the Peyote activities have also participated in heavy drinking. More recently the Baptist Indian Mission provided an alternative for a few residents of the pueblo. Led by a former heavy drinker from a Tewa Pueblo, this church takes an active stand against heavy drinking and provides reinforcement against heavy drinking for its membership. A third alternative has been ceremonialism within the Pueblo. Men who are recognized as heavy drinkers within the pueblo are able to stop their drinking while participating in ceremonial activities. A final alternative is the development of economic activities within the area in which residents of the pueblo can participate. This would relieve the boredom which is frequently cited as the primary cause for heavy drinking among the young men of the pueblo.

4. The pueblo rules against public drunkenness and disorder must be consistently enforced within the pueblo by pueblo officers. Governors who are "hard" on drinkers do appear to influence the amount of heavy drinking at the pueblo.

5. The members of the Taos Pueblo Council and other leaders of the community must recognize their responsibility and influence as models for enculturating the young within the pueblo. The attitude "Men higher than me are drinking" perpetuates heavy drinking and encourages the younger residents to actively participate. These influential individuals must be involved in any program within the pueblo if it is to be successful.

B. Treatment of problem drinkers:

1. The unit of treatment may be a group, the drinking partners, rather than an individual. The approach of Alcoholics Anonymous has generally failed for residents of Taos Pueblo since individual heavy drinking is rare. For most residents heavy drinking is a social event, and the individual who refuses to participate in heavy drinking is likely to lose the friendship of all other participants.

2. Heavy drinking must be recognized as an "environmental problem" at Taos Pueblo. Several residents of the pueblo have received treatment at Turquoise Lodge, the state alcoholic treatment center. Upon returning to the pueblo, most of these individuals have renewed their heavy drinking. Several young men who frequently participate in heavy drinking at the pueblo refrain from all drinking when working away from the pueblo. Any program for treating the heavy drinker must recognize this "environmental problem," since the treated individual will probably return to this same environment.

3. As an educational process, the program of treatment should focus on the unacceptable behaviors associated with heavy drinking rather than on physiological effects of alcohol. Alcohol is not considered to be "bad" or "evil" by most residents of the pueblo, and drinking by adult men is culturally acceptable behavior. Heavy drinking, however, can lead to unacceptable behaviors. Individuals should learn to control their heavy drinking in order to better control their own behavior, thus lessening the occurrence of "not knowing" behaviors.

4. A successful program for controlling heavy drinking will assist in the treatment of problem drinkers. This is related to the "environmental" aspect of heavy drinking at Taos Pueblo. Without a more adequate program for control, treatment for most problem drinkers will be unsuccessful.

REFERENCES CITED

Abel, A. H.
  1915   *The Official Correspondence of James S. Calhoun.* Washington: Government Printing Office.
  1916   The Journal of John Greiner. *Old Santa Fe* **3**:189–243.
Adams, E. B. and Fr. A. Chavez
  1956   *The Missions of New Mexico, 1776.* Albuquerque: University of New Mexico Press.
Bennett, W. C. and R. M. Zingg
  1935   *The Tarahumara.* Chicago: The University of Chicago Press.
Bloom, L. B.
  1937   Bourke on the Southwest, XI: Chapter XX, at Taos in 1881. *New Mexico Historical Review* **12**:41–7.
Dozier, E. P.
  1966   Problem Drinking Among American Indians: The Role of Sociocultural Deprivation. *Quarterly Journal of Studies on Alcohol* **27**:72–87.
Garrard, L. H.
  1938   *Wah-to-yah and the Taos Trail.* Glendale: Arthur H. Clark Co.
Gregg, J.
  1954   *Commerce of the Prairies.* Norman: University of Oklahoma Press.
Hoover, J. E.
  1965   *Crime in the United States.* Boston: Beacon Press.
Parsons, E. C.
  1936   *Taos Pueblo.* General Series in Anthropology, Number 2. Menasha: George Banta Publishing Co.
Seigel, B. J. and A. R. Beals
  1960   Pervasive Factionalism. *American Anthropologist* **62**:394–417.
Smith, A. M.
  1966   *New Mexico Indians.* Santa Fe: Museum of New Mexico.
Stewart, O. C.
  1964   Questions Regarding American Indian Criminality. *Human Organization* **23**:61–6.
Underhill, R. M.
  1946   *Papago Indian Religion.* New York: Columbia University Press.
Worcester, D. E.
  1951   *Instructions for Governing the Interior Provinces of New Spain, 1786.* (Bernardo de Galvez): Albuquerque, University of New Mexico Press.

4

Drinking as an Expression of Status: Navajo Male Adolescents[1]

Martin D. Topper

Navajos and whites are both seriously concerned about the economic, social, and medical consequences of heavy drinking on the Navajo Reservation. There are, of course, many other problems that Navajo people face. In many ways the drinking is as much a symptom of these other problems as it is a problem in itself. In this paper adolescent drinking, "problem drinking," and some proposed causes of "Navajo alcoholism" will be discussed. Because many Navajos who drink do not drink like Anglo-Americans, this chapter will also approach some of the theoretical issues that have been raised about the nature of the phenomenon of drinking and its proper ethnographic description.

Martin D. Topper was appointed clinical anthropologist for the Navajo Area Mental Health Program of the U.S. Public Health Service in 1978. He has a Ph.D. in anthropology from Northwestern University and has conducted research on American Indian mental health and family life. His general interests lie in the area of applied anthropology, culture and communication, and psychological anthropology.

[1]The data on Navajo drinking patterns used in this report were collected over a period of two years. The study was conducted both in the western portion of the Navajo Reservation and in several Anglo communities which surround it. The most intensive period of research occurred during the summer of 1969. At that time, a three month investigation into the cultural patterning of Navajo drinking was conducted. When I realized that the investigation covered only the summer patterns of Navajo drinking, I collected further data on drinking patterns while pursuing a different research project from October 1970 to August of 1972, which was supported by both the Doris Duke Foundation and the National Institute of Mental Health. This support allowed a thorough examination of the elicited data by observation and further elicitation.

SETTING: THE RESERVATION

The Navajo Reservation lies within the states of Arizona, New Mexico, and Utah (see Figure 4.1). Kluckhohn and Leighton (1958:49) list the area of the Navajo Reservation as over 18,000,000 acres. This is an area larger than the nation of Hungary. However, the reservation is located on the arid Colorado plateau and much of it receives ten inches of rainfall or less per year. This means that the capacity of the land for agriculture and grazing is quite limited. In addition, the summers are very hot. Daytime temperatures may reach 110° F. and higher. Thus, it takes a long time for the range to recover from the summer's grazing. At times, the range may become so poor that the heavy rains of August cause considerable erosion. Over the years this erosion has taken a heavy toll and the remaining land is badly overgrazed.

DINE': THE PEOPLE

The Navajos call themselves *Dine'*, which means "the People." They are a people who are undergoing rapid cultural change. The past two decades have been decisive. Since 1950, the percentage of Navajo school age children attending school has risen from 40% to more than 95%. At the same time, the total population has grown from 60,000 to over 150,000 (Aberle 1966:369; the *Navajo Times* 1971). Since 1960, paved roads have opened the interior of the reservation to high-speed traffic. The tourist trade has correspondingly increased. The number of pick-up trucks owned by the Navajo has also increased. At the present time, it would be safe to estimate that over 75% of all Navajo households have a motor vehicle of some type. And most of the others can rely on the occasional use of a relative's vehicle. Finally, the Navajo economy has undergone great changes. In 1940, nearly all of the income on the reservation came from either on-reservation wage employment, craft productions, agriculture or animal husbandry, or federal government subsidy. Only a small percentage of the income came from wage labor off of the reservation (Heath 1964:130–1). By 1958, over half of the Navajo income came from off reservation sources, primarily wage labor employment or social security or other welfare or retirement benefits (Kluckhohn and Leighton 1958:60). The population had simply outgrown the capacity of the reservation to support it—in spite of the natural resource industries that have developed on the reservation since 1950.

The employment situation on the Navajo Reservation had become so critical by 1971 that the tribal chairman officially estimated that 65% of the Navajo work force was unemployed. Robbins (1975:6) estimates

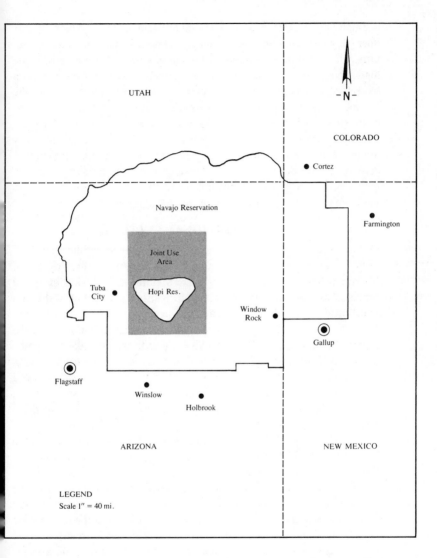

Figure 4.1   Map of Navajo Indian Reservation and surrounding communities

unemployment at 35% and underemployment at 56%. Much of this unemployment could be found among young men who had recently returned from military service or who had graduated or completed some high school. Most of the Navajos who are employed on the reservation work for the Bureau of Indian Affairs, the Public Health Service, or the Navajo Tribe. Others work for natural resource industries, for traders, or for small businesses (gas stations, etc.) which may be found throughout the reservation. But the number of jobs available is still very limited. Furthermore, there is a strong aversion among a large number of Navajos to take up permanent residence off the reservation where jobs are more plentiful. Many refuse to live in urban areas because these are so unlike the environments to which they are accustomed.

THE TRADITIONAL CULTURE

One could not easily pick two cultures which are more unlike than those of the traditional Navajo and the modern Anglo-American. Traditional Navajo culture, like many non-Western cultures, had kinship as the primary basis of its social organization. Kinship was reckoned through matrilineal clans. A child became a member of his mother's clan. However, the child also inherited rights in his father's clan, i.e., the clan of his father's mother. Kluckhohn and Leighton (1958) describe three smaller kinship units that functioned on a more day-to-day basis as units of mutual aid and cooperation: the biological family, the extended family, and the outfit or localized clan segment. When a crisis arose in a biological family, its members had a wide variety of relatives on whom they could call for aid.

Traditional Navajo economy was based on agriculture and animal husbandry. Agricultural land was located near streams, rivers, and artesian wells where irrigation was possible. The Navajo grew corn, beans, squash, and melons. Some Navajos were lucky enough to have orchards as well. Animal husbandry mostly involved the raising of large herds of sheep and goats, but some horses, pigs, and a few cattle were also kept. Since the sheep and goat herds were large (many average close to 200 animals) and the summers were hot and dry, the average Navajo family usually had two sheep camps; one for winter and one for summer. One sheep camp simply would not suffice because year-round grazing would ruin the pasture in any one area. In addition, the summer sheep camp had to be located near a permanent source of water, since the sheep had to have water at least once a day during the summer.

Although agriculture and animal husbandry were the mainstays of traditional Navajo economy, rug-weaving and other craft industries brought in a necessary supply of petty cash. This was used to buy manufactured items and processed foods from Anglo traders. The traditional Navajo were not totally self-sufficient. They needed money to buy flour, tools, sugar and other items produced by the larger American industrial economy. These items made their lives easier, but they did not greatly alter the Navajo lifestyle. It is only since World War II that major changes in the Navajo economy have forced many Navajos to become more like Anglo-Americans by entering the wage labor market.

Finally, traditional Navajo religion was and still is extremely important in the daily lives of many Navajos. The traditional religious system was based on a hierarchy of deities, monsters, and Holy People, of whom the sun-carrier was the most important. Many of the religious ceremonies, called "sings" or "chant ways," were supplications to the sun. The Navajo believe that by performing the proper ceremony one could compel specific deities into curing someone by reestablishing the ceremonial balance between the sick person and the forces of nature. The sings were almost always performed over a person or a group of persons who had become ill by upsetting this ritual balance. Reichard (1950:81–2) describes the many, many ways in which an individual could transgress against the forces of nature and become ill. When this happened, a diviner would be summoned. There were several types of diviners, but the one which would be most often called was the hand-trembler. The diviner would perform the ritual, and then he or she would prescribe a specific sing (ceremony) and give the name of the singer who was to perform it. The sing would then be performed four times over a period of several months or years to insure the complete recovery of the patient. Each repetition of the sing could last from one to nine days. The longer sings usually cost a considerable amount in money and goods, and it could take several years for the patient's family to accumulate the wealth to have the four repetitions performed.

Today, the traditional religion is continually under attack from various Christian missionary groups. In addition, the Native American Church is attracting a large following. There is a considerable amount of anguish produced in individual households as its members become converted to the many different missionary churches. Often there will be persons of three or four religious persuasions within a household, and severe arguments may occur. However, in times of extreme crisis, the hand trembler is often called in, and a sing is performed by a traditional singer "just in case." The traditional system still serves as a religious basis for many households, even though its members may belong to other religions as well. This double (in some cases triple) membership is analogous to the use of the Public Health Service doctor and the singer to cure an illness. If one power for curing is good, then two are even better!

A DEFINITION OF DRINKING

Due to the variety of theoretical positions taken on the nature of drinking, this study begins by developing a composite definition of drinking that views drinking as a phenomenon that exists at the cultural, social, and individual levels.

Drinking is composed of a culturally patterned set of behaviors. These behavior patterns are relevant to a set of culturally defined values that determine such concerns as who may drink, who may drink together, where the drinking is to occur, the type of liquor appropriate for the occasion, the role relationships between the various drinkers, the topics discussed during any particular drinking event, and the particular activities characterizing any specific drinking occasion. Furthermore, this value system usually includes a taxonomic definition of the various types of drinkers. This taxonomy will indicate the difference between the "normal" and the deviant drinker if such a distinction is made in the culture being studied. These values may be seen to operate by observing the manner in which the drinker uses his immediate environment and by observing how he structures his drinking behavior with regard to those who drink with him. Finally, these values are apparent in the statements the drinker makes about his own drinking and the drinking of others.

This definition of drinking supports both groups which have argued the question of the cultural patterning of drinking behavior versus the environmental determination of drinking patterns (see Topper 1970, 1976). Clearly, cultural drinking patterns are developed for specific environments. It is when the drinker takes his or her culturally learned, environment-specific drinking patterns and tries to adapt them to the drinking patterns and environments of another culture that real trouble can ensue. Therefore, Graves (1967) is partially right when he says that the Navajo gets into trouble in a bar because it is a strange environment. But this difficulty is also caused by the fact that the Navajo has a specific set of learned drinking behaviors that are not appropriate to the barroom situation and to the pattern of drinking behaviors associated with it. Thus, it appears that both cultural pattern and environment play important roles in the success or failure of a person trying to drink in a cultural context foreign to his own.

DRINKING PATTERNS:
A MULTILEVEL PHENOMENON

This investigation of Navajo drinking patterns was developed from the theoretical position of linguistic anthropologists. The project was designed to test specific hypotheses about language and culture that had been set forth by Werner (1966), within the substantive context of Navajo drinking patterns. The work of Mandelbaum (1965) and Lomnitz (1969) has been used in developing a model of the cultural patterning of drinking behavior. In addition, however, a component derived from the psychodynamic analysis of drinking by Robert Levy (1958) is included. Although it is very clear that drinking often has a socially cohesive function, the loss of memory and the special drinking behavior patterns associated with the ingestion of large quantities of alcohol among the members of many cultures clearly indicates its usefulness for the acting out of repressed frustrations. The reinforcement of social ties and the release of pent-up aggression through culturally approved drinking behavior offer many drinkers temporary solutions to the psychic stresses facing them. These solutions often give the individual drinker enough release from the stresses of his daily life so that he may cope with them when he returns to a state of sobriety. Evidence for this escape or "discharge" function of drinking (see R. Levy 1958) appears in the statements of Navajos themselves and of mental health workers on the Navajo Reservation. In fact, many persons dealing with mental health on the reservation go so far as to claim that drinking is a native pharmacological attempt to seek release from chronic depression (Dr. Steven Proskauer, personal communication).

For these reasons, limiting the discussion of Navajo drinking to, say, the interrelation of drinking patterns and social structure offers an inadequate method of explaining drinking as a cultural event. Drinking must be seen both as it functions socially and psychologically for the individual and as it serves to maintain society. To do otherwise would be to fall back on an unsatisfactory model for the operation of cultural systems in which social structure is the primary focus. A culture is not only a functioning set of related social institutions; it is also a group of individuals mutually seeking a systematic solution to the problem of survival. Within the cultural framework, each individual must play his part and cope with the psychic stresses that accompany it. Therefore, drinking is viewed here on three basic levels: the individual, the social, and the cultural.

The theoretical position underlying this study emphasizes the verbal elicitation of data from informants both when they were drinking and when they were sober. Aside from this, it was also felt that clues to the determination of the drinking patterns of the informants could be found in the environments in which they drank. Therefore, a two-fold approach toward data gathering was adopted.

It is important to stress at the very beginning that this study focuses on Navajo youthful drinkers; hence, the reader should keep in mind that there are many Navajos who are abstainers and many who are only moderate drinkers. It should not be assumed that heavy drinking is pervasive over the entire population.

The first step taken in the gathering of the data was a series of interviews with Navajo drinkers when they were sober. During these interviews a taxonomy of Navajo categories or types of drinkers was elicited. The informants were then asked to classify themselves according to these taxonomies.

Next, the informants were asked to give sequential descriptions, called "verbal action plans," for both the drinking behaviors in which they participated and those which they had only heard about. The verbal action plans were developed by Werner (1966) along the model of a computer flow chart. The informants were asked to list, step by step, all of the things which they did during the course of drinking. In a later interview, they were asked to give detailed step-by-step descriptions for behaviors composing each step of the plans that were previously elicited. This reelicitation procedure was continued until the informant felt that he had provided all the detail he could. In this way, a plan was developed that had several levels of detail. These various levels showed the depth of knowledge that each individual informant possessed about the various aspects of the drinking behaviors being discussed. The plans themselves showed the cultural patterning of the behavior in question.

The differences in the plans given by various informants provided valuable information on the differences in their personal experiences. This yielded considerable insight into the personality of each individual informant, since the experience that a person has with a particular behavior sequence indicates the degree to which he has been willing to talk about the behavior sequence in question. This willingness to talk also reflects on his personality. For example, one of the teenage boys included a statement about how girls were seduced after the dances in his verbal action plan. Another omitted this topic entirely.

Once the informants had provided plans for the drinking of their peer group, they were asked to tell what they could about the drinking patterns of individuals who fit into the other taxonomic classes. In some cases, informants had observed the drinking of members of another category and could describe the drinking behavior sequences of other types of drinkers in great detail. However, when they spoke of drinking by groups that they had never observed, their knowledge was more superficial.

TAXONOMIES, VERBAL ACTION PLANS, AND DRINKING ENVIRONMENTS

These interviews suggested that the social and physical environment in which drinking occurred had a great deal to do with the determination of the behavior patterns of the drinkers. During the first interview session, an informant asked which drinking event he was supposed to describe. He commented that Navajos drink in a variety of places, and that when drinking occurred on the reservation, it was in conjunction with some specific activity. Thus, the first task with respect to the verbal action plans became the gathering of a list of the times and places at which drinking occurred both on and off the reservation. Informants were asked which categories of drinkers fit which drinking situations. After this, verbal action plans for the drinking behaviors of the various categories of drinkers in specific environmental situations could be elicited.

The observational aspect of the field methodology then became very important. Informants recognized that the setting of the drinking activities influenced the way in which they drank. Therefore, it was important to try and discover the relationship between the environment of the drinking and the behavior of the drinkers. This was done in two ways. First, informants were accompanied into these various environments where drinking normally occurred and were asked to explain how drinking in these environments might occur. Secondly, observations of how the informants were using the environment were made in environments where drinking was legal. As the same event recurred, patterns in the drinking behavior of informants were discernable.

THE INFORMANTS

With some exceptions, the primary informants for this study were young Navajo men. They ranged in age from fifteen to thirty. The sample was small; verbal action plans were elicited from six male informants, and assorted information was received from approximately thirty other young men and from about ten Navajo females (aged 14–30).

Based on these data, the picture of Navajo drinking presented here is one-sided. Most of the informants fit into one native taxonomic category: *ashiiké da'adlą́ąnii* or "young men who drink." Some of the informants had recently become old enough to be called *hastóíí da'adlą́ąnii,* or "older men who drink." However, these men felt that they could still be categorized as young men. The transition between the two statuses is quite gradual.

Although male informants were primarily used, their conceptualizations appear to constitute a quite accurate description of Navajo drinking in general. Drinking among the Navajo is predominantly a male-oriented and male-dominated set of behavior patterns. Women rarely drink by themselves, and when they drink with men, the men generally determine the plan for the activities. When the women drink they try to maintain order and prevent extreme arguments by helping separate men who appear to be on the verge of fighting; but women take little active role in the patterning of the actual drinking behavior. On the other hand, Navajo women often take an active role in initiating any sexual behavior associated with drinking.

Because Navajo drinking is very much male-oriented behavior, and because drinking is often more a part of the social life of a young Navajo man than it is for an older Navajo man (see Levy and Kunitz 1974:135–7 on late life abstention), this chapter will concentrate on the *ashiiké da'adlą́ąnii.* These are the individuals who are experiencing the greatest difficulties in dealing with Anglo culture. They have the highest suicide rates (J. E. Levy 1972:598), the highest arrest rates, and an extremely high unemployment rate. For them, drinking offers an escape from the stress of living between two cultures by allowing them to return to an acceptable, traditional escape behavior. Although this behavior is defined as acceptable according to Navajo norms, it is deviant by white standards. The young Navajo male's attempt to seek release through liquor often backfires in the culture-contact situation and creates severe problems for him (see below). The times which young Navajo men choose for their drinking are often very traditional in their lack of regard for the timing of events in the Anglo world. This can mean the loss of a job or even worse. Ultimately, it may lead the young man to drinking behavior that is considered deviant even by Navajo standards.

THE TAXONOMIC CATEGORIZATION
OF NAVAJO DRINKERS

In the course of this study, several taxonomies were elicited. No single taxonomy included all of the possible categories into which Navajo drinkers could be placed. From these partial taxonomic categories of drinkers, a composite taxonomy, meant to represent the knowledge of the ideal, omniscient Navajo informant, was created (see Figure 4.2). Werner and Fenton (1970:540) have proposed the adoption of this position in the study of cultural knowledge. It allows the investigator to view the knowledge of the individual informant against the totality of knowledge which is available to members of his culture.

There are many reasons why an informant will not be able to give a taxonomy that contains the totality of the cultural knowledge about a taxonomic domain. His experience may be limited. He may simply not remember part of it. Or his personal beliefs may have forced him to deny part of it. For example, one informant steadfastly refused to recognize level three of the composite taxonomy (Figure 4.2), which distinguishes between moderate drinkers and alcoholics. He had been a policeman who had to enforce reservation prohibition laws, and before that he had been a very heavy drinker. So he gave two taxonomies. One was composed of levels one and two, and the other was composed of levels one and four. It was not until other informants were questioned that these two taxonomies could be combined and the domain of "drinkers" could be unified. Once the domain was clearly defined, and the composite taxonomy was drawn, it was shown to other informants who agreed that it was a proper categorization. However, many felt that it was excessively detailed.

Level One: Da'adlą́ąnii ("Drinkers")

The first question asked of each informant was, "What do you call people who drink? Is there one Navajo word which could apply to all of them?" On every occasion the answer was, "Yes, the word is *da'ad-lą́ąnii*. It means 'the drinkers.'"

The informants were then asked to list the defining characteristics of these people. They stated that they were simply people who drank alcoholic beverages. It was also said that these people were not as morally upstanding as they might be. When asked why this was so, the response was "Because they are drunks!" When queried as to whether all *da'adlą́ąnii* were alcoholics, informants replied that both alcoholics and socially acceptable drinkers were *da'adlą́ąnii*. It was the fact that a person drank at all which marked him with the unpleasant characteristics of the term *da'adlą́ąnii*.

This seeming confusion of classification arises from two sources. The first is the Navajo view of categorization. Unlike Anglo-Americans, the Navajo strongly stress the relationship of two categories

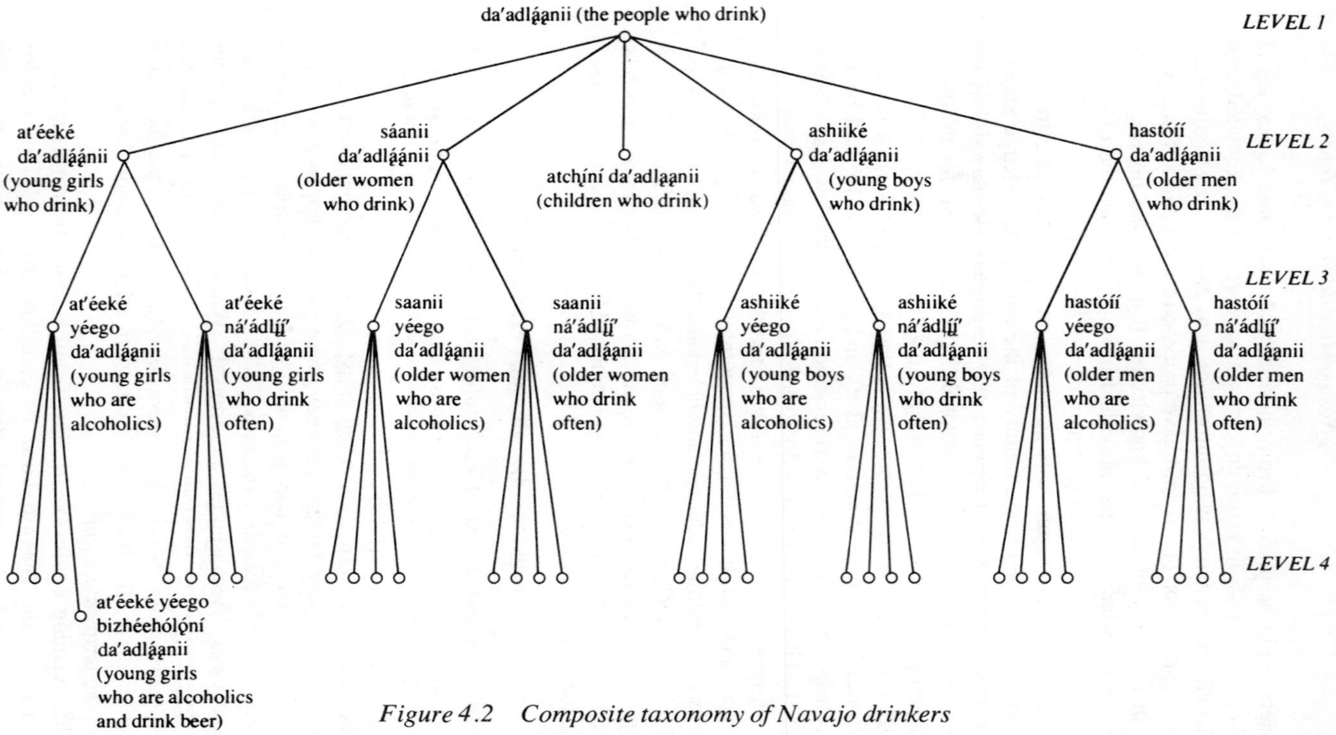

Figure 4.2 Composite taxonomy of Navajo drinkers

LEVEL 1

da'adlą́ąnii (the people who drink)

LEVEL 2

at'ééké da'adlą́ąnii (young girls who drink)

sáanii da'adlą́ąnii (older women who drink)

atch̨íní da'adlą́ąnii (children who drink)

ashiiké da'adlą́ąnii (young boys who drink)

hastóii da'adlą́ąnii (older men who drink)

LEVEL 3

at'ééké yéego da'adlą́ąnii (young girls who are alcoholics)

at'ééké ná'adlíį' da'adlą́ąnii (young girls who drink often)

sáanii yéego da'adlą́ąnii (older women who are alcoholics)

sáanii ná'adlíį' da'adlą́ąnii (older women who drink often)

ashiiké yéego da'adlą́ąnii (young boys who are alcoholics)

ashiiké ná'adlíį' da'adlą́ąnii (young boys who drink often)

hastóii yéego da'adlą́ąnii (older men who are alcoholics)

hastóii ná'adlíį' da'adlą́ąnii (older men who drink often)

at'ééké yéego bizhéehółǫ́ní da'adlą́ąnii (young girls who are alcoholics and drink beer)

LEVEL 4

if they are both related to a common third category. This holds even if the relationship is not strong (Oswald Werner, personal communication). Reichard (1950:3–12) gives a good description of this. Things or ideas sharing common attributes are, in many cases, considered to be identical by the Navajo. Therefore, drinkers may be separated into alcoholics and normal drinkers, but they can also be "the same." A second reason for the overlapping of the categories for the alcoholic and the normal drinker is due to the influence of the white man. There are numerous Christian sects which send missionaries to the reservation (17 in Tuba City alone!). Many of these strongly denounce the use of alcoholic beverages. In their attempts to missionize, they offer the Indian a better life and/or eternal salvation if he would but give up such sins as the use of alcohol. This attitude was long reinforced by the myth of the drunken Indian. The myth was fostered during the last century and gained credence under the previous laws of the U.S. Government and the states of Arizona and New Mexico, which made it illegal to sell liquor to an Indian (Heath 1964). Even today, the Navajo Tribal Council upholds this attitude by making it illegal for anyone to sell, transport, or possess alcoholic beverages on the reservation.

Since drinking is frowned upon to this degree, it may surprise some that it occurs at all! There are many explanations of why the Navajo drink. The missionaries ascribe the use of alcohol to the active presence of a supreme evil spirit whom they call "the devil." Informants merely said that they did it because it was fun and because it allowed them to "get away from my problems for a little while." Reichard (1950:123–34) also provides an explanation. In her statement on Navajo ethics, she says that a Navajo is expected to transgress against firm moral positions. This is especially true of minor crimes that return immediate rewards. It is the act of getting caught that is the dishonor. When this occurs, the Navajo then goes about elaborately atoning for his transgressions.

When this general principle is applied to drinking, it is easy to see why the Navajo drinks and risks arrest. Drinking is no great crime. The odds are that the Navajo drinker will not get caught, and in all probability he will have a good time. If he gets too drunk and becomes belligerent, he will be arrested and/or receive a stern lecture from a concerned medicine man. The drinker will admit his guilt, pay his dues, and life will go on as usual. As long as his drinking does not greatly disrupt the life of his family, it will be accepted as a more or less unfortunate aspect of his personality.

Level Two Categories

On level two of the composite taxonomy (Figure 4.2), the domain of drinkers is broken down along the dimensions of age and sex. When asked why this was so, the informants replied, "Because people of different ages and sexes drink differently, and because people tend to drink with others of their own age and sex, but this is not always so."

The attributes of the various taxonomic categories on this level were culturally defined. Sex may be a "biological reality," but Navajos did not use sex alone to define the categories on level two. Sex was combined with relative age and behavior pattern to create the definitions. For example, there is the category *áłchíní da'adlą́ą́nii* which means "children who drink." With respect to this category, sex is neutral. When asked why, informants said, "It is because children are young, and they all drink in the same way. Their parents give them a little bit when they are drinking." Therefore, the seemingly undeniable "facts" given by the "biological realities" of sex and biological age are combined with culturally patterned behaviors to form a categorization that is culturally relevant rather than universal.

The category *ashiiké da'adlą́ą́nii* ("young men who drink") was separated from *hastóíí da'adlą́ą́nii* ("older men who drink") on grounds which were also culturally defined. There was no definite age at which a young man became an older man. Most of the informants agreed that it was a gradual transition occurring sometime between the ages of thirty and forty. Usually this was accompanied by the establishment of a successful marriage and the fathering of several children. However, the primary differences between the two categories lay in the very divergent drinking patterns displayed by their members. These variations had two primary forms of expression. First, there are the differences in the events at which the two categories of men drank. Young men drink at the western stomp dances or cat dances. These are teenage dances similar to those found in any American high school. They also drink at the traditional "Squaw dances," at "Yeibichei dances," on afternoons when they ditch school, on afternoons during summer vacation when they have nothing else to do, or before sports events sponsored by the local high school or community center.

Older men tended to drink at religious ceremonies (including the squaw dances), on pay day, and when they were in the company of friends or relatives who simply "feel like it." There is obviously some overlap in the events at which older and younger men drink. The categories represent tendencies to drink at specific events rather than absolute behavioral prescriptions. The informants recognize this, and they say, "a young man is *ashiiké da'adlą́ą́nii* because he usually drinks like a young man, although sometimes he may drink like his older relatives when he is with them.''

In addition to the difference in the types of events at which younger and older men drink, there is a definite difference in the patterns of drinking displayed by these two types of drinkers. These differences are partly due to the environment in which the drinking occurs. Since drinking is illegal on the reservation, the environment of the place where drinking occurs has a great deal of influence on the behavior patterns of the drinkers (see Topper 1970 and below). Therefore, the type of drinking event and its physical and social environment are clearly important to the creation of the distinction between old men and young men who drink. In the extreme example, it is clear that anyone who has seen the drinking of a young man at a western stomp dance inside a high school gym could never confuse it with the pattern of the older men at a shooting-way chant (see verbal action plans below). The remaining two categories on level two are *at'ééke da'adláąnii* and *sáanii da'adláąnii*. They refer to young women and older women who drink. Since most of my informants were males, the data on these two categories are the least complete. However, there is enough information to supply a few of the attributes of these categories.

At'ééke da'adláąnii refers to young women who drink. These were almost always defined as unmarried girls who were in high school or college. Young women from twenty-five on up who were married and had several children were usually excluded from this category, unless they were non-traditional. This indicates that the changing situation on the reservation is at least tacitly recognized for both males and females in this taxonomy. Young men who drink at the stomp dances and young women who seek to be "modern" and drink with their husbands at house parties were both placed in the categories for the less mature drinkers. One can clearly see that the adoption of the traditional Navajo attitudes toward drinking and traditional drinking behaviors is very important for the movement of an individual into the categories for the more mature drinkers. The really significant aspect of this point is that it comes from a categorization given by young men who represent some of the most acculturated members of the Navajo Tribe.

Since the Navajo woman usually marries and bears her first child much younger than her Anglo-American counterpart, it is logical that she would acquire the status of a mature woman much earlier. The category *sáanii da'adláąnii* could include very traditional women who are as young as twenty-five. However, most young women will not admit to entering this category until they are well into their thirties. This is partly because most Navajo women do not normally adopt (or re-adopt) traditional dress until that age. The word *sáanii* has been used traditionally to indicate women over forty. And even though a very traditional young woman may drink in the manner of an older woman, her reluctance to be called by this term is understandable. When they were pressed on this point, the informants usually said that they would just say that they were *da'adlą́ąnii* since "it is all the same anyway." As with the shift from the young men to older men, the shift from young women to older women occurs gradually.

Level Three Categories

The distinction defining the categories on level three (Figure 4.2) is perhaps the most difficult to clarify in the entire taxonomy. It is the distinction between the normal drinker and the alcoholic. The difference between the two categories is not based on the amount of liquor the drinker consumes. Nor is it made on the frequency with which the drinker drinks. This is in spite of the notion among many Anglo-Americans on the reservation that stresses these two factors as indicators of Indian addiction to alcohol.

When faced with the difficulty of trying to uncover the Navajo definition of an alcoholic, we finally asked informants to describe how an alcoholic drinks. At this point, a clear distinction appeared between the normal drinker and the alcoholic. The results obtained were much the same as those which Lomnitz (1969:294) found among the Mapuche. The alcoholic was defined as an individual who drank alone. By drinking alone, the Navajo violated most of the norms of Navajo drinking. The lone drinker was considered selfish because he did not share his liquor with his friends and relatives. He wanted it all for himself. His drinking usually occurred at times which were not defined as being acceptable for drinking. He could often be found down at the bootlegger's house when he should have been at work. He usually hoarded the money he earned or received through welfare and used it for drinking rather than for the support of his family. He showed a marked disrespect for valuable items that belonged to himself or his family. And he frequently engaged in extra-marital sexual relations.

Although it is clear that there is a cultural definition of the Navajo alcoholic, the difficulty of classification for specific individuals on level two may also be found here on level three. The norm defined here is rarely achieved by any drinker. A person who behaves in the manner of an alcoholic on rare occasions will be considered to be an untrustworthy drinker, but he will be tolerated. It is the person who frequently drinks in this manner who is the alcoholic. As noted above, the amount of liquor consumed or the frequency of drinking has nothing to do with the

Navajo definition of an alcoholic. It is the individual who frequently denies the social proprieties of drinking who is the alcoholic. He is a threat to the stability of his household as well as thought of as an unreliable person.

Since drinking norms have much to do with the events at which drinking occurs, the normal Navajo drinker will not be discussed here. Instead, normative drinking at specific drinking events will be described in a later section of this chapter.

Level Four Categories

Level four of the composite taxonomy (Figure 4.2) contains the most detailed set of categories. Because these categories are very intricate, one would be led to believe that they would be very useful in describing specific individuals. However, the exact opposite is true. These terms are rarely used. When asked why, informants gave three reasons. The first was that it was just easier to use the cover term *da'adlą́ąnii*. The second was that it was quite difficult to get any kind of liquor on the reservation except wine. In fact, one could usually buy only one brand of wine from bootleggers. Therefore, it seemed silly to many informants to talk about a drinker from the standpoint of what he or she drank, although some did. Finally, some informants also said that, "Some of these guys will drink anything that they can get their hands on! They may like beer better than wine, but if wine is all that they can get, then they will drink it."

Although the categories on level four are clearly defined along the lines of what the drinkers prefer to drink, the variety they express has little correlation with the degree of variety in observed behavior. Instead, these seemingly empty categories express the possibilities that may be found. In this way, the taxonomy may include every possible drinker instead of only the majority of drinkers.

TAXONOMY: A SUMMARY

Figure 4.2 is an idealized view of the semantic domain of Navajo drinkers. The categories it contains are clearly defined according to the Navajo conceptions about the behavior patterns of Navajo drinkers. However, the taxonomy is a cultural idealization. Therefore, it is a model rather than an absolute yardstick by which the activities of each and every Navajo drinker may be measured. This does not mean that the model is invalid. It simply means that there will be some individuals who do not easily fit into any of the categories below level one. Human behavior does not remain constant. A drinker may change categories many times throughout his or her life span. These shifts are gradual.

Thus, at any one time, there may be a considerable number of individuals who seem to be hard to classify. When this happens, the level one term is used until the change is complete. In this way, Figure 4.2 classifies the majority of Navajo drinkers within a limited set of categories, but it also allows for the inclusion of all drinkers regardless of how atypical they may be at any specific point in time.

VERBAL ACTION PLANS

Examples of all verbal action plans for the drinking behavior of the various categories of Navajo drinkers in this study would add unnecessary length to the text; therefore only a couple of examples will be included to illustrate their structure. These plans represent the informants' view of the drinking behaviors they ascribe to various categories of drinkers. Since these behaviors are relevant to the environments in which they occur, the plans will be discussed with respect to the category of individuals who are drinking and the specific environment in which the drinking occurs.[2] The plans will be presented according to the level of Figure 4.2 from which they were elicited.

The verbal action plan (see Figure 4.3) is read from left to right. Each culturally defined act is represented by an arrow. The connecting sequencing relationship (Werner 1969) is represented by a circle which joins two arrows representing action sequences. Each arrow is a separate step in the plan and represents the informant's own statement. A number of decision tables follow the verbal action plan in Figure 4.3 in order to illustrate alternative courses of action. For example, Figure 4.3 would be read as follows: Step 1, *dajilzhish baanidiildee'go* ("there is an occasion"—a chance), *áádóó* ("and then"); Step 2, *bik'is béiyikai* ("his friends come"), etc. At Step 4, a choice point is found at the sequencing relations (see decision table number 1). It is a complex one. The boys either decide to go to an off-reservation bar or they go to a bootlegger on the reservation. If they decide to stay on the reservation, they must then decide whether to buy the liquor in the dance parking lot or go to the bootlegger's house.[3]

---

[2]The sample verbal action plans in Figures 4.3 and 4.4 contain only a single pathway through the informant's knowledge of possible plans. This is due to a lack of space. The complete set of data which includes all possible plans may be obtained from the author.

[3]In later studies of verbal action plans, we have used computer decision tables to more adequately describe these decision situations. However, for this chapter, it was not possible to reelicit the decision complexes for these plans since some of the informants are now deceased.

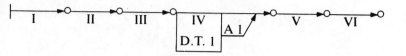

I.   There is an occasion (a western stomp dance).
     dajilzhish baanídiildee'go
II. He meets his friends.
     bik'is beiyikai
III. They pitch in.
     béeso beinił
IV. Decision Table #1
     A 1: They go to a bootlegger (in the parking lot).
           nichxǫǫ'ígíí chidí yeenideeyeehígíí yanidayiiłnii
V.   They go to a bootlegger (in the parking lot).
     nichxǫǫ'ígíí chidí yeenideeyeehígíí yanidayiiłnii
VI. They buy wine (Tokay).
     nichxǫǫ'ígíí nayiiłnih

Decision Table #1

unelicited	unelicited
They go to a bootlegger (in the parking lot). *nichxǫǫ'ígíí chidí yeenideeyeehígíí yanidayiiłnii*	
They go to the bootlegger's house *nichxǫǫ'igii beehólónígíí yich'į' iigháàh tónaneezdizígóó*	unelicited
They drive to an off-reservation bar (gray mountain) *dzilbáíígoo iigháàh*	

Figure 4.3   How young men drink in groups (at the stomp dance) (pp. 121–25)

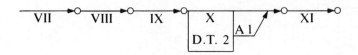

VII. They drink it behind a hill.
   dahyisk'id yine' iikah
VIII. They return to the dance.
   da'azhishgóó anákáh
IX. They stagger around to show they are drunk.
   bil honiidohgo na'niłliish leh
X. Decision Table #2
   A 1:   He gets arrested.
      bidiiltsood
XI. He gets arrested.
   bidiiltsood

Decision Table #2

unelicited	unelicited
He gets arrested. *bidiiltsood*	
He feels sick (in the head). *bitsiits'iin neezgai*	unelicited
The dance ends. *dajilzish ałtso baana'asdee'*	

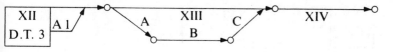

XII. Decision Table #3
A 1: The boy fights the police.
ashkii báŋáchįįh

XIII. The boy fights the police.
ashkii báŋáchįįh
A. The policeman asks the boy if he is drunk.
siláago ashkii neiyídiłki' "nit hooneezdoiiś?"
B. Two cops put the drunken boy in hammer locks.
ashkii bił hooneezdoiisíí naakih siláago ch'iihbiiłnááh
C. The drunken boy is thrown into the rear of the squad car.
ashkii bił honeezdohígíí siláago bichidí bikéé'déé'
biih bi'diilgháąh

XIV. He is taken to jail.
Siláago bahooghangóó bidigééh

Decision Table #3

unelicited	' unelicited
The boy fights (the police). *ashkii baháchįįh*	unelicited
The drunken boy goes quietly. *ashkii bił honeezdohígíí* *doobáháchį'da*	

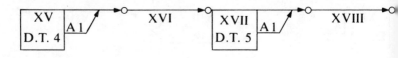

XV. Decision Table #4
   A 1:   He is tried.
          baahwiinit'įįh
XVI. He is tried.
   baahwiinit'įįh
XVII. Decision Table #5
   A 1:   He is convicted.
          baanahoót'ááh
XVIII. He is convicted.
   baanahoót'ááh

Decision Table #4

unelicited	unelicited
He is tried. *baahwiinit'įįh*	unelicited
He is not tried. *doobahwiinit'įįhda*	

Decision Table #5

unelicited	unelicited
He is convicted. *bahnahoot'ááh*	unelicited
He is acquitted. *bideidichi'*	

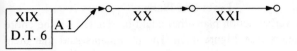

XIX. Decision Table #6
    A 1: He is fined.
          beeso neidééh
XX. He is fined.
    beeso neidééh
XXI. He goes home.
    hooghangóó anádááh

Decision Table #6

unelicited	unelicited
He is fined. *beeso neidééh*	unelicited
He is imprisoned. *siláago bighangóne sidáalheh*	
Both. *éídoodago t'áá álhah*	

Level One Plans

There were no verbal action plans that could be elicited for the entire domain of drinkers (see Figure 4.2). The informants said that there were so many ways to drink that they would have to know the age and sex of the drinker and where the drinking occurred before they could describe their behavior.

Level Two Plans

Informants were able to provide drinking plans for all five of the categories of drinkers on level two. Since the informants were mostly teenage boys, the sequences which include women are, with rare exception, poorly defined. Another interesting point is that the informants distinguished between off- and on-reservation drinking patterns on this level, providing plans for drinking in both settings. There were some marked similarities in some of the drinking behaviors displayed on and off the reservation. But these similarities seemed to disappear when Navajos were allowed to go inside the bar and drink (see below).

Level Three Plans

Only one new verbal action plan was generated on level three of the taxonomy of drinking types (Figure 4.2). This was the plan for the "alcoholic," hence it is included in this study (Figure 4.4). Since the distinction between the moderate drinker and the alcoholic was largely made on the basis of behavior, it may be very useful to compare the verbal action plans for these two categories to see just what these differences are. This may be especially important for the therapist who is to treat the "problem drinker." It can give him an idea of where the drinker "went wrong" according to his peers. It can also give the therapist an idea of the difficulties that the patient may encounter acquiescing to the behavior patterns the therapist wants him to adopt.

The two verbal action plans included in this chapter clearly indicate the differences between the behaviors of the "normal" Navajo drinker (Figure 4.3) and the Navajo alcoholic (Figure 4.4). The young man going to the western stomp dance begins his drinking sequence with the occurrence of a dance (Figure 4.3). The alcoholic begins his drinking with having a "problem" (Figure 4.4). The second step for the young man going to the stomp dance is to gather his friends, but the alcoholic decides to really get drunk, and more than likely he will go to the bootlegger's home alone. Further comparisons are obvious.

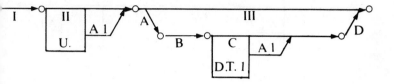

I. He has a problem.
   (Informant included step 1 in English version, but
   not in Navajo version of the plan).
II. He decides to get really drunk.
   t'áádoole'é biniighe l'niidlį́įh
   U.   Unelicited decision table.
III. He goes to the bootlegger.
   nichxǫǫ'ígíí nahniihgóó iighááh
   A.   He knocks on the door.
          hooghan bidáádilkał neidiiłs'į́įh
   B.   He asks "Do you have wine?"
          "nichxǫ́ǫ́'i nee hóló?"
   C.   Decision Table #1
          A1:   He buys (Tokay) wine (same as D).
   D.   He buys (Tokay) wine.
          nichxǫǫ'ígíí neyiiłnih

Decision Table #1

unelicited	unelicited
He buys (Tokay) wine. *nichxǫ́ǫ́ígíí neyiiłnih*	unelicited
He may pawn something (with the bootlegger if he is really desperate). *yahnínídláh*	

Figure 4.4   *How older men drink alone*
             (pp. 127–29)

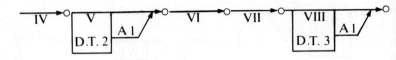

IV. He goes over the hill.
   haná'ąągnoo iigháah

V. Decision Table #2
   A1:   He drinks the wine fast.
         nichxǫǫ'ígíí tsįįłgo yidlįįh

VI. He drinks the wine fast.
   nichxǫǫ'ígíí tsįįłgo yidlįįh

VII. After he gets drunk he staggers around.
   bił honiidohgo na'niltł'ish łeh

VIII. Decision Table #3
   A1:   He passes out.
         naa'iiléeh

Decision Table #2

unelicited	unelicited
He drinks it fast. *nichxǫǫ́ígíí tsįįlgo yidlįįh*	unelicited
He may go from place to place and drink a little bit at each one. *ałch'íídígo yidlįįh*	

Decision Table #3

unelicited	unelicited
He gets arrested. *yah'abi'dilt'eeh*	unelicited
He passes out. *naa'lileeh*	
He goes home. *hooghangóó anádááh*	

IX. He passes out.
    naa'iilééh
X. He goes home.
    hooghangóó anádááh

An interesting point arises from the fact that informants only gave a plan for an alcoholic who was an older man. Although they admitted that a young man could be an alcoholic, they felt that this was a remote possibility. They felt that this person would drink very much like the old man who was an alcoholic. However, they could not imagine that any of their peers could be alcoholics, no matter how often they drank. Bouts of heavy drinking are normal for a young Navajo man. These could go on for a day or two, but as long as he drank with his "buddies," the young man was merely a drinker and not an alcoholic.

Since the informants were mostly young males, very little data could be obtained about young women or older women who were alcoholics. The informants admitted that some women could be alcoholics, but they thought that these would be those who are very old and husbandless. They felt sorry for these individuals who they believed turned to alcohol addiction for escape and companionship.

Level Four Plans

No new verbal action plans were elicited for the categories on level four (Figure 4.2). The informants felt that the differences between the way one drinks beer and the way one drinks whiskey or wine were too minor to require the addition of an entirely new plan. They said that the plans that were already given would suffice, with very minor changes.

RESERVATION DRINKING PATTERNS
AND THEIR ENVIRONMENTS

The effect of the environment on the determination of drinking behaviors of Navajo drinkers on the reservation is clearly shown by the
differences in plans given for young men drinking at stomp dances and
for young men drinking at squaw dances. The three factors in the
ecological milieu of the drinker that appear to have the greatest influence
on the determination of Navajo drinking patterns exhibited on the reservation are: 1) the fact that most drinking occurs out of doors; 2) the fact
that the possession, drinking, sale, or transportation of liquor by
Navajos on the reservation is illegal; and 3) the fact that the Tribal
Police are generally not overzealous in their enforcement of the prohibition laws which have been passed by the Navajo Tribal Council.

The combined effects of prohibition and reasonable enforcement by
the Tribal Police are best seen in the patrolling patterns that the police
employ at western stomp dances and at squaw dances (enemy way ceremony). These two events are both regularly held during the summer and
western stomp dances are also held in the winter. Dances are traditionally occasions at which men meet young women who are eligible for
marriage and where old acquaintances with both men and women are
renewed. Drinking, especially among men, has always been an important aspect of the squaw dance and has been carried over to the western
stomp dances which have developed recently.

The Western Stomp Dance

The patrol patterns used by the police at the western stomp dances are
primarily aimed at preventing the sale of bootleg liquor in the parking
lot and preventing drinking and fighting inside the places where dances
are held. Police are stationed in the parking lot, in the lobby of the
dance hall, on the dance floor, and sometimes in the projection booth
above the dance floor. In addition, the police patrol the halls and men's
washroom. Guards are also posted at the fire exits near the stage to
prevent people from bringing their friends in without paying and/or to
prevent liquor from being brought in. There is not enough manpower to
patrol the vast stretches of desert surrounding the community centers or
the backyards around the schools where stomp dances are held. Therefore, a group of teenagers from the dance could obtain a bottle of wine
in the parking lot and disappear to drink it in a relatively safe place
before entering the dance hall (see Figure 4.3, decisions VII and VIII).
Some bootleggers take advantage of the concentration of police patrols
at the dance hall by operating a shuttle service to where they have their

"stash" hidden. For example, a bootlegger can fill his car with customers several times during an evening. It is also possible for the drinkers to walk to many of the bootleggers' homes and purchase liquor before or after they have arrived at the dance.

The verbal action plans for drinking at the western stomp dance clearly indicate informants realize that there are several ways of drinking at this event. The choice of where drinking will take place usually depends upon how much the drinker is willing to risk arrest and how much alcohol he has already consumed. The more intoxicated a Navajo gets, the more risks he usually takes. The more conservative plans for drinking are very similar to those for older men drinking together (see note 2). The plans usually involve a group of drinkers either going over to the bootlegger's house and drinking there, or buying some liquor and going "over the hill." However, the more risky plans are entirely new elements in Navajo culture. They involve drinking in the parking lot outside of the dance hall and/or drinking inside the dance hall. These plans (not included here) show an increasing awareness of the police as they change location from the area around the bootlegger's house to the dance hall itself.

It is interesting to note the evasive behaviors performed in the washroom and on the dance floor. First liquor is hidden in trousers, usually tucked under the belt with coats buttoned over. When the boys enter the washroom, they go into a stool stall, where they can hide and drink the liquor. The boys then drink the bottle quickly and go straight into the dance area. If they drink on the dance floor, they hide behind the bleachers. This is extremely risky, since there are usually police in several places on the dance floor. Therefore, it is clear that the drinker's behavior pattern becomes more and more a response to the patrolling of the police and less an expression of traditional Navajo drinking behavior. When the drinking moves to the dance floor, it becomes a highly structured avoidance behavior rather than a casual sharing of the bottle. The locus of the socially cohesive element of the drinking shifts in the main from chatting while passing the bottle to "making the rounds" of the dance floor with a buddy after the bottle is finished. No one stops to chat while drinking in the washroom or behind the bleachers.

Since it is possible to drink outside the dance hall, one may wonder why the drinker risks arrest by drinking inside. In some evenings as many as 10 arrests may be made at a western stomp dance. Most often these involve boys under the age of eighteen. However at the time of this study these boys were not subject to prosecution for drinking under the tribal law. When this factor of the "statutory" or "legal" environment is coupled with the poverty of the drinkers and the dance rule of no readmittance without the payment of an additional admission fee, it is easy to see why the financially strapped drinkers who want to stay fairly drunk would bring liquor into the dance. A system of behavior designed to avoid the police has been the result of this conflict between desire, absence of funds, and environmental restrictions.

It is clear that the chief determinants of teenage male drinking patterns at the western stomp dance are the patrol patterns of the Tribal Police and the desire to drink at the dance. Most of the young men want to "get a little torn down," but they do not want to get "thrown in" and miss the dance. Therefore, they carefully pattern their activities so that they can simultaneously show off their bravery by drinking at the dance and still stay out of jail.

The Squaw Dance (Enemy Way Ceremony)

Squaw dances are held out in the desert near the sheep camp of the person for whom the dance is held or one of his relatives. On some occasions, the first of the three nights of ceremonial dancing may be held in a semi-urban area like South Tuba. The dances are usually several miles from the nearest hard-surface road. This makes it difficult for the Tribal Police to assign more than one or two squads to provide security and prevent fighting. This is not true of the western stomp dances, which are held in buildings located only a few hundred yards from the police stations. The differences in the settings of these two dances force the police to use different tactics, which in turn affects the milieu of the drinkers.

At the squaw dance, the police concentrate their patrolling to the circle of cars parked around the dancing area. The dancing area includes the "parking area" and the fire where the dancing and ceremonial singing occur. The police do not frequently patrol the desert away from this area. They are few in number and could be easily overpowered if they patrolled these remote areas singly or even in pairs. They wisely elect to attempt to prevent fights near the fire and to catch the bootleggers as they sell their liquor in the parking area.

The drinkers pattern their behavior so as to avoid detection by the police. They usually meet at the squaw dance and "pitch in" to purchase a bottle or two of wine. Then one of their members takes the money and approaches the bootlegger. The rest of the group usually waits some distance away (usually 100 yards or more). This is done to avoid suspicion and also because the bootlegger normally refuses to sell to groups of individuals for the same reason. In order to sell his load of liquor as fast as possible the bootlegger must remain in the parking area where the drinkers can find him. But he takes no chances because this is the area which the police patrol most thoroughly. After he buys the wine, the buyer rejoins the group and they quickly "go over the hill." They often go as far as 500 yards from the parking area before they find "a safe place." This is usually on the far side of a hill or behind a group of trees. Even though this makes the drinkers very difficult to find, they sometimes drink up quickly and return to the dance area. If they elect to stay out and talk for awhile, they may still drink quickly and get rid of the bottle. Once back in the dance area they may talk with their friends, join the singing competition, or join in the dancing if there is any going on.

It is quite clear that while the patrol patterns of the police do not prevent all drinking, these patterns do allow them to prevent excessive drinking from occurring in the area of the dancing. It also provides for a maximum of police surveillance in the dance area where the majority of people come into contact. This is also the place where the potential for large-scale fighting is greatest. Those fights that occur in the more remote areas are, of course, usually not stopped by the police. However, the Navajo drinker on the reservation is often suspicious of his drinking companions and rarely drinks with a man who is not either related to him by clan or by long-standing acquaintance.

The verbal action plans for the western stomp dance and the squaw dance (not included here) clearly reflect the difference in tension between these two environments. For the western stomp dance, young men hide liquor in their pants and drink in stool stalls or under the bleachers in the gymnasium (see note 1). The squaw dance is quite different. The men do not attempt to hide the bottle. They simply walk behind the hill and look for the best cover. Then they drink the wine. Sometimes they drink it very slowly with each drinker holding the bottle for several minutes or so. Often there is a considerable amount of discussion. The young men talk of their prowess in sports or in the rodeo, and the older men discuss religious mythology.

The verbal action plans also show the importance of the environment for planning of behavior of the informant (actor) in both situations. When a new environment has been created (i.e. the dance hall), a new set of behaviors is required to assure that the drinker will not get caught by the Tribal Police. But when the teenager drinks at the squaw dance, he uses the age-old pattern developed by the older men. This does not mean, however, that the categorization of drinking types is inapplicable. Young men still prefer to drink among ''their own kind'' and they do not discuss religious mythology as the older men do.[4]

THE BARROOM:
AN OFF-RESERVATION EXAMPLE

The drinking patterns expressed by Navajo men of all ages off of the reservation are also largely determined by the milieu in which the drinker finds himself. But the ecological elements comprising this milieu differ greatly from those found on the reservation. For this reason, the verbal action plans and the drinking patterns displayed by Navajo drinkers off the reservation also differ greatly from those seen on the reservation, and there is no difference between the plans for young men (*ashiiké da'adlą́ą́nii*) and older men (*hastoi da'adlą́ą́nii*). In fact, the ecological milieu of the drinker may be seen to vary between bars in the same town. This results in the expression of different drinking patterns by Navajo customers in the various bars.

Five ecological factors appear to influence and in a large part determine the drinking behaviors of Navajos in off-reservation and semi-urban areas: 1) drinking usually occurs in bars (enclosed areas); 2) the liquor laws in the towns are different from those on the reservation; 3) these laws are strictly, often overzealously, enforced by the police; 4) the drinker cannot control the composition of the group in which he drinks; and 5) the bartender, with the backing of the local police, sets the limits for ''acceptable behavior'' in the bar.

---

[4]This example demonstrates the usefulness of the verbal action plans in conjunction with the taxonomy as a method for the investigation of drinking behavior and its environments. The taxonomy indicates the categories into which the informants place all people who drink. It also provides definitions for the various categories by listing the common attributes of those people who are included in them. The plans provide additional detail about the persons assigned to a category. They indicate precisely how the behavioral attributes of the categories have arisen from the drinking behaviors of the people they include. In addition, the plans give the investigator a clear image of the drinker's emotional state. This information is derived in two ways. First, it can clearly be seen in activities such as the avoidance behaviors which the drinkers express toward the police. Secondly, the information comes in the form of parenthetical inclusions at specific points in the plans. Informants often include details which cannot be expressed as sub-sequences of the plans, but which they feel are nevertheless important aspects of the behavior that is occurring. In this way, the investigator can get an idea of how the informants feel about what is happening as well as their in-sequence description of how they behave in a given situation.

These five factors combine to make the barroom situation a very hostile environment for the Navajo drinker who has learned to drink on the reservation. In fact, one wonders why a Navajo who is used to drinking in the open environment of the desert with his friends and relatives would want to enter a bar to drink. It would seem that he would prefer to drink in the safety of his room. There are two primary reasons why a Navajo goes to a bar. The Navajo man who goes off the reservation to seek seasonal or permanent employment turns to the traditional pastime of drinking with other Navajos as a release from the pressures of boredom, isolation, and frustration of life among the people of a largely foreign culture. It is also true that while bar liquor is more expensive than packaged goods, the bar prices are still 200–500% cheaper than the prices charged by the bootleggers on the reservation. This second aspect of the barroom environment attracts many of those Navajos who are chronic alcoholics (by both Navajo and white definitions) to the bars set up on the fringes of the reservation and to the "lower class" bars in the small towns and cities nearby. The fact is that the low price of liquor in these bars is quite attractive to Navajo men who find most other forms of recreation in white society very foreign and expensive.

The Bartender and the Determination of Navajo Barroom Drinking Patterns

Of the five major factors in the ecological milieu of a Navajo drinking in a bar, the role of the bartender in the determination of "acceptable" behavior has the greatest influence upon the behavior patterns displayed by Navajos in the bar. This definition of what is acceptable depends in turn on the bartender's attitude towards Indians in general and his understanding of what the Navajo consider to be "proper" drinking behavior. The result of the attitude of the bartender is the creation of a barroom situation which may range from the total exclusion of Indians after they have purchased packaged liquor, to limited tolerance, to almost complete tolerance of all but the most aggressive behaviors. For example, in one verbal action plan involving a barroom situation, a man was forced to sneak out to the corral behind the bar to be able to drink as he wanted to.

Another example of extreme racial prejudice was found in an off-reservation Utah town. In one bar, the bartender would readily sell liquor or food to a Navajo, but he would then proceed to clean the bar where the Navajo had placed his hands or his money. This was usually followed by a stern lecture in a hostile voice. On one particular occasion, the bartender threatened to call the sheriff because he claimed he had seen a Navajo man giving the liquor to his "grandson." The end result of this hostile attitude was that the Navajos hid behind some bushes, played cards, and drank in the empty lot next door to the bar.

The situation in a Colorado town was somewhat different. The local bartenders and owners would allow Navajos in their bars, but all of the bars except one enforced rigid codes of behavior. If the Navajo did not conform, he was immediately thrown out. The net result was that most of the Navajo patronized the one bar in town that catered to Indian business. It was the only bar at which traditional Indian songs were heard and bottles were passed between friends. Most of its Indian customers recognized it as the only place where they could drink and have any freedom to express their idea of proper drinking behavior. The owners of the other local bars saw this Indian bar as a protection for their properties. More than once some of them stated, "Thank God they have a place of their own. Otherwise we'd really have trouble here." The underlying motivation for this attitude may have been racial prejudice, the refusal to tolerate a different point of view, or the desire to protect the bar and its furnishings. Whatever the case, a definite attempt was made by most establishments to restrict the more traditional drinking behaviors of the Navajo customers, primarily by the policy executed by the bartender.

Other Ecological Factors
in Barroom Drinking

Even in the one bar where the bartender was the most tolerant, the other four major factors in the bar environment served to prevent traditional drinking patterns from being expressed. For example, in this and the other bars the spatial relationships were proxemically wrong for the Navajo drinker (see Hall 1959 for a discussion of proxemics). The Indian bar had several booths along the west wall and a bar along the east wall with a long bench between the two. The overall effect of this was to split the drinkers up into small groups. Usually the largest of these groups had about four members. Most reservation drinking groups have from five to fifteen participants, who usually stand or sit in a circle so that there is a large amount of face-to-face social interaction. When they finish drinking at the squaw dances, the drinkers form even larger groups for the singing contests. Drinking is always accompanied by a large amount of joking, loud laughing, and general "horse-play" involving close physical contact and a considerable number of drunken displays such as staggering. The barroom is not suited for any of these behaviors. The Navajo drinking in the bar sits next to his friends if any are present. He talks in low tones. If he is more traditional than most or if he has no friends at the bar, he usually withdraws to one of the booths and drinks by himself, which is the kind of drinking behavior displayed only by "alcoholics" (*yéego da'adlá̧ą̧nii*) on the reservation!

In addition to being in unfamiliar surroundings, the Navajo has no choice as to the other occupants of the bar. Therefore, he is usually in the company of total strangers who are often of different racial and tribal affiliations than his own. For example, the Indian bar in a Colorado town was patronized by poor whites, Mexican Americans, Utes, Navajos, and some occasional blacks. The hostility these groups have for each other became clear in a number of fights observed by the author and from statements of drinkers in the bars. Furthermore, the Navajo define a larger area of personal space in their "space bubble" than Anglos (Oswald Werner, personal communication). This is especially true of Navajos in the presence of strangers. This makes for an intensely hostile situation when they are confronted at close quarters with their traditional enemies the Utes and the none-too-friendly blacks, whites and Mexican Americans. It is little wonder that fights may easily occur between individuals who have become intoxicated in an attempt to escape both the unhappiness and frustration of life in a foreign culture and the strangeness and hostility of the bar environment (see Graves 1971, for a description of the psychological pressures exerted by the urban environment on Navajo migrants).

Finally, the difference in the laws concerning drinking and their strict enforcement lead to a drastic change in the drinking patterns of the Navajo male when he enters a bar. When the field research was done, it was illegal in Arizona, Colorado, and Utah for a person under 21 to purchase liquor or occupy a bar. Therefore, there were no publicly observable teenage drinking behaviors among off-reservation Navajos. In fact, there were few places for a youth to go and drink, even if an adult bought the liquor for him. Few young Navajos had cars and all of the local land off of the reservation was owned by whites who were not receptive to a group of intoxicated Navajo teenagers. The situation described above in the Utah town was a rare case in which the teenagers were drinking in the company of adults. Minors who drink and the adults who buy the liquor for them are normally subject to prosecution for which heavy penalties are usually imposed.

In general, the local white police are extremely efficient—even overzealous—in policing Indian events involving drinking. Arrests are so frequent at such large events as the Indian pow-wows and ceremonials held off the reservation that large detention centers for drunken

Indians are usually set up. The police form the ultimate sanction which may be imposed by the bartender to ensure that his standard of barroom behavior is met.

THE BARROOM: A SUMMARY

Although it proved difficult to elicit verbal action plans for barroom behavior, those that were gathered clearly indicate that the barroom is a hostile environment. One informant was not allowed to remain inside the bar and another informant said he always got into an argument after he became drunk in a bar. Thus, the bar is clearly a hostile place and the Navajo drinker recognizes it as such.

The Navajo drinking in an off-reservation bar is a very isolated individual who is withdrawn toward strangers and tries extremely hard to establish social relationships with other Navajos. His behavior toward people to whom he tries to relate will largely be determined by the attitude of the bartender toward such activities as the singing of squaw-dance (or other traditional) songs, the use of loud voices, and exhibition of display behaviors through which the Navajo drinker indicates his drunkenness to his friends. Non-Navajos in the bar will further inhibit the behavior of the Navajo drinker. The mutual lack of understanding between different cultural groups in the bar will influence the behavior of all concerned by limiting the displays of drunkenness in order to avoid intergroup enmity. Even so, the hostility generated by the presence of several groups of drinkers of different and often antagonistic racial and cultural origins, may lead to vicious fighting, arrest, and incarceration.

THE YOUNG NAVAJO MALE:
A PROFILE OF YOUTHFUL DRINKING
IN A CHANGING CULTURE

The verbal action plans, the taxonomy of drinking types, and the compassionate attitudes displayed by the Navajo Tribal Court and the Tribal Police toward the young male drinker clearly indicate that although liquor is prohibited on the reservation, it is, within limitations, a culturally acceptable method of having a good time and venting frustration. As long as a young man drinks in a culturally appropriate manner, his drinking will not be a major concern to his family. They may tease him and laugh about his drinking, but "as long as he knows when to stop, it's okay." One also hears that, "You have to get a bit torn down before you can start to enjoy yourself," and "It helps me to get away from things."

It is clear that the Navajo recognize that liquor is a useful escape for the drinker. But this still leaves several questions unanswered: Why is the young Navajo male escaping? What is he escaping from? Why are Navajo teenage boys involved with drinking? It is difficult to answer all of these questions fully, but at this point some definite trends have appeared in the data.

The Functions of Drinking on the Reservation

In an effort to discover why Navajos drink, informants were asked to list the reasons why they thought a Navajo male might drink. They came up with the following:

1. Introduction to traditional drinking by parents at ceremonies
2. The social pressure of friends and relatives when the bottle is passed
3. Drinking for pleasure
4. Demonstration of manhood
5. Unemployment
6. Loss of responsibility
7. Loss of personal pride
8. To forget the drinking of friends or relatives
9. Sexual frustration
10. Family arguments

From this list, it is clear that Navajo drinking has both a socially cohesive function and an escape function. The social cohesion function is apparent in the first three reasons. Children are introduced to drinking as something pleasureful associated with the family. Usually it is the parents or some other close kinsman from the child's outfit who introduces the Navajo boy to drink. Often this introduction occurs at sings during those times when there is no ceremonial activity going on. The drinking is taught to the boy as something that relatives should enjoy together. They are told that "it is good to drink with your relatives (clansmen) because they are your friends, and you should share those things which you enjoy with them."

When the boy becomes older, he begins to go to the western stomp dances with his kinsmen and the friends that he has made at school. Very often they will decide to go to the bootlegger's house before going to the dance. Since even cheap fortified wine costs at least \$3 a pint from the bootlegger, it is extremely expensive for one person to drink alone. So the young men "pitch in" and buy a pint or two together. This pooling of resources is a very important aspect of Navajo life. At many religious ceremonies, the relatives are asked to give what support they can so that the person who is ill may have the most elaborate form of the chant that he or she needs to get well. At other times, such as when a dam has to be built, relatives may be asked to provide labor. But whatever the need happens to be, when a kinsman or a friend is asked for aid he must make an effort to provide something.

When the young men get together to pitch in and buy a bottle of wine, they are reinforcing the ties they have to each other as kinsmen. Every time they pitch in to buy liquor, the bonds of mutual assistance and mutual identity holding them together grow stronger. A relative who drinks with you will be the person who will give you money for a sing when you become ill. He will herd your sheep if you go away. And he will help you haul water if your well runs dry.

The Escape Function of Drinking

Reasons four through ten represent a different function of Navajo drinking. They indicate some of the pressures confronting the individual in his daily life. The informants specifically stated that these reasons represented the kinds of problems from which drinking allowed them to escape. In many cases, the informants felt that most of these problems were more relevant to men who were older than they were. However, even the teenage boys admitted that they drank to "show off" their manhood. Few of the younger boys had problems with unemployment or with unhappy marriages, but they did admit that many of their friends and relatives who were only slightly older had such problems. They also listed the drinking of others and their own normal adolescent sexual frustrations as being reasons to drink. Therefore, all of these reasons apply to the persons who are *ashiiké da'adlą́ąnii* as well as to those who may be placed in the category *hastóíí da'adlą́ąnii*. However, it is evident that individuals drink because they have problems arising from different combinations of these reasons. They drink to both discharge their repressed emotional energy and to experience the narcotic effect of alcohol, which helps them to get "torn down" and to relax or to get "drunk" and to forget.

Even though reasons four through ten are quite different and very specific, one common thread appears to run through all of them: the maintenance of a viable male image. This is a very serious problem facing many young Navajo men today. The problem arises from various sources, but underlying it is the fact that the young Navajo man is the one who suffers the most from the stresses of culture contact and culture change on the reservation (J. E. Levy 1972). This is especially true of the present generation of young Navajo men since they are the ones who have had the fullest formal introduction to Anglo culture. Many of these young men are either high school dropouts or have high school diplomas. Some of them have spent a considerable amount of time living off the reservation in boarding schools or in the homes of Mormon or other white foster parents. Through their text books and through their personal experiences, these young men have learned the male role in the dominant white society. They have seen fathers who were the primary decision makers in the family. They have seen the economic power that the white male has within the family. And they have seen how economically and socially independent the individual white American domestic family is from its kinsmen on both the father's and mother's side. In fact, they have even had to learn a different set of kin categories in order to understand the white man's kinship network.

All of this is very strange to a young Navajo man who was raised in a traditional context for the first few years of his life and who must return to the reservation to begin life when school is over. The traditional society stresses the biological family, the extended family, and the "outfit" as its major economic units (Kluckhohn and Leighton 1958:105–11). In fact, the more traditional families extend these ties of mutual social and economic aid to the entire clan of the child's mother. Some Navajos would even include many of the father's clansmen. Most of the individual domestic families on the reservation are not financially independent at the present time. A Navajo man who has a steady job has a great number of relatives who are continually asking him for financial support of some kind. This does not allow him to accumulate the amount of capital which he would need to live at an Anglo standard of living. He often simply cannot maintain the life style which he has been taught in school is "normal" for the "average American household."

A second problem facing the young Navajo man with respect to the white world is the fact that the Navajo are traditionally a matrilineal and matrilocal people. Descent is reckoned through the mother. A Navajo man owes his first loyalty to his mother's people. His wife and perhaps even his children are both related to him through affinal ties (Witherspoon 1970; 1975). Furthermore, a married Navajo male lives with his wife's people. Because of this, he is often not the head of the household. The authority in the family lies with the wife and her parents. The man may have a job and bring home his paycheck but it is his wife and her family who most often have the say in how it is spent. In addition, the Navajo man must continually refuse or inadequately honor the requests of his mother's people for financial or other forms of support.

If his father-in-law needs him to herd sheep and his mother wants him to help with the shearing, the Navajo man must often refuse his clan to keep peace in his marriage. When this has gone on for some time, the Navajo man finds himself more and more dependent upon his father-in-law.

Finally, there is the problem of unemployment on the reservation. The Tribal Chairman stated frequently between 1971 and 1978 that the unemployment rate on the reservation often reaches 65% (as quoted in the *Navajo Times*). At best, many Navajos are only seasonally employed. The rest of the time they occupy themselves with doing odd jobs for their wives' or mothers' relatives. Often the only pay which these men receive is a warm meal and perhaps some extra food to take home. In an economy where there is little cash and many minor but time-consuming tasks to be done, one cannot expect frequent cash payment. Therefore, the average young Navajo man often simply cannot bring home a regular paycheck like the average Anglo father.

All of this leads to great frustration for many young Navajo men. If they are to live on the reservation, the chances are few that they will be able to occupy the male role which their white school teachers have taught them. Even if they have been lucky and have been able to master the English language and graduate from high school, there may be no jobs available for them to fill. When there are jobs, they are usually of the manual-labor type that offer low pay and little opportunity to put a high school education to use.

Off-Reservation Frustrations

If a young Navajo man tries to leave home for extra training or to obtain a job in large cities like Denver, Los Angeles, or Phoenix, he may have great difficulty in convincing his wife to go with him. She is more secure within the social structure of the Navajo family than he is. Very often she would rather settle for some degree of poverty than the uncertainty of living in the low-income areas of the big cities amid so many people of different racial and cultural backgrounds. Her family will often put up firm resistance to her going with her husband. She may have several children and her relatives will argue that there will be no one to take care of them if she becomes ill. Finally, they will say, "After all, he is only one man and there are many young men around here who will treat you better. We are your relatives and your place is here on the reservation with us." Navajos marry quite young and it is not uncommon for them to have been divorced at least once due to problems like these. The end result of this may be that the young man who goes to the city goes alone.

Finally, the young Navajo man may be faced with difficult religious problems when he leaves the reservation. It is hard to find anyone from the Native American Church (Peyote) with whom to worship in Denver. And it would be nearly impossible to have a singer come out and do a shooting-way chant in a YMCA hotel room. If the young man becomes ill and returns to the reservation for a cure, the hand trembler (a native diviner) will usually diagnose his problems as arising from the polluting influences of the white man. This may be quite true if the illness is largely psychosomatic in nature. When he is treated for his illness, the singer will attempt to convince the young man that the only way for him to remain healthy is to return to the reservation and "live like a Navajo."

Drinking: One of Many Solutions for Psychic Stress

The young Navajo male must find some solution for these difficult situations on and off the reservation. There are many possibilities and drinking is only one of them. Some of the others are religious conversion, complete abandonment of the Navajo way of life for some type of career in the big cities, or the adoption of a completely traditional way of life. Often some of these solutions are combined to meet the needs of the individual. Some people have chosen to go to the cities and have joined their Indian companions in the local bars. There are others who have adopted the native way of life and who drink according to the "old" norms. Those who experience religious conversion usually deny drink but often those individuals join the Native American Church (see Levy and Kunitz 1974:134–7).

Each of these solutions, except simple drinking, offers the Indian a change in his social environment and an altered mental outlook on life. The return to the traditional life and traditional drinking patterns represents a repudiation of the white man's culture and any attempt to get along in it. It also means a reduction in the number of contacts that the young man has with Anglos. Conversion to a "white religion" means the acquisition of many new contacts from within the church groups. Often it involves at least a partial ostracism from the convert's family. This is largely due to the conflicts created when the convert attempts to take the family into the new church with him. This ostracism is never complete, but it does allow the convert to maintain enough distance from his relatives so that he can begin to acquire some capital.

The abandonment of the family is the most extreme of any of these positions. It is also the least successful. The peer group that the young Navajo male has in the city is extremely unstable. Often a young man will go to the city and begin to make good, but he will then become very lonely. When this happens, he begins to take to the bars to look for Indian friends. He soon finds the bars to be a hostile environment, as already noted. Most of the friends he makes are transients who stay awhile and then move on. As he becomes lonelier, the Navajo man drinks more frequently. Finally, he begins to miss work and then loses his job. Graves (1971) has pointed out that this pattern may repeat itself several times before the young Navajo man gives it all up and returns to the reservation for good.

Simple drinking offers a different kind of solution to the problems of the young Navajo male. It allows him to maintain the same social contacts and remain in essentially the same position with regard to the white man's culture and in regard to his own. Drinking allows him to maintain contact with his mother's people without sacrificing his marriage. When they have a ceremony, or when there is a squaw dance he can seek out his maternal relatives and share his bottle with them. Although money is short, he can usually scrape up enough to treat some of them on occasion.

By drinking with his relatives and his high school buddies he can also temporarily escape from the reality of his failure to fulfill his expectations of "supporting his family" like a white man. They will all go down to the bootlegger's place together and drink up as fast as they can. They will stay out and talk about various subjects until they either become sober and go home or they lie down and "sleep it off." In short, they will have created a social group from which the white man is excluded. They will often drink so much that their problems will seem to disappear in the darkness of the moonlit desert. They will reinforce their manhood by talking of local sports and bragging of their prowess in the rodeo. And the next morning, they will return home to their wives or go off to whatever jobs they have been able to find.

Although this solution is a workable one, it is definitely not foolproof. It does allow the young man to vent a tremendous amount of frustration. It lets him drink and demonstrate his manly ability to "handle it." It also leaves him with a hangover. This may prevent him from getting to work and lose him his job, if he has been lucky enough to find one in the first place. At best, simple drinking offers only a temporary solution. It does not do anything to change the dependency relationship between a man and his wife's relatives. It also does nothing toward getting an unemployed man a job. It merely gives a traditionally acceptable "out" that he can use as a means of temporarily getting away from a very stressful situation.

Eventually this drinking pattern becomes obsolete for a Navajo man. As his children begin to grow up, he gains more status within his wife's family. He begins to gain more responsibility. As his wife's parents age, they become more willing to turn the responsibility of caring for the sheep herd over to him. If he and his wife have been industrious, they will have used some of their income from occasional wage labor to build up a small herd of their own. His children may contribute to the family by occasionally doing some wage labor. And finally, when his daughters begin to marry, it will be his turn to be at the receiving end of the father-in-law/son-in-law relationship. In short, he will have become more traditional. He may still drink, but a great deal of the insecurity that made the drinking psychologically essential will have disappeared. His drinking will take on an almost purely social function. The drinking of his youth will have served its purpose by buying him the time that he needed to mature socially.

However, there are many individuals who will not be so fortunate. If the drinker allows his drinking to interfere with his holding a job, or if he cannot find work at all because he is known as a drinker, his wife may try to leave him. He may seek another wife, or he may try to reform his drinking habits. If he tries to find another wife, the odds are that he will fail to find a wife who is not a heavy drinker, and he may turn to the bottle so heavily that he will become a chronic alcoholic, even by Navajo standards. He will begin to drink alone and hang out at the bootlegger's house or at one of the numerous bars that can be found on the margins of the reservation. When this happens, his chances of surviving even into his early forties are remote.[5]

CONCLUSION

In this chapter a methodology has been presented for the study of drinking behaviors. It has viewed the phenomenon of drinking on three levels: the cultural, the social, and the individual. It combines the elicitation techniques of cognitive anthropology with a functional analysis of what drinking does to help bolster both the individual and the culture in the struggle for survival. This use of diverse theoretical viewpoints is necessary if drinking is to be seen, as it must, on a wider level than that of mere social or psychological "function." It is a cultural phenomenon. Thus the data to be used in the analysis of drinking must be relevant to the culture of the drinkers. This means that a cognitive

---

[5]Since this chapter was written, four of the original informants have been killed in alcohol-related accidents.

approach is imperative as a first step to any other research by other methodologies (see Spradley 1970, 1971 and Topper 1976).

The application of this cognitive methodology and its analytical scheme to drinking behavior has revealed that Navajos define "problem drinking" differently than do Anglo-Americans. Because of these different definitions and the misunderstandings they foster, the complexity of the Navajo drinking "problem" is magnified many times. Even if Anglo-Americans and Navajos were totally aware of the differences in definition, however, other areas of cultural conflict generate further difficulties, which act as obstacles to the understanding, tolerance, and treatment of "problem drinking" on the reservation. Considerable space has been taken to discuss some of these major problems. It is hoped that this chapter may be useful in helping explain the Navajo version of the causes, patterns, and functions of "problem drinking."

REFERENCES CITED

Aberle, D. F.
   1966   *The Peyote Religion Among the Navajo.* Chicago: Aldine.
Graves, T. D.
   1967   Acculturation, Access, and Alcohol in a Tri-ethnic Community. *American Anthropologist* **69**:306–21.
   1971   Drinking and Drunkenness Among Urban Indians. In *The American Indian in Urban Society,* J. Waddell and O. M. Watson, eds., pp. 275–311. Boston: Little, Brown and Company.
Heath, D. B.
   1964   Prohibition and Post-Repeal Drinking Patterns Among the Navajo. *Quarterly Journal of Studies on Alcohol* **25**:119–35.
Kluckhohn, C. and D. Leighton
   1958   *The Navajo.* New York: Natural History Press.
Levy, J. E.
   1972   Navajo Suicide. In *The Emergent Native Americans,* Deward Walker, ed. Boston: Little, Brown and Company.
Levy, J. E. and S. J. Kunitz
   1974   *Indian Drinking: Navajo Practices and Anglo American Theories.* New York: John Wiley and Sons.
Levy, R. I.
   1958   The Psychodynamic Functions of Alcohol. *Quarterly Journal of Studies on Alcohol* **19**:649–59.
Lomnitz, L.
   1969   Patterns of Alcohol Consumption Among the Mapuche. *Human Organization* **28**:287–97.
Mandelbaum, D. G.
   1965   Alcohol and Culture. *Current Anthropology* **6**:281–8.

Navajo Times
1971   A newspaper published weekly by the Navajo Tribe in Window Rock, Arizona.
Reichard, G.
1950   *Navajo Religion, A Study of Symbolism.* New York: Bolingen Foundation, Random House.
Robbins, L. A.
1975   Impact of Power Development on the Navajo Nation. *Lake Powell Research Bulletin* **7.**
Spradley, J. P.
1970   *You Owe Yourself a Drunk.* Boston: Little, Brown and Company.
1971   Adaptive Strategies of Urban Nomads. In *Culture and Cognition: Rules, Maps, and Plans,* J. P. Spradley, ed. San Francisco: Chandler.
Topper, M.
1970   The Determination of Navajo Drinking Patterns by Police Policy and Behavior and by Racial Discrimination in Tuba City, Arizona, Cortez, Colorado, Monticello, Utah, and Kayenta, Arizona. Paper presented at Central States Anthropological Society Meeting.
1976   The Cultural Approach, Verbal Plans, and Alcohol Abuse. In *Cross-Cultural Approaches to the Study of Alcohol,* M. E. Everett, J. Waddell, and D. Heath, eds. The Hague: Mouton.
Werner, O.
1966   The Basic Assumptions of Ethnoscience. MS, Northwestern University.
1969   On the Universality of Lexico-Semantic Relationships. MS, paper presented at the Annual American Anthropological Association Meetings, New Orleans.
Werner, O. and J. Fenton
1970   Method and Theory in Ethnoscience and Ethnoepistemology. In *A Handbook of Method in Cultural Anthropology,* R. Naroll and R. Cohen, eds. New York: Natural History Press.
Witherspoon, G.
1970   A New Look at Navajo Social Organization. *American Anthropologist* **72**:55–65.
1975   *Navajo Kinship and Marriage.* Chicago: University of Chicago Press.

Drinking As a Measure Of Proper Behavior: The White Mountain Apaches[1]

5

Michael W. Everett

Man and alcohol have been associated for some time, certainly several thousand years. Aggression and violence have disrupted human communities since prehistoric times. Yet the relationship between the three variables—man, alcohol, and conflict—remains obscure and puzzling. The object of this chapter is to analyze this relationship for a single culture—the White Mountain Apaches. After a brief introduction to Western Apache culture, an ethnographic account of White Mountain Apache drinking behavior is presented. Following this, the Apache domain of "trouble" is characterized, and the relationships between this domain and that of drinking per se are explored.

But there is another dimension of the problem that assumes paramount importance: the uses to which inquiries concerning alcohol are put. A significant contribution to the body of human knowledge can certainly be made in this regard. Yet the useful application of this information does not necessarily follow. Who is better qualified—and justified—to define "useful application" than those individuals most directly involved? Where efforts are being made to modify, adjust, or change patterns of alcohol use and abuse, this is a new, powerful, and

[1]Research upon which this work is based was supported by U.S. Public Health Service grants (MH 17923-01 and MH 22186-01) and a faculty research grant from the University of Kentucky. Helpful comments on an earlier version of this paper were provided by Keith Basso, Stephen Kunitz, John Honigmann, Nancy O. Lurie, Robert Weppner, Martin Topper, Philip Greenfeld, and William Willard. Thanks are also due William Marquardt and Gary Thomas for bibliographic assistance.

yet threatening notion. Some have taken the position that cross-cultural specialists already possess the requisite knowledge to effectively cope with problem drinking in their own terms, regardless of the particular views of drinkers and problem drinkers themselves. Others have argued that the cultural meanings of drinking behavior and problem drinking must be utilized in the understanding and control of these activities. In the concluding discussion of this chapter, evidence is presented in support of this latter position.

THE CULTURAL MATRIX

To view drinking behavior outside its cultural context is untenable, for the manufacture and consumption of alcoholic beverages are inextricably integrated into other conceptual and behavioral domains. For White Mountain Apaches, these complex relationships are compounded because alcoholic beverages are an important component of traditional Apache culture and have been for perhaps several hundred years. Thus, contemporary Apache drinking behavior and problem drinking are not simply the products of recent Anglo-European intrusion, oppression, and deprivation, but are the outcomes and by-products of long-term adaptation to both traditional Apache culture and an alien, more recent white one (Everett 1972a).

White Mountain Apaches occupy the northern mountainous homeland of the Western Apaches proper (see Figure 5.1). Traditionally, the White Mountain bands hunted deer and antelope, gathered wild plant foods such as the acorn and mescal, and planted corn and beans in the high river valleys (Goodwin 1942; Buskirk 1949). These seasonal pursuits kept residential units scattered, but concentrated enough to permit the control of arable land by localized kinship groups. More than 50 nonlocalized unilineal groups or clans functioned to provide a geographic network of cooperative kin relations that could be activated on economic, social, and ceremonial occasions. Subsistence tasks were undertaken by groups of kinsmen, relatives constantly visited each other's camps, and community rituals and curing ceremonies were sponsored by kin relations. In all these activities, the native corn beer *tulpai,* acquired originally from Mexican Indians, served as a social lubricant (Goodwin 1942).

With the advent of the Spanish and the introduction of the horse, Western Apache culture was irrevocably altered. Raiding sorties were mounted into Mexico, and booty plundered from Mexican and Indian villages provided an important adjunct to the Apache subsistence system (Basso 1971). Both raiding and warfare between Apaches and

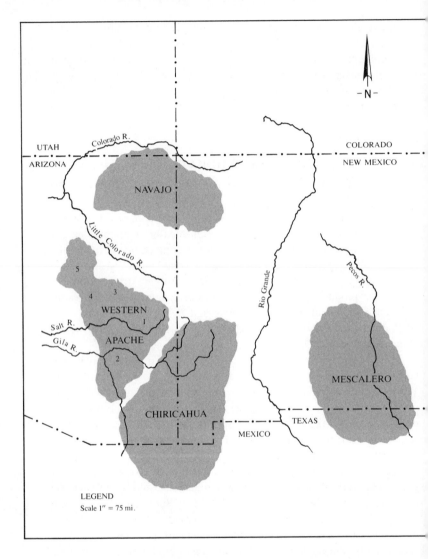

*Figure 5.1   Pre-Columbian Southern Athapascan territory, indicating
discrete Western Apache sub-groups: 1) White Mountain,
2) San Carlos, 3) Cibecue, 4) Southern Tonto, and 5)
Northern Tonto (from Everett 1971a)*

Pima, Papago, and Navajos were considered threatening to Anglos in the mid-1800s, and systematic pacification campaigns were organized against Western Apache and Chiricahua bands. White Mountain Apaches quickly established amiable relations with Anglo military authorities, and, as allies, were permitted to continue an essentially aboriginal lifestyle well into the present century (see Spicer 1962).

Early adaptation to Anglo economic, social, and religious institutions and the beginnings of reservation life were marked by an apparent lack of disruption and disorganization in traditional Apache culture. Seasonal wage labor replaced raiding activities, and settlement patterns crystalized around the agency town, trading posts, government schools, and missionary churches and schools (see Figure 5.2). But even in the late 1930s, large segments of the reservation population, engaged in traditional subsistence pursuits, observed reciprocal kin obligations, and participated in communal ceremonies and individual curing rituals (see Goodwin 1942; Basso 1970a). This is not to say, of course, that acculturation was nonexistent or painless, for there is evidence to suggest that deprivation was being experienced by some segments of the population, but not enough to distort severely the tenaciously persisting core of aboriginal Apache culture (but see Reagan 1930).

In the 1940s and 1950s, however, conditions changed. Traditional economic endeavors were no longer viable, and were subordinated to government seasonal, unskilled wage-labor enterprises, to various Anglo social-welfare programs, and to credit arrangements at local Anglo-owned trading posts. Jobs were few, cash economy needs could not be met by working males, and reciprocal kin obligations redistributed cash resources below the subsistence level. Both men and women attended school and were exposed to the attitudes and values of an Anglo wage-labor economy. Women began to move out of domestic spheres into competition with males for employment. Reciprocal kin obligations fractured, and conflict arose among close consanguineal kinsmen and spouses caught between opposing demands. Intergenerational conflict compounded the readaptive process, and parent-child relations diverged in almost every respect.

The role of alcohol in this process is not at all clear. Anglo observers have long noted an association between alcohol and various forms of interpersonal conflict, physical violence, homicide, and suicide (see Reagan 1930; Goodwin 1942). All existed prior to Anglo contact, but linkages are difficult to identify (Everett 1972a). There is no mistaking the long association between alcohol, fighting, and killing; these have

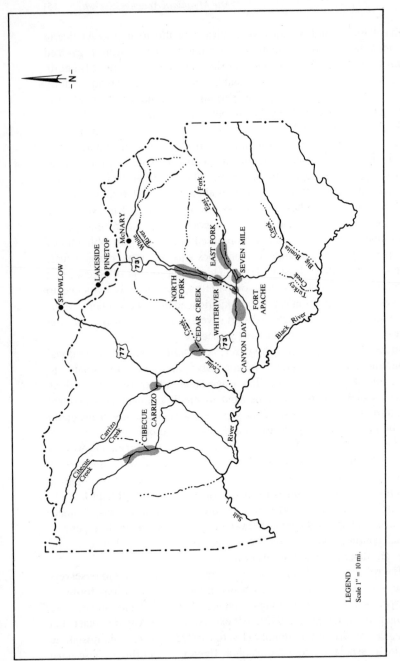

Figure 5.2   Fort Apache (White Mountain Apache) Indian Reservation in 1971, showing 10 official districts
White areas indicate communities; stars and tribal headquarters (from Everett 1971a)

LEGEND
Scale 1" = 10 mi.

simply taken on new forms and meanings in recent times. White Mountain Apache suicide and alcohol, however, appear to involve some radical shifts from earlier patterns.

"DRINKING"

For White Mountain Apaches, people either "drink" or they do not. Potentially, it can be said of any individual, "he drinks" or "she doesn't drink." "He used to drink" is also a common and quite meaningful description. For the Anglo observer, confusion is generated when it is discovered that the label for "drink," *iidłąą'*, is normally used with an object to indicate consumption of nonalcoholic beverages, while in isolation it always refers to liquor of some kind. When one Apache says to another, "do you want a drink?" there is no mistaking the alcoholic referent. The semantic domain *iidłąą'* is thus partitioned in the following way. To the query *iidłąą' datehii?* ("drink, what kinds are there"), Apaches usually respond by numerating various alcoholic beverages. Thus, even though the category *iidłąą'* consists of both alcoholic and nonalcoholic beverages at the most specific level of discrimination, there appear to be two covert, unlabeled categories corresponding to this dichotomy (see Figure 5.3).

The existence of such categories can be readily demonstrated through the use of several sorting techniques (see Berlin, Breedlove, and Raven 1968). When Apaches are asked to select from among three types of beverages—both alcoholic and nonalcoholic—the one item most "different," they easily isolate intoxicating from nonintoxicating drinks. When asked to distinguish between an alcoholic beverage and a nonalcoholic one, the response is invariably that the former "makes you drunk." Thus, though there are no monolexemic labels for "alcoholic drinks" and "nonalcoholic drinks," these categories clearly exhibit cognitive saliency. Perhaps because of the absence of such labels, Apaches have shifted the cover term *iidłąą'* down one level and use it to refer to the category of intoxicating drinks.

What then is the character of this category? In response to the query *iidłąą' datehii?*, Apaches usually list some subject of five different alcoholic beverages: *tułpai, tuu łitsogii* ("home brew"), *bia siłkozii* ("cold beer"), wine, and *tuunčįį'* ("whiskey"). Two—*tułpai,* and *tuu łitsogii*—are domestic. *Tułpai,* the only traditional Apache drink, is manufactured by mixing ground and sprouted corn kernels with water, allowing the mixture to ferment, and then adding a number of herbs or "medicine" for health and strength. In the recent past, a variant of

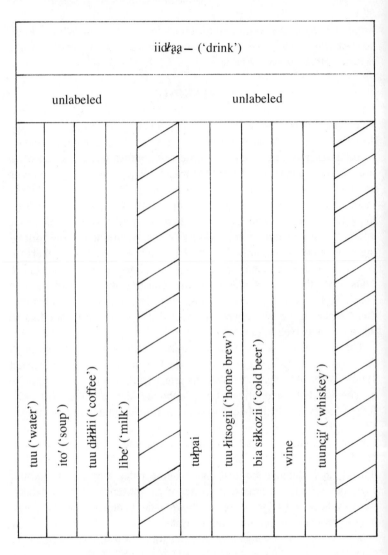

Figure 5.3 Taxonomy of Apache domain of iidłąą'— or "drink."
Hatch marks indicate the position of unextended taxa

tułpai, without the medicine, but with sugar and yeast added, was made "to make you real drunk." Today, some people add whiskey to *tułpai* to strengthen it (see Hrdlicka 1904; 1908). Only mildly intoxicating *tułpai* also plays an important role in traditional economic (ceremonial) exchange activities.

Tuu łitsogii or "home brew" is a concoction of malt syrup, sugar, yeast, and water. It is the most recent of several intoxicants brewed specifically for and by a low-income, heavy-drinking population. Officially, home brew is illegal, but many Apache households, even those of nondrinkers, manufacture it for labor exchange and personal use. The longer it ferments, the stronger the mixture becomes. Its alcoholic content can be as much as twice that of *tułpai.*[2] But Apaches say that people are unable to let it brew for long. Several variants of home brew exist, some characterized by substitutes for key ingredients, such as fruit juice for malt syrup. Others, like the use of additives, such as snuff, tobacco, and aspirin, are intended to heighten the intoxicating effects of the beverage.

Bia siłkozii, wine, and *tuuncįį'* are all commercially available. Of the three, beer is the most popular, and when they can afford it, people prefer it to home brew. Beer is purchased by the quart bottle at the local tribal tavern and package store and is bootlegged by Apaches as a highly lucrative economic venture. Apaches used to make a kind of grape wine, but no longer do so. *Tuuncįį'* or "whiskey" is not popular among Apaches, partly because of its cost, and partly because its packaging and strength are not conducive to group drinking, as are beer, home brew, and *tułpai.*

White Mountain Apaches conceptualize this set of alcoholic beverages in terms of discriminable attributes by which one beverage can be distinguished from another. Through an analysis of these attributes and their interrelations, it becomes possible to assess the meaning and significance of both individual beverages and relationships between these. First, the five types of alcoholic beverages are presented to informants in sets of three for a total of ten different combinations. Then, informants are asked to specify which of the items is "most different" and to justify the choice on the basis of the criteria employed in the decision. Some combination of twelve different attributes is usually revealed.

---

[2]No reliable quantitative measures of alcoholic content exist for *tułpai* or "home brew." Local police estimates put *tułpai* at about half the alcohol content of commercial beer, while because of the time factor in fermentation, "home brew" is thought to range anywhere from "very weak," like *tułpai,* to "real strong," perhaps to the level of cheap wine.

Six of these—availability, strength, preference, effect, source, and manufacture—are used by most Apaches to discriminate between types of liquor in terms of one or another attribute, such as wide or limited availability, strong or weak in strength, etc.

Table 5.1 summarizes the five alcoholic beverages as they are rated by Apaches.

TABLE 5.1   Attribute ratings of five Apache alcoholic beverages.

Alcoholic Beverage	Availability a		Strength b		Preference c	
	wide	limited	strong	weak	popular	unpop.
	1	2	1	2	1	2
tułpai		●		●	●	
home brew	●		●			●
cold beer	●		●		●	
wine	●		●			●
whiskey		●	●			●

Alcoholic Beverage	Effect d		Source e		Manufacture f		
	makes sick	not make sick	Indian	white	home	buy	trade
	1	2	1	2	1	2	3
tułpai		●	●		●		●
home brew	●			●	●	●	
cold beer		●		●		●	
wine	●			●		●	
whiskey	●			●		●	

A careful inspection of Table 5.1 provides some insight into relationships between different kinds of alcoholic drinks. Home brew, wine, and whiskey clearly share at least five of the possible six attribute values. Beer is somewhat intermediate, but *tułpai* shares with the others only one to two values. In other words, common attribute values indicate that wine, whiskey, home brew, and to a lesser extent beer, are conceptually more similar than *tułpai*.

How is this conceptual distinction important? Presumably it has behavioral implications, such that drinking behavior involving *tułpai* is somehow different from that involving other alcoholic beverages. Two other factors are relevant here. First, *tułpai* is frequently referred to as "food" or nourishment, and its herbal additives are termed *izee* or "medicine." Second, individuals who say they do not "drink" nevertheless drink *tułpai*. In other words, drinking *tułpai* is not the same as drinking home brew, clearly an alcoholic beverage; it is more akin to eating food. Thus, it is commonplace to hear a parent admonish his child, "here, drink some *tułpai,* it is good for you." Alcoholic beverages, then, are defined in cognitive terms which are directly relevant to drinking behavior. This relationship is perhaps most clear with respect to the setting or context of drinking activities.

Apaches classify drinking situations into two basic categories: appropriate and inappropriate. In other words, in some situations, drinking is considered acceptable behavior, and it is expected that people will behave in terms of this standard, except, of course, those who do not drink under any circumstances. In other situations, drinking is viewed as inappropriate and unacceptable. The ratio of inappropriate to appropriate drinking situations is not high. Apaches say that one shouldn't drink in view of others who might object. Nowadays, consumption of alcoholic beverages in a public place is unlawful, according to local tribal statutes. Thus, Apaches perceptively note that drinking in view of policemen is inappropriate, since this form of behavior can and usually does result in arrest and incarceration. Much of the time, this prohibition is contingent upon the zeal of the law enforcement officers themselves, as illustrated in the following account, considered quite humorous by the person involved:

> A person should not drink in front of police. They might catch him and put him in jail. One time, they caught me on Blueberry Hill. I had just opened a can, and the policeman snuck up behind me and grabbed that can. He told me to get in the car. Then he took me to jail. The next day, a friend put up $25 bond for me. I went to court the next Monday and got 15 days or $15 for one open can, and I hadn't even taken one drink yet!

In addition, it is considered disrespectful to imbibe in front of those who abstain or strongly disapprove of drinking, namely Christian Apaches and Anglo missionaries both termed *inaašut*.[3]

Both of these prohibitions apply to all situations in which there is the potential for drinking; actual drinking behavior is constrained by these limitations. In addition, these rules apply to situations in which it is considered appropriate to drink. Thus, in the situations to be described below, normal drinking behavior is either postponed or interrupted

---

[3] Some Apaches, especially the young, are concerned with Anglo attitudes toward Indians. They object to behavior that Anglos disapprove of or that might cause whites to think less of them as Indians. Hence, these people consider drinking and drunkenness in front of whites inappropriate behavior.

when it becomes necessary to temporarily observe one or the other of the two drinking prohibitions. Moreover, in some situations, such as public dances, acceptable drinking behavior is structured by the necessity to observe these rules. Thus, the drinking prohibitions are not meant to serve as deterrents to drinking, but function simply to redefine the parameters of appropriate drinking behavior.

White Mountain Apaches specify at least six distinct situations in which it is considered appropriate to drink (see Everett 1971b). Three of these are important social occasions: *gojiitał* ("dance"), *daiyąą'* ("party"), and *nahastą'* ("wake"). The others are permutations of a common theme: *goshjįyųų'* ("my place"), *X goḥįyųų'* ("X's place"), and *dawotehe* ("everyplace"). It is important to note that, although these situations may vary considerably in structure and content, they all have two things in common. First, except as affected by drinking prohibitions, the consumption of alcoholic beverages is an appropriate and acceptable activity or accompaniment to other activities. Second, there exist rather specific rules for each of these situations regarding *how* drinking is to occur. In other words, Apaches expect that when drinking takes place in one of these situations, it will proceed according to a formal plan for behavior shared by the participants in the activity.

Gojiitał ("dance"). There are at least three kinds of dances in which Apaches participate. They may vary in terms of structure and purpose, but all share a number of common features. Perhaps most notable is that large numbers of people are present, some participants, others simply as spectators. Some are given drinks in exchange for their services. If it is a curing ceremony, the medicine man and those who assist him receive drinks from the host. A meal is usually served, sometimes only to the participants, and drinks are exchanged for assistance in preparing food, chopping wood, and hauling water. A medicine man's assistant described the situation this way:

> We were sitting around, drinking cold beer, as we ate. The medicine man went back to sleep again. About 7:30, three of us present were given beer to drink, then they got a bucket of home brew. Whoever is helping in the ceremony usually gets served. Most of the people were relatives but there were other persons there, too. They were given drinks for helping with cooking, for chopping wood, carrying water, cutting beef, or peeling potatoes. We drank a bucket of home brew and some cold beer as the singing went on. Whoever is a singer is given two or three cups to drink. Every other person that is sitting around, is given one cup. The medicine man gets the most. Helpers like me and C get one cup. Singers drink first, then persons sitting on the side drink.

Much of the time, too many people, especially nonparticipants, are present, and drinks are distributed sparingly. Usually, large quantities of home brew are prepared, and this is intended for marginal participants and spectators, while beer is reserved for central figures in the activity. In either case, bootlegging is prevalent and is the source of liquor for a large proportion of those present. One man gave this account of *gojiitał* drinking behavior:

> Down near the campfire they were dancing. Many people were gathered around to watch while some others were dancing. Drinking was going on somewhere outside but not inside near the fire. Outside the circle where the cars are parked people were looking around to buy some beer from the bootleggers. Only the people on the outside buy and drink it. Some people bring wine, whiskey, *tułpai*, and home brew to the dance. They hide it inside their pickups. If someone needs a drink, he goes to the pickup to buy it. Friends will usually get together and go up for a drink. Friends take turns buying the drinks.

Daiyąą' ("party"). A party may be given for a number of reasons. Some are intended solely for drinking, while others involve a combination of both eating and drinking. Some are part of a ceremonial complex in which, prior to a dance, several parties are given by the members of two kin groups. The formal exchange of food and drinks—five gallon cans of *tułpai* and cases of beer—is an integral part of this pattern (see Basso 1970a). Others may simply celebrate an important social event, such as a birthday, a wedding, or a high school graduation. Rules governing consumption vary. Where drinks are exchanged between kin groups, the recipients are expected to invite their hosts to share the liquor, and there is much formality, as illustrated by the following case:

> We gave him half a cow. After that we gave him flour, salt, baking powder, and sugar. Then we gave him about four cases of cold beer and about 15 cans of *tułpai*. All of this goes on as they eat. One person is responsible for getting beer and *tułpai* but he picks someone else to pass out drinks. We call on each other to drink together, even if we don't know each other.

But if the party is intended specifically for drinking, even though the ostensible occasion is a birthday or some such event, rules guiding drinking behavior are less rigid. One man gave this account:

> The drinking party starts at noon. If they can't afford it, they don't feed the guests. They will just serve from ten to twenty gallons of home brew. People will just sit around in the shade and the bucket is

put out for them to help themselves if they get thirsty. They will use a big malt syrup can as a cup. They take the first drink at the bucket, then take another dip and take it back to the shade.

Nahastą' ("wake"). At a wake, relatives and friends maintain a solemn nightlong vigil over the remains of the deceased. Wakes for adults are normally two-night affairs, but those for infants and young children may be only one night in length. Paying one's respects and grieving are highly formalized gestures. Like dances, many people attend wakes. It is considered standard for a midnight meal to be served to all who are present. Thus, food must be accumulated and prepared, wood and water hauled, and so on. For all these tasks, drinks are exchanged, and not on a voluntary basis. It is imperative that drinks be distributed to those who help out, simply so they will continue to be of assistance. As one person put it:

> The people help out because they expect a little bit to drink. If you don't have anything, they will just drop in for five minutes. But if you have some beer or *tułpai*, they will help you chop wood, haul water, and all the jokes they know they will tell you.

Low-key humor is an important component of *nahastą'*, and Apaches say that handing out drinks functions to encourage people to stay all night, to stay awake, and to relieve periods of mourning and grieving with tales of humor and ribaldry. The following account gives some indication of how all these factors operate to provide solace and support for the relatives of the deceased:

> Guests are given drinks to encourage them to stay longer. Otherwise, after the midnight eating is over, they might go home. Then there would be nobody around in the morning at the place where the wake is. Drinks help to keep all the people there awake until the morning. If everybody left, the host would be left all alone to watch the body.

Rules for drinking behavior at a wake can be rather complex, depending upon the circumstances. Drinking prohibitions prevail when pertinent and may be accompanied by further restrictions, as indicated in this instance:

> At a wake, it is okay to drink if no missionary is around. If there is one there in the circle, then you have to drink outside the fence. But if they are not there, it is okay to drink inside. Veterans shouldn't drink inside the bench of veterans. If they want to drink, they have to move out to where other people sit. For civilians, it is okay to drink inside the bench.

Dawotehe ("everyplace"). Those who drink anywhere are jokingly referred to as *ƚįį bigan diskit* or "camels." The referent is not so much the perpetual search for liquor as it is the amount of alcohol consumed once a source has been located. One man, himself a camel, described the behavior pattern this way:

> You can tell a camel by how much he drinks. If a man drinks too much, people call him a camel. He picks up a cup and drinks it all down. I would wake up at three or four in the morning with a hangover, so I would run off looking for home brew. When it cools down, then you go drink some more.

Since camels are heavy drinkers, on a full-time, permanent basis, most of the money they acquire is quickly spent on liquor. The seasonal and odd jobs they hold provide little in the way of ready cash. Thus, camels wander on regular circuits through the community in search of free drinks. These can be had in exchange for labor at parties, dances and especially wakes.

Home brew is the camel's "water," since it is cheap and easy to make. A large percentage of camps in every community have home brew on hand daily. Because of their physical conditions (i.e. hangovers) and because etiquette demands it, camels are usually offered home brew when it is available and uncommitted. Needless to say, camels use this to their advantage. A young man, well on his way to becoming a camel, said this:

> If you don't have any money, you can't get a drink, so some of your friends might give you drink. If they buy it, they give you some. But it doesn't matter if you don't have a friend. If you have a hangover, you can go check each house. If a guy uses some sense, he can see someone heating up water in the evening. That's the first place to stop in the morning to get home brew.

Gosƚįiyųų' ("my place"). This situation is a particular expression of *dawotehe* in which the residents of a camp manufacture and/or consume liquor on the premises. Availability and commitment are central here. If and when drinks are available at camp, they are usually committed to two somewhat different activities. The first is simply social drinking involving the residents of a camp and acquaintances who just might happen by. But Apaches emphasize another pattern, perhaps because of its redeeming economic value. In most camps, cash is rare. There always exist menial tasks that cannot be handled effectively through traditional kinship channels. Home-brew ingredients can be gotten on credit at local trading posts, and enough liquor can be manufactured to hire several workers, usually camels, for these jobs. Even nondrinkers and Christian Indians consider this a viable economic alternative. The pattern is described this way by one informant:

> Home brew is made if someone needs workers for chopping wood, carrying water, looking for a donkey, irrigating, making a shade shelter, or hoeing. You look for two or three guys and make about 10 or 15 gallons. You give two and a half gallons to each. In the morning, they might take one gallon with them to work but if they don't want to, they might fill up first and then go to work. They then come back about noon time and eat, then start drinking.

X gołįiyųų' ("X's place"). When Apaches speak of drinking at another camp besides their own, they tend to characterize these activities in terms of friendly reciprocity.

In general terms, this pattern is identified with social drinking in the context of *gosłįiyųų'*. But Apaches usually specify a particular camp when they use the term *X gosłįiyųų'*, and the referent is both to the prevalence of heavy drinking and to the pattern of accessibility. Although they may be purchased outright on a cash basis, drinks are regularly traded or gotten on credit. Three Apaches gave these accounts:

> If you don't have money, you can get groceries at the store on credit and trade them off for drinks. If I got new boots, a hat, or a knife I can pawn them until the next day, then get them back for $2.

> You can pawn flour, sugar, meat, or any canned goods. If you have five pounds of sugar and one package of yeast, you can get one gallon of home brew. One egg and one piece of meat for one gallon. One carton of Coke will go for half a gallon. Two cans of pork and beans and one can of Spam will get one gallon.

> A lot of people buy drinks by pawning things like billfolds, watches, or groceries. If you are working, you can get credit until payday. If I told a friend I was getting paid next Friday and promise to pay him back on Saturday, he will give me two gallons. That much costs $5. Then when I pay back, I will get one more gallon free.

These do not, of course, exhaust all the possible Apachean drinking situations. But they do account for those which are most prevalent. One pattern not represented here, due partly to its emergent, nontraditional nature, is private, domestic drinking. Found predominantly among those who hold full-time, permanent jobs, domestic drinking is characterized by one or more cans of beer within the confines of the household and primarily for the purpose of relaxation. Its asocial nature is striking in contrast to the situations described above, and is explained by Apaches in terms of successful adaptation to a wage labor economy.

"DRINKING" AND "TROUBLE"

The Apache term *naǫnt'lok* labels the notion "trouble" or "things to be avoided." The domain of "trouble" includes everything from "sickness" and "witchcraft" to "going to jail" (see Everett 1970). Potentially, any of these can be associated with or caused by drinking. But when Apaches are queried, "What kinds of trouble come from drinking?" the usual response is a rank ordering of four types of trouble in terms of prevalence: *iłkediddi'* ("bad talk"), *nałįįnesįį'* ("fighting"), *atiziste'* ("suicide"), and *yozesii'* ("killing"). Each of these can be directly related to drinking, but it is much more common for drinking to generate bad talk which then causes fighting, suicide, or killing. Thus, central to an understanding of problem drinking is the phenomenon of bad talk.

Iłkedidii' or "bad talk" is a label that apparently covers a number of conflict situations in which heated verbal exchanges usually occur between adversaries. In some cases, confrontation is absent, and the pattern simply involves one person saying "bad things" about someone else to other people, essentially a form of gossip or rumor-mongering. In others, a public announcement of grievances occurs. But the classic form of bad talk involves an antagonist confronting either an individual or a group of people and shouting insults and curses. Why is this form of conflict so significant? One man explained it this way:

Apaches do not like bad words used against them. Working people might be cussed out by their boss. If so they just walk off the job. Apaches do not grow up with these hard words. If you are missing an arm, or if you limp, or if you are absent-minded, people throw it up to you. Apaches are like that. Whatever your personality is, whatever you are, people kid you about it.

The six drinking situations discussed earlier provide somewhat different contexts for bad talk and subsequent forms of trouble, and Apaches rank them according to which exhibit the "most" or the "worst" trouble. *Gojiitał* or "dance" is almost always ranked first. The group *daiyąą-dawotehe-X gołįįyųų'* ("party"-"everyplace"-"X's place") is ranked second, while *gosłįįyųų* ("my place") and *nahasta'* ("wake") are thought to involve the least amount of trouble. All of these manifest the same basic pattern, different only in quantitative terms.

Two features appear to set aside dances as likely places for trouble to occur. First, a large number of relatively unacquainted people are present. Second, the prevalence of *benawodizigiz* or "drunkenness," as compared to simple drinking, is high. One man described trouble at a dance in these terms:

> I never did get a chance to see the dance. It was too crowded. But I didn't want to take a chance outside, either. Somebody might hit me, you know. There is a lot of drunken business outside, under the shade trees just beside the river. Drinkers are fighting each other. The boys especially go crazy. They all talk about girls every time they get drunk. If somebody insults another guy's girlfriend, there will be trouble. It is dangerous because there are a lot of boys and girls running around outside drunk, trying to buy more beer.

Also of concern here is the expectation that trouble will not cease with bad talk, but will proceed to fighting or, even worse, drinking and drunkenness will generate fighting directly without any warning by way of bad talk.

Apaches note that drunkenness per se is not solely responsible for trouble. They point out that camels are careful not to get involved in trouble, for if they do, they jeopardize interpersonal relations by which drinks are procured. But this is no guarantee that camels will not foment trouble once inebriated. Another variable becomes preeminent in the process: casual verbal dueling in the form of teasing, boasting, and joking, frequently with a sexual referent. A heavy-drinking man of about 45 gave the following account:

> When people get together to make a little talk, it could lead to trouble if they start teasing each other. Pretty soon someone gets mad. Even friends can get mad and start fighting. If I teased a guy about doing it to his girl right there and he said he wasn't, I would keep it up until he would get mad. Or if I said I gave my friend the money I owed him and he said I hadn't done it yet, then I would get mad. Ladies get jealous when their husbands go around with other women. They start talking like they were joking about it but they would soon get mad. There is a lot of arguing over who does something best. If I tell a story about my doing something, the other guy might say I was lying even though it might be true. He just wants to be better than me. Trouble starts this way.

The relationship between drunkenness, humorous repartee, and trouble is perhaps best illustrated when heavy drinking occurs and there is an emphasis on joking and teasing. Only a thin line separates harmless banter from bad talk. Apaches say that this line becomes obscured for those who are intoxicated; innocuous verbal jousting is interpreted by the drunk as intentional derision and condemnation. A 25-year-old person described the situation this way:

> Drunks don't know what they are doing. You may make fun or joke about something but drunks don't know it and get mad. If I told a guy I saw him with a girl last night, or I saw him fall off a horse or bull in a rodeo, then I started laughing, he will get mad when he is drunk. If not, he would let it go.

What, then, is the pattern of problem drinking with regard to bad talk and fighting? Drinking is essentially a social activity, characterized by intense affective and emotional content perhaps best expressed by the English term "conviviality." Verbal play in the form of humorous repartee is an important feature of drinking situations, especially where this is prescribed behavior, as at wakes and at dances (Basso, personal communication). But intoxicated persons interpret this harmless banter as a serious personal challenge or a severe threat. The responses of such individuals are anger and bad talk.

The relationship between drunkenness, bad talk, and physical violence is more complex. Simply because bad talk occurs in the context of drinking activities does not mean that it will inevitably lead to subsequent fighting or other forms of trouble. Indeed, Apaches indicate that much of the time the process ceases with bad talk. Two mechanisms intervene. Physical constraints can be applied by observers. But this is a rarity. Although drunkenness is considered inappropriate behavior in virtually all settings, little is done to prevent its occurrence. At dances, parties, and wakes, speech making by respected community leaders usually involves a request that guests drink prudently and avoid excess, especially if a medicine man is attempting to treat a patient. Sometimes, an individual will be refused drinks because "he has had too much." But once drunkenness occurs, it is handled cautiously. Only rarely is the intoxicated person confronted directly, and then usually by another drunk. One strategy is to get the drunk to go to sleep; thus camels are rarely refused food and drink. The general pattern, then, involves a set of indirect preventive or avoidance measures which it is hoped will cope effectively with drunkenness.

The same is true for bad talk and fighting; most Apaches are hesitant to intervene in a verbal assault between a drunk and an adversary. Avoidance is the key feature in preventing bad talk from generating physical violence, but not, of course, on the part of the antagonist. The avoidance strategy may operate once bad talk occurs or even in response to initial physical attack. In either case, appropriate conduct calls for the victim to "just walk away." Said two informants:

> When a sober guy runs into a drunk who wants to argue, he is going to walk off. He will think that trouble might start so it would be best to go home.

> When I first started bullriding, everybody was glad about it. Now they all hate me. Last week, this guy got six boys after me. He is only a loudmouth. He hit me two times in the face, but I didn't do anything. I just walked away. If you know its going to end that way, you just have to walk away when you know he's jealous.

The rationale here is unmistakable: an individual who is drunk is not in full possession of his senses and thus is not aware of what he says or does. He is completely unresponsible for the consequences of his own behavior. Thus, the drunk is deviant in two respects. Potentially, he can say and do virtually anything and, as a result, is highly unpredictable and dangerous, especially to people at whom he directs bad talk. Moreover, the drunk cannot be held responsible for the consequences of his actions while intoxicated; it was the alcohol that caused the trouble. The situation was characterized this way by two Apaches:

> When the drinking was going on, something went wrong. Everyone there was drunk and didn't know what they were doing. The next morning, they all came around and shook hands. They said they were sorry and didn't know what they were saying. They apologized to each other.

> When people are drunk, they don't know it. When they sober up, they apologize again. They may not even remember drinking or being drunk and wonder later on why they were fighting. They might shake hands.

The relationship between sobriety, drinking, and drunkenness is critical in Apache problem drinking. No measures are taken to prevent drunkenness, and when it occurs in conjunction with bad talk, onlookers hesitate to intervene because of the unpredictability of the antagonist. The victim of verbal assault is also aware of the potential danger, and usually seeks to avoid it, *if he can*. If he is sober, and can reflect on the possible meaning of the developing situation, he can take positive steps to avoid further trouble. Characteristically, avoidance takes the following form. The victim stands quietly, eyes cast ground-ward, awaiting the end of the verbal onslaught. When it ceases, he simply turns and walks away (see also Basso 1970b). But if he is incapable of sober reflection because he is intoxicated, then the avoidance strategy is impaired, and further trouble can be expected to erupt.

Clearly, rationality, in Apache terms, is the dominant feature of the drinking-bad-talk-fighting configuration. But how are killing and suicide integrated into this set of relationships? At the moment, little is known about White Mountain Apache homicide, except that it appears to be the most persistent of all aboriginal social pathologies (Everett 1972a). Basically, killing occurs in three forms. It can be the unintended consequence of fighting, i.e., the result of drunken violence. It can occur in conjunction with suicide. And it can simply be an act of premeditated violence, usually involving drinking but not drunkenness. In the latter case, responsible judgment is clearly operant, readily apparent in the homicidal strategy. The following accounts illustrate each type:

F is married to G's brother, who had been beating her up, so F came over to beat up G. They were drinking there. They started fighting. F is a big woman and kicked G real bad. A few days later, G started to bleed and then she died. The death was ruled an accident, but F's husband has been throwing this up to her, about killing his sister.

H was drunk and got into a fight with this woman. She said he was working witchcraft on her 15-year-old daughter. She started arguing with him about it. She was talking too much, so he hit her. She said she was going to report him for it. He went home and shot himself. After he shot himself, his wife went over looking for the woman, who was hiding. The girl returned from school. H's wife asked the girl where her mother was, saying she was going to shoot her. When she couldn't find her, she killed the girl instead. Then she tried to hang herself, but her sisters stopped her.

J told his wife they were going up to the corn field to work. He wasn't drinking. He put his rifle in the truck. Her mother was scared and told the woman not to go. But they went. J accused her of running around. He was jealous. He got his rifle, and they started fighting. She grabbed the gun and shot him. Then she started to run away. But he picked up the gun and killed her. J died later at the hospital.

Retaliation, revenge, "getting even" are all important factors here. The offense may be actual or presumed and can be characterized by anything from gambling arguments and interference in quarrels to jealousy, which is the dominant motive. In any case, the association of killing with alcohol, so far as Apaches are concerned, is a meaningful and expectable relationship. Moreover, the direction of physical aggression against an antagonist or adversary is consonant with the long-standing tradition of "getting even."[4] But there is another way that retaliation can occur, in which physical aggression is directed against the victim by himself, and, in the process, his antagonist incurs emotional injury. This is the Apache definition of *atiziste'* or "suicide," which is thought of as a voluntary "killing of one's own body" (Everett In press).

With regard to its association with alcohol, suicide is somewhat similar to killing, except that drunkenness appears to be absent from the configuration. As in the other major forms of trouble, drinking generates bad talk. The emotional reaction of an adversary to bad talk is "not to care for his life" and a desire to inflict punishment on his antagonist in the form of guilt and responsibility for his death. One Apache put it this way:

> In the old days, a person could murder someone he was mad at. But now he will be arrested and punished. Now the only way to show a person how much he has hurt you is to go kill yourself. That will show him.

Conflict between spouses, usually involving jealousy, is a frequent suicide motive. Other consanguineal kin may generate trouble, such that self-destruction becomes an appropriate coping mechanism. Three such instances were described like this:

> K was married to my son. They and their two kids lived with us. There was a dance at the community building. K's husband was dancing with another girl. K came home and took a small can of kerosene from the house. She walked over there between those two trees. She poured it on herself and then burned herself. She must have been jealous. She was not drinking because she belonged to the Miracle Church.

> L was my 24-year-old brother. He was living with my husband and me. He went over to his brother's camp to watch them play cards. No one would give him a drink. L asked his brother. He said no and

---

[4] Goodwin (1942:550) notes emphatically that this factor dominates interpersonal relations in Apache society, virtually to the exclusion of all else.

talked bad to him. L left and came here. Only the kids and me were here. He told me that he was feeling bad because his brother talked against him. He took a rifle and said he was going to take it back to the owner. Then he shot himself.

M was my wife's son. He was about 15 years old. He was trying to ask for a drink from his mother's sister, right across the road. She told him no. He told them he was going to go home, get his gun, and kill himself. He got a 30-06 and shot himself in the forehead.

In each case, there are two key features. Bad talk, usually involving drinking, occurs. The victim responds to this verbal attack with anger and a desire to retaliate. He makes certain that the responsibility for his death can be unmistakably laid to his adversary, frequently by announcing his intentions beforehand, as in the last case above. Another incident clearly illustrates the notion of revenge:

N lived with her parents. She was about 17. She was staying with her boyfriend at her mother's camp. Her mother did not want them together. She and N fought, and she ran the boy off. After she burned herself, N said to her parents, ''I hope you are happy now as I won't be seeing him anymore.''

Retaliation is not always the goal of a self-destructive act. When it is not, the gesture is usually just that, an attempt involving the obvious nonlethal application of a common technique, such as a drug overdose.[5] The intent is clear: reconciliation between adversaries, initiated by the one responsible for bad talk in response to the suicidal gesture. Said one Apache:

O burned herself after an argument with her husband. He lost his job and started drinking. He beat her. Since she burned herself, they have gotten back together because he feels very sorry for how he treated her, and he has gone back to work and is supporting his family.

Since it is the potential victim who designates the purpose of the impending act in response to the precipitating conflict situation, his adversary must take full responsibility for preventing a possible suicide.

---

[5]Most gestures involve drug overdoses, shooting, or burning. In each case, the substance ingested is small and the wounds inflicted superficial. In addition, there have been, with one questionable exception, no successful suicides by overdose. Clearly, an attempt, rather than the real thing, is the intended goal of such behavior (see Everett In press).

The outcome cannot be predicted with certainty, but most antagonists, if capable of sober reflection, are not willing to gamble. Thus, the threat of a possible suicide, even if only an attempt, is a powerful level in interpersonal relations. A mother of three teenagers described the dilemma this way:

> It's really hard when you have teenagers. They think they are so grown up. They want everything we didn't have as kids. You just don't know what they're going to do. When they're big, you can't stop them. So you try to give them what they want, like these motorcycles. If you don't, they'll say, "I'm going to kill myself." You really get afraid of them. If you talk to them or beat them, they get mad and kill somebody or themselves.

DISRUPTION, TOLERANCE, AND CONTROL

For White Mountain Apaches, the man-alcohol-conflict relationship is a readily understandable and predictable aspect of contemporary reservation life, perhaps even to the exclusion of all else. There exist a set of conceptual notions regarding these variables against which actual behavior is constantly measured. The less the degree of variation in cognitive expectation the closer the fit between conceptualization and actuality. In the Apache case, there are few surprises; overt behavior only infrequently deviates from what is expected. Drinking behavior is regularized in readily apparent and understandable ways. Rules or standards for appropriate conduct act to generate these forms; if a particular activity does not conform to cognitive expectation, it becomes difficult to interpret in culturally meaningful terms. In other words, the significance of Apache drinking behavior and problem drinking depends upon their orderly and predictive character; when this is absent, the usual response is to attribute orderliness to the activity such that it can be satisfactorily interpreted. Thus, Apaches will frequently account for an activity whose details are unknown by saying, "Well, he must have been drinking."[6]

---

[6] It matters not that behavior may not in fact result from this kind of decision-making process. Indeed, there must exist a kind of feedback mechanism from deviant behaviors to cognitive expectation. The failure of consistency theory to account satisfactorily for *all* behavior supports this contention. But the validity of the cognitive paradigm is not at issue here. Apaches act as if it were a true and accurate representation of reality. They readily verbalize cognition-behavior comparisons. And, perhaps most importantly, they commit themselves emotionally to the belief that sets of standards or rules must in fact underlie actual behaviors or must at least be utilized in attempting to interpret and thus understand each other's actions.

Clearly, the man-alcohol-conflict paradigm as conceptualized and utilized by Apaches is explanatory as well as descriptive. Its descriptive function is analytical in the sense that the abstract model can potentially be superimposed on virtually any domain of human behavior for possible interpretation. But this interpretation not only involves the ordering of a set of disparate variables into a coherent and thus meaningful whole; it also includes the specification of causal relationships between these variables, such that explanation and prediction become possible. From the Apache point of view, the man-alcohol-conflict paradigm constitutes a device by which to account for past, present, and future activities, so that these become knowable, understandable, and thus culturally sensible.

But there are exceptions. Sometimes adult behavior does not conform to Apache expectations. One reaction of observers is to force the activity into the prescribed mold, especially when its details are unknown or unclear. Another response is resort to contingency rules, secondary or situation standards that apply only under special circumstances, such as an unusual physical setting, uncertain interpersonal relations, and peculiar personality characteristics. Regardless of how or why the exceptions occur, their significance is of paramount importance to the existing model as a feedback mechanism; they indicate the direction and magnitude of change occurring in the system. Thus, as behavioral exceptions occur, the conceptual paradigm is continually adjusted to adequately account for these and to maintain the integrity and coherence of the phenomenal and ideational systems.

Perhaps the most tension is created in this relationship in transgenerational terms. Although some of the conceptual structures of adult Apache are shared by adolescents, it is exceedingly difficult to account for the drinking activities of youngsters using the adult paradigm (Everett 1972b). Some overlap is unavoidable; the character of the socialization process is such that children learn about adult drinking behavior at a very early age. But new and different forms are created in peer-group settings, environments which not only exclude adults but are often hostile to their presence or interference (Everett 1973). Adult Apaches complain that their children do not "act right," i.e., behave in terms not acceptable to adults. This is particularly true with respect to drinking behavior and problem drinking; teenage gangs roam at night in search of liquor and violence, and anyone abroad, especially adults with drinks, is in potential danger of at least a severe beating. This is a worrisome state of affairs for adults and parents, one which makes little or no sense to them, but over which they would like to exert some control. In this context control means modeling adolescent drinking behavior after its adult counterpart, such that the same man-alcohol-conflict paradigm serves both groups.

The simple fact that cognitive expectation and behavioral reality converge to within acceptable limits does not necessarily mean that the particular activity has any positive value or that Apaches wish to retain it unchanged. By definition, "trouble" is to be avoided, not prevented; presumably, as long as it does not affect one's self, the fate of others is of little or no concern. But such is not the case, for both drinking per se and concomitant trouble can be and usually are disruptive to normal interpersonal relations. Thus, the camel would appear to be a harmless individual, if not to himself then certainly to others and thus of little bother to anyone. The problem, of course, is that the camel does not exist in vacuo or only in a group of his peers; he is part of the community at large, a position in an intricate kin network whose effective functioning depends upon relatively smooth interpersonal relations, especially in economic terms. By his behavior, he abrogates familial and kinship responsibilities, something which can be especially disruptive when alternatives to cooperative kin relations are nonexistent or ineffective. For this, the camel is held responsible and, as a result, frequently becomes the target of domestic conflict and discord.

Forms of trouble are difficult to rate in terms of their disruptive potential (see Everett 1970). Some are conflict-producing in their own right. Killing, for example, deprives a kin group of a useful and active member and involves at the same time sudden and traumatic severance of strong affective ties. Suicide generates similar economic and social disruption, especially for surviving kin not directly involved in the event. When bad talk and/or fighting flare up, they mean a halt to previously important and sometimes imperative cooperative relations between the adversaries, particularly if these are kinsmen. In each of these instances, conflict resolution strategies are called into existence in order to restore a kind of uneasy equilibrium at least to the point that necessary economic prerequisites can be met. But sometimes an initial form of trouble generates further trouble, as in the drinking-bad-talk-fighting paradigm. Some forms of trouble can be ranked in terms of their potential for producing further trouble; bad talk, fighting, and killing are particularly dangerous in this regard (Everett 1970). This is not really surprising in the case of killing, in view of the aboriginal pattern of retaliatory homicide and clan feuds. But, the important question for Apaches is, can conflict be mediated without recourse to further conflict?

One effective strategy is tolerability, which mitigates the "get even" maxim or at least defers it until a more advantageous time and place where retaliation can occur. Real tolerance, i.e., acceptance of willful wrong-doing without malice or ostensible objection, operates along kin lines. Regardless of the inherent rightness or wrongness of the act, kinsmen can be expected to cooperate, and one kinsman is not likely to tolerate an act of ill will or aggression against a relative.[7] The reaction of the community at large may be overt disapproval, but a "hands off" policy usually prevails. In addition, tolerability of disruptive behavior is inevitably a function of intoxication. As was noted in the drinking-bad-talk-fighting paradigm, those not in control of their senses due to intoxication are thought to be unaware of the conflict they generate, be it verbal or physical. Thus, in a very real sense, they are not responsible for their behavior or its consequences. It is the alcohol that is the culprit. On this basis, tolerance is frequently extended to disruptive behavior that would normally be avenged (see McAndrew and Edgerton 1969).

There is one dimension of tolerability that is counter-productive with regard to the conflict resolution function: fear of reprisal. Retreating in the face of a drunken verbal assault may be considered a prudent ploy, but there exists a thin line between this and tolerance of an act for fear of violent reprisals. Young Apache men are especially concerned that their masculinity not be impugned and are thus more likely to be imprudent vis-a-vis conflict resolution involving tolerability than their adult counterparts. It is from one generation to the next where tolerability and fear of reprisal become inextricably linked. Adults and parents do not understand the drinking behavior and problem drinking of adolescents, nor can they readily predict the consequences of such behavior. Adolescent drinkers utilize this uncertainty as a lever in their relations with adults and promote, frequently intentionally, a real sense of physical fear in their elders. The result is anxious, concerned adults whose fearfulness causes them to openly tolerate adolescent disruptiveness (Everett 1973).

What, then, of "control"? How is this notion integrated with the meaning of Apache alcohol use and abuse? Perhaps most striking in this regard is that control is not an absolute phenomenon, an immutable yardstick against which all behavior is measured. Control is viewed as

---

[7]It is impossible to overestimate the importance of this principle, for it is both the strength and the weakness of Apache society. The united front it presents is impenetrable. Yet it has the disadvantage of precluding individual merit except on grounds of kinship. It has functioned in the past and will continue to function as a highly adaptive response to the demand for impersonalness from the white world.

differentially applicable; it is appropriate for some of the people some of the time, and the circumstances and conditions are, outside an Apache frame of reference, virtually impossible to articulate cohesively—a well-appreciated fact in both Apache tribal and Anglo court systems. Thus, it is not a question of simply eliminating alcohol on the reservation or incarcerating every wrongdoer. The Tribal Council is unlikely to repeal the sale of commercial liquor because it is a major source of revenue, and, except in the instance of a serious crime, almost every individual who is jailed can call upon a relative for assistance in obtaining his release. Thus, control of alcohol use and abuse must be viewed in perspective as only one in a set of priorities; for Apaches, unconditional and absolute control is not a reasonable or even appropriate objective with regard to problem drinking.

TRIBAL ALCOHOLISM AND MENTAL HEALTH PROGRAMS: SELF-DETERMINATION AND THE FUTURE

The primary question then becomes, who is to decide these matters? The question is only partly open to debate. Adoption of Anglo legal codes has automatically provided for control of certain forms of disruptive behavior. But Apaches use recourse to the court system as a kind of retaliation in much the same way that other forms of "getting even" function. Simultaneously, the decision-making process is complicated by a conflict in priorities. Through the mid-1970s, substantial amounts of federal government money were available for the treatment and prevention of "alcoholism," "mental illness," and related phenomena. The problem, of course, is that these are Anglo notions, and they have a particularly Anglo frame of reference; individuals, rather than patterns of cognition and behavior are the focus of attention, and cultural meanings tend to be ignored as irrelevant or considered curious and bizarre. Apaches are aware of the lack of fit between these approaches and native reality. Their reaction is to perceive such programs as instrumental devices, which may or may not achieve their stated goals, but which can effectively be put to social and economic ends; they provide needed jobs for kinsmen. As long as they continue to do so, they are valuable; when this function ceases, they become expendable, unless, of course, such programs begin to operate in terms that are meaningful to their Apache hosts and clients.

Several factors appear to mitigate this possibility and are thus likely to precipitate the imminent demise of tribal mental health and alcoholism programs, at least in their present forms. Perhaps the most prominent of these is the increasing amount of conflict produced by program activities that do not focus on community conceptualizations of "drinking" and "trouble," tolerance and control, and thus are in themselves inappropriate and unacceptable. Community support as a result is at best negligible, and program opposition is frequently overt and intense. Partly, this conflict is due to the character of staff training programs and subsequent program development and management. Without exception, the training process is couched in Anglo frames of reference using standardized social scientific protocol accompanied at times by generous portions of religious and moralistic zeal. Hence, program goals, strategies, job descriptions all generate and perpetuate community wide disagreement, confusion, and conflict.

Another element threatens to accelerate the process: funding. Increasingly, less federal money is becoming available for Indian mental health and alcohol programs. Monies are being channeled through state and local governments and private agencies. With the loss of direct federal support has come increased demands for program evaluation and accountability—in non-Indian terms. In view of the program-community discrepancy noted above, Anglo notions of responsible program management practice become virtually impossible to achieve. Coercion has to some extent been successful in the past; program funds and staff positions can be cut if sponsoring agency regulations are not assiduously observed. But there is developing hostility to this kind of treatment on the part of Apache program staff members—usually phrased in terms of Anglo domination and Indian militancy. Even though they are caught continually between the community and their jobs, program personnel find themselves aligned with the former, more aware of their own job inadequacies, and determined to take some positive action to resolve the impasse.

But what action? As the tribal programs become more sensitive to community opinion and needs, the discrepancy widens between them and Anglo funding demands. Tribal coffers are one as yet untapped resource. Human resource development, however, is relatively low on the socioeconomic priority scale in tribal affairs. Political decision making is not likely to divert large sums of money away from lucrative business enterprises into treatment, rehabilitation, and education programs designed for individuals whose behaviors are only marginally deviant in traditional Apache terms.

The future course of such programs is not bright. Yet the situation is far from hopeless, for as emergent tribalism and pan-Indianism intensify, all health-related reservation programs are being forced to redirect their efforts along culturally meaningful lines. Resultant "alcoholism" and "mental health" programs may resemble only slightly their predecessors. But if these are acceptable and effective in local community terms, then that is sufficient justification for their existence. Tremendous amounts of time, energy, and money have been expended on programs that are not sensitive to local cultural conditions; their poor success record stands in moot testimony for such grandiose effort. A program designed in culturally meaningful terms can only improve on these past performances. If it does not, the cost will be small and the returns will come in the development of Apache self-confidence and self-determination.

White Mountain Apaches live in an orderly world, one consisting of rules and standards for appropriate conduct, principles that provide the basis for weighing and evaluating these and whatever sanctions are considered suitable for their maintenance and control. There is evidence to suggest that some components and relationships in this system—especially in regard to drinking behavior, conflict, and problem drinking—have been present since aboriginal times. As adaptation to an essentially Anglo world proceeded, adjustment began to disarticulate some aspects of Apache life while others tenaciously persisted. Contemporary Apache life is a not-too-cohesive admixture of the old and the new. Understandably, Apaches are comfortable with the former and uncertain about the latter. This applies to drinking and the problems it generates as well as to reciprocal kin relations and curing rituals. No amount of coercion will convince Apaches that drinking, fighting, homicide and suicide are inherently pathological attributes of human existence; their meaning and significance derive from the Apachean experience. As that experience is broadened, diluted, and Anglicized, interpersonal conflict and coping behavior inexorably change. But these changes are merely adaptive transformations and unmistakably Apachean in character. Efforts to understand Apache "drinking" and "trouble" outside this frame of reference must be considered, from an Apachean point of view, as a major obstacle in the developing course of modern tribalism and pan-Indianism.

REFERENCES CITED

Basso, K. H.
    1970a   The Cibecue Apache. New York: Holt, Rinehart, and Winston.
    1970b   To Give Up On Words: Silence in Western Apache Culture. *Southwestern Journal of Anthropology* **26:**213–30.

Basso, K. H. (editor)
1971   *Western Apache Raiding and Warfare: From the Notes of Grenville Goodwin.* Tucson: University of Arizona Press.
Berlin, B., D. Breedlove, and P. Raven
1968   Covert Categories and Folk Taxonomies. *American Anthropologist* **70**:290–9.
Buskirk, W.
1949   Subsistence Economy of Western Apache. MS, Doctoral Dissertation, University of New Mexico, Albuquerque.
Everett, M. W.
1970   Pathology in White Mountain Apache Culture. *Western Canadian Journal of Anthropology* **2**:180–203.
1971a   White Mountain Apache Health and Illness: An Ethnographic Study of Medical Decision Making. MS, Doctoral Dissertation, University of Arizona, Tucson.
1971b   Drinking, Talking, and Fighting: An Apache Dilemma. MS, paper presented at Annual Meeting of American Anthropological Association, New York.
1972a   American Indian "Social Pathology": A Reexamination. MS, University of Kentucky.
1972b   White Mountain Apache Inter-Generational Problem Drinking. MS, paper presented at annual meeting of American Anthropological Association, Toronto.
1973   Anthropological Expertise and the "Realities" of White Mountain Apache Adolescent Problem Drinking. MS, paper presented at annual meeting of Society for Applied Anthropology, Tucson.
In   Conflict, Adversaries, and Retaliation: Suicide Among the White
press   Mountain Apache. In *Cross-Cultural Studies of Suicide,* Ari Kiev, ed.
Goodwin, G.
1942   *The Social Organization of the Western Apache.* Chicago: University of Chicago Press.
Hrdlicka, A.
1904   Method of Preparing Tesvino Among the White River Apache. *American Anthropologist* **6**:190–1.
1908   Physiological and Medical Observations Among the Indians of Southwestern United States and Northern Mexico. *Bureau of American Ethnology Bulletin No. 74.* Washington.
McAndrew, C. and R. B. Edgerton
1969   *Drunken Comportment.* Chicago: Aldine.
Reagan, A.
1930   Notes on the Indians of the Fort Apache Region. *Anthropological Papers of the American Museum of Natural History* **31**:28–345.
Spicer, E. H.
1962   *Cycles of Conquest: The Impact of Spain, Mexico, and the United States on the Indians of the Southwest, 1533–1960.* Tucson: University of Arizona Press.

PART THREE

Contemporary
Assessments
By Native American
Observers and Public
Health Workers

Introduction

In this section we wish to incorporate the views of Native Americans and those directly involved in Indian alcohol and public health programs. The first selection is by Fernando Escalante, a Yaqui, who has been active in local alcohol programs for urban Indians in Tucson. As a native member of the Yaqui community and as one who knows the local scene intimately, Escalante is able to blend this background with his training in sociology in assessing Native American drinking in terms of reference group theory.

Richard Cooley, in the next essay, departs from academic protocol and speaks "off the cuff" about his reactions to various Indian alcohol programs. His experience with training Indian alcoholism workers and his utilization of their comments and opinions in setting forth his ideas provide a valuable perspective. Regrettably, Richard Cooley died in the spring of 1976 in the midst of active involvement in Indian health programs.

While not directly related to alcohol problems per se, the remarks by Miller and Ostendorf on Indian mental health programs touch upon a frequent correlate of alcohol abuse. Their emphasis on culturally aware and locally sensitive mental health programs is also essential in alcohol action programs. Focus is on local community involvement and the training of local workers who understand local problems. This is not to say that local Indian people do not want professionals; rather, local people can be used to direct professional services into locally meaningful response.

The last selection is by Ron Wood, a Navajo. Wood reiterates the importance of keeping in mind cultural variation and differences among the tribes when implementing treatment programs in urban areas. It is a temptation to lump all Indians into a single category and to treat their apparent similarities in drinking styles as if they were all the same phenomenon—Indian drinkers. Wood sees as a danger for Indian urban programs their inability to compete for either clients or monies with Anglo-American programs. He also notes that being Indian or being a recovered alcoholic are not sufficient in themselves for preparing alcohol counsellors for working with Indian clients.

6

Group Pressure
and Excessive
Drinking
Among Indians

Fernando Escalante

It is a recognized fact that the phenomena of excessive drinking and alcoholism are prevalent in all socioeconomic classes of the United States, encompassing all racial, ethnic, and nationality groups and cultures. In view of this, one would tend to wonder if any one group is more susceptible to the disease of alcoholism and to excessive drinking than others. Studies of American Indian drinking problems seem to indicate that Indians may have an especially severe problem with excessive drinking and alcoholism. Factors leading to this problem among Indians and other minorities are many, but as yet no single causal variable has been isolated. Perhaps the cause of excessive drinking among Indians may be the influence of particular group norms. Perhaps the causal variables are related to unique aspects of history and the way particular Indian societies are treated by the white man. One significant causal factor might be the underdeveloped socioeconomic conditions that have characterized many American Indian societies.

American Indians share with other minorities similar conditions of low socioeconomic status: discrimination, poverty, poor housing, lack of education, and other deprivations that rank the Indian at the bottom of the stratification scale. The problems connected with excessive

Fernando Escalante is a member of the Yaqui community in Tucson, Arizona. He received a B.A. in Sociology from the University of Arizona in 1972 and has been active as a counsellor in local alcoholism programs.

drinking among Indians and other minorities are many—problems with the police, with employment, with handling aggressiveness, with spouse and family, with friends, and with the non-Indian community in general.

Dozier (1966:72) states that a greater proportion of the American Indian population drinks to excess than is the case for the rest of the American population. The majority of criminal acts committed by Indians occur under the influence of alcohol, and the Indian arrest rate for all alcohol-related crimes is the highest in the country. Dozier (1966:75) says, "Since drinking and criminality seem highest among Indians of all groups in the United States, it is pertinent to ask whether conditions of deprivation are, or have been more severe among these people; whether, for example, unusual circumstances among Indians could cause acute conditions not encountered among other groups." The causes of Indian excessive drinking must be looked for in particular social and cultural circumstances.

This chapter formulates a hypothesis and pursues some theoretical considerations about excessive drinking behavior of American Indians in terms of the significance of specific social organization and cultural content. The hypothesis is: the greater the degree of group pressure, the greater the incidence of excessive drinking. Social control and group norms of American Indians influence excessive alcohol consumption and deviant behavior to a greater degree than do American Indian individual personality characteristics having to do with anxieties, fears, frustrations, conflicts, tensions, insecurities, dependencies, and immaturities. A qualifying statement is needed in relation to this point: "Among all those who drink to excess, whether Indian or non-Indian, there is a background of emotional troubles, frustrations and disappointments" (Dozier 1966:74). While emotional problems do influence excessive drinking, my argument is that they are not the primary causes of drinking among American Indians. Obviously, emotional problems can facilitate excessive drinking and lead to other mental health problems. But these personality factors are not the prime initiators of drinking activity. Drinking is a learned habit and a valued way of engaging in social life. In order to understand the nature of American Indian drinking, it is necessary to raise and to try to answer several questions. This chapter is both a theoretical and a speculative attempt to deal with these questions.

A comparative analysis of the drinking experiences of several American Indian tribes will be considered, using studies already published.

Also, my own personal experience with alcoholism and my current work with urban Indian problem drinkers will be considered in formulating and arriving at some tentative conclusions.

THE PROBLEM

The World Health Organization defines alcoholics as ''those excessive drinkers whose dependence on alcohol has attained such a degree that they show a noticeable mental disturbance or an interference with their mental and bodily health, their interpersonal relations and their smooth social and economic functioning; or who show the prodromal signs of such developments'' (Moss 1970:1).

In relating this definition to American Indian drinking, several specific questions can be raised. Are there any outstanding characteristics of Indian drinking that can help to identify its major causal factors? Why are some Indian people excessive drinkers while others within the same cultural setting are not? Does Indian social organization have any significant effect on an individual that may encourage him to resort to excessive drinking? Is it the emotional instability of particular individuals or is it the power of the group of individuals that explains drinking? Is Indian drinking that is learned early in social life later influenced by sociopsychological and economic conditions?

In searching for a clue as to why American Indian people collectively have a high rate of alcoholism and excessive drinking, we need to look at several individual tribes and analyze their drinking experiences and drinking patterns. Generally speaking, Indian populations are scattered on and around reservations with an ever-increasing number moving to urban areas. Each tribe has its own culture, language, religious beliefs, legends, dances, and myths, and is exposed to different laws, regulations, and local social environments and social institutions.

Studies of Indian drinking problems may try to discriminate between drinking experiences on Indian reservations and the excessive drinking problems of Indians in urban areas. It must be remembered, however, that a good majority of urban Indians are not strictly urban; about half are reservation Indians who have chosen to remain in an urban setting. It is my opinion that as far as drinking is concerned there is actually no great difference between urban and reservation Indians. Perhaps liquor is the common bond that joins all Indian groups. The literature supports a relationship between group influences and drinking whether on a reservation or in an urban setting where Indians congregate. This relationship will be discussed in detail later.

There has been much speculation about the origin of excessive drinking among Indians and a number of historical reasons for it. Each individual tribe probably has its own unique history in this respect. It is a commonly held idea that one of the reasons behind excessive Indian drinking is that Indians have been kept like prisoners on reservations, being deprived of hunting, warring, and fighting which, in the old days, served as a means of getting rid of tension, anxiety, and frustration. Because of such treatment, Indians today have turned to liquor to solve emotional problems. But this explanation is not applicable to all tribes since not all Indian people were hunters or warriors. Many Indians were farmers, fishermen, and basketmakers. Hamer (1965:285) lists some of the motives for drinking:

> It . . . a) gives the individual a means for coping with an unpredictable universe; as well as an escape from anxiety about the expression of overt aggression; b) permits persons temporarily to assume desirable status positions when there has been interference with, and inadequate substitute for the traditional social structure; c) serves as a means for categorizing groups in an acculturative situation by rendering the behavior of one predictable by the other; and d) provides a kind of solvent of tension which helps, periodically, to bring the white and Indian communities together on a basis of friendship.

SEARCHING FOR A COMMON FACTOR

While these theories about American Indian excessive drinking are reasonable, they are not totally convincing. Since these considerations are not applicable to all Indian tribes or people, I will try to examine factors I think to be common to all Indian groups. First, I want to demonstrate that aboriginal Indians changed from nondrinkers to drinkers during early contacts with white men. I will follow closely DuToit's thinking as to how culture change processes brought Indians under the influence of alcohol. He states that

> . . . under conditions of stress and frustration and with the loss of institutionalized forms of interaction, an individual or a group of individuals may innovate and substitute a heretofore deviant form of behavior in order to obtain a feeling of unity, and to share and alleviate the frustration and anxieties that they feel. This form of behavior in time comes to be accepted by the majority of persons in the group, and, instead of being deviant, it now becomes the mode. Even though it still has disorganizing effects upon specific aspects of domestic and community life, it is accepted (DuToit 1964:17).

Who the individual was who first made this substitution because of certain similarities he thought to be real, will probably never be known, but the fact is that most individuals in this group, whether they are consciously aware of it or not, feel that these drinking parties serve a function, and supply something to their daily life which they need very much (*ibid.*, p. 23).

DuToit's basic point is that drinking and excessive drinking have become accepted and become a way of life by the general Indian population. The major influencing factor in excessive Indian drinking, therefore, is the social milieu or drinking culture, not the emotional state of the individual Indian. Dozier (1966:72) believes "that group or gang-type drinking among Indians represents a greater problem in terms of crime rates and community disorganization than addicted drinking." He goes on to say that persons drinking alone are rare in most Indian communities and that solitary drinkers are considered deviant by the community in general. Moreover,

Many instances of American Indian drinking behavior judged pathological by the dominant American society may not be so considered by the Indians who engage in it. Indeed, they may think of their drinking bouts as simply a form of recreation and relaxation and have no desire to eliminate such behavior (Dozier 1966:83).

Lemert (1958:92–3) states that among the modern day Holalthko, Tlahoose, and Sliammon, drinking is a group affair with no cases of solitary drinkers in evidence. The eventual goal of these Indians is to get drunk and to get drunk fast. While these Indians do speak out against drinking, they do not apply any social punishment against it. "The heavy drinker in the Indian community does not become socially isolated as a consequence of his drunkenness, nor does his behavior lead to a broken marriage and loss of family support. Furthermore, the values of his group actually uphold and sanction his behavior" (Lemert 1958:103–4). Heavy drinking and alcoholism could be very disorganizing in every phase of the life of an Indian when seen from the side of the dominant white society. But to the majority of Indian drinkers, heavy drinking does not seem to be so pathological or abnormal.

Some alcoholism studies have demonstrated that individuals of diverse social backgrounds respond differently to types of frustrations arising in everyday living. Here again we might point out that the causes of drinking among American Indians are somewhat different. In the majority of cases, alcoholics from white middle-class or upper-class backgrounds drink because of emotional problems, while with the Indian "alcoholic," it is more a group or social pressure to drink that is the dominating influence.

Curley (1967:116) points out that drinking behavior "... must be viewed as behavior which becomes institutionalized through a process of learning." He says that a Mescalero Apache boy's first introduction to liquor usually takes place in a social group setting. At first he is not actually pressured to drink, but is expected to get drunk like his peers. For the adolescent Apache and for the adult Indian there is very little or no recreational activity. The boys engage in some sports, but for the majority of boys and adults, drinking is one form of social activity that is most readily available, and its main attraction is that it takes place in groups. Apaches seldom drink alone. They drink to get drunk or until they have no more money to buy drinks. It does not matter if it is in a bar, tavern, or out in the open. Moderate social drinking is rarely practiced among the Apache. Their goal is to get to the extreme point of drunkenness, that is, unconscious. "The drinker is not seen as any sort of marginal man operating on the periphery of the social order, but he is as much a part of that order as the next Apache" (Curley 1967:129). Drinking brings some spark of interesting activity into Apache existence: "... the danger of being arrested; the long automobile ride to a bar; the fighting; and the occasional sexual adventure ..." (Curley 1967:130). Thus, it seems that to the Mescalero Apache, drinking is an enjoyable sport just as traditional sports are enjoyable and appealing to non-Indian people.

As has been stressed earlier, Indian drinking usually occurs in groups, and Navajos seem to be no different than other Indian groups. Heath says that large gatherings were the most frequent occasions for heavy drinking, i.e., religious ceremonies, pow-wows, rodeos, fiestas, and dances (Heath 1964:124). He mentions that a Navajo who has a bottle of liquor will usually try to find some drinking friends who will share the bottle with him. When he finds friends to share his liquor, the usual pattern is for the owner of the bottle to take a small drink and pass it on to his friends. It has been said that to turn down a drink is to turn down and offend your friend. Sometimes with these drinking bouts, it is not uncommon to have fights with stones, sticks, knives, and guns. Heath reports the following Navajo reasons for drinking: "just to feel good"; "some liquor is good at a ceremonial"; "helps your voice in singing"; "there's nothing else to do"; "when a Navajo fellow gets a hold of liquor, he just wants to get drunk on it. He doesn't want to mess around with drinking—just get drunk quick" (Heath 1964:127). Heath claims that such statements are representative of most of the excessive drinkers and that usually drunkenness is not disapproved of except when it interferes with religious events and mutual obligations.

For the Navajo drinking culture as well as for the rest of the American Indian drinking cultures, drinking is mostly spontaneous and drinking affairs are not planned events. For example, in an Indian setting, an individual may start out to visit some friends or to go to a store. On the way he may meet one or several individuals drinking who offer him a drink but he refuses. The refusing individual will try to explain why he cannot drink at this particular time. If the drinking companions accept his explanation, then he is left alone. But if the explanation is refused, he is pressured, coaxed, pleaded with, ostracized, and even physically threatened. Usually if there are several individuals, each one tries his own way of trying to persuade the individual to drink. An explanation of having to go to work the next day is usually not accepted. The individual is thrown verbal persuasions such as "one drink won't hurt you," or "I have to work too and I am drinking." Usually he will reluctantly take a drink and hang around for some more, or else he can leave at the risk of being called names.

This persuasive method of getting someone on the road to drinking seems to be common to all drinking tribes. Savard (1968:913) reports that in the Navajo drinking group,

> any attempt to refuse a drink from a member of the fellowship was countered by a concentrated, unrelenting pressure to drink. This was expressed in slashing accusations, sarcasm and threats of physical harm. They were commonly accused of rejecting the drinking companion by rejecting his liquor. "What's the matter that you won't take my drink?" was one of the most frequent remarks. Sarcasm frequently took the form of, "Who do you think you are, a preacher—you a Christian or something?"

Savard states further that

> in some instances several of the group would point out that on the basis of the man's past performance he would eventually give in and drink anyway, so why didn't he cut out the nonsense and take the drink without so much delay and fuss (p. 913).

Apparently with the Navajos as well as with other Indian groups, the importance of having a ready and willing supply of drinking peers is considered very important. For the drinker, the relationship between drinking friends and liquor is the nucleus that forms and satisfies his needs rather than the craving for alcohol alone. Savard found Trice's observation pertinent in this case: "The unique ingredient in the process of alcoholism is the fit between the vulnerable personality traits and drinking group values and goals'' (p. 911). In groups like these, the use of liquor, drinking, and drunkenness is not something to be looked down on. The drinking fellowship influences and offers the excessive drinker a means to facilitate and to participate in social interaction. Savard says that there are clues that point to the fact that ''... alcohol was used more to ease social participations than as a means of escape'' (p. 913). For some Indians as well as with other people, alcohol is or could be used as a ''means of escape.'' But for the majority of Indian excessive drinkers, escape drinking would be the exception rather than the rule.

Many of the alcohol-related problems due to excessive drinking and alcoholism should not be viewed as evidence of conflict and frustration between the individual's emotional problems and the larger Anglo social system. Rather, the Indians' problem with excessive drinking has become a way of life, influenced by Indian peer-group pressure to conform to the Indian way of drinking, which usually is to drink in order to get drunk. In the process, the drinking group influences many Indians to act in a deviant, antisocial manner, such as fighting, stealing, destroying private property, and generally disturbing the peace. All of this deviant behavior is greatly influenced by the drinking group, and the deviant behavior is facilitated by the degree of intoxication of the individual. But not all tribes experience the same problems with drinking.

Devereux (1948:249) discovered a somewhat unique situation in the Mohave drinking culture:

> It was found that drinking is today integrated with Mohave culture and with Mohave psychology as well. The absence of high levels of anxiety and the preservation of certain basic cultural attitudes probably explain why, on the whole, the intoxicated Mohave is not aggressively antisocial, and why Mohave society has fairly successfully withstood the ravages of alcoholism observed in many other American Indian tribes.

The reason this unique situation has developed is that drinking performed in a social setting usually does not end in severe drunkenness. There seems to be no objectionable behavior connected with drinking, and if a person does drink to excess, the tendency is to pass out quickly. Sometimes there is not enough alcohol to get enough people drunk, and parties or dances usually do not end in fights. Drinking on the whole is not considered a manly act and ''excessive drinking is freely criticized'' by the Indians. There is no doubt that Mohave culture is in a unique situation when compared to the mode of drinking of other Indian tribes. But as we have seen in these other groups, this situation is influenced by culture norms and expectations.

GROUP NORMS

In Indian social drinking groups in general, norms and behavior pertaining to drinking are generally clear and unambiguous. Either you drink or don't drink, but because of circumstances beyond control, a great many Indians have grown up with little or no contact with Indian drinking groups. Obviously, these Indians do not have the same values, attitudes, or norms that drinking Indians have. If an Indian has not been exposed to the social control and group norms of the Indian drinking group, his role performance will conflict with his own different norms. He can either conform to the dominant Indian group norms or face the consequences of the sanctions, which impose collective standards of action and belief. This collective pressure is induced by ridicule, disapproval, and disdain. Clearly, if the individual is perceived as somewhat different, then his role will be expected to differentiate from the Indian drinking society. Therefore, if an Indian has not been exposed to the social control and group norm expectations of the drinking group and if he wants to be approved and belong to the group, then the group pressure and norms will prevail and influence his favorable response toward excessive drinking, regardless of his personality makeup.

The pattern of drinking behavior leading to excessive drinking, to problem drinking, and for many, to alcoholism, is a symptom of the complex interactional process inherent within the total Indian social system. The whole social field includes the socialization processes that introduce the individual to the drinking behavior and consequently to a personality that will conform to the drinking group's norms and pressures. Every Indian community, whether urban or reservation, has its own drinking and nondrinking groups. This setting is the society in which social control and group norms greatly influence a stable or unstable individual toward drinking and consequently into excessive drinking and "deviant" behavior by some set of standards. Communication of the norms through social control and interaction between individual and group tend to condition and, therefore, to lead to a learned behavior of excessive drinking.

The Indian, if he has been raised in an Indian community, will have been exposed to the Indian norms, values, and folkways. Through the process of socialization, his personality will have adapted and organized his habits, attitudes, and traits according to the norms of the particular group that has been most influential in his life. His personal emotional problems will facilitate his excessive drinking, but even if there is an absence of emotional problems—which is possible—group pressure and group norms may be so strong that an Indian will have no trouble falling into an excessive drinking experience. Under these circumstances, it does not matter if an Indian's personality is stable or unstable; he will fall under the influence of social pressures and plunge into drinking. If an Indian was not socialized in an Indian community, then this socialization process is not applicable.

The American Indian drinking group, like every other social group, has its own range of appropriate conduct made permissible by its normative expectations and value orientations. In general, the value orientations of a significantly large number of American Indians toward excessive drinking do not consider this excess as pathological or as an attribute of an unstable individual. Some groups of Indians regard excessive drinking as a way to relax and enjoy themselves, as recreation, and as a means to facilitate socialization; in general, excessive drinking is a way of life. Dozier (1966:78) says that under the influences of alcohol there is a tendency to form and feel an Indian social solidarity and, consequently, to interact in laughing, joking, shouting, using profanity, fighting, and indulging in general "boisterousness"—with deviant forms of behavior such as housebreaking, stealing, destruction, and general vandalism as side effects of drinking.

As Homans (1958) and Merton (1938) have suggested in discussion of social structure anomie, the greater the frequency of interaction and communication in an American Indian drinking group, the greater the tendency to become more "cohesive." The more "cohesive" the group, the greater the change the members can produce in the behavior of other members. This "cohesion" exerts a definite pressure on an Indian who is a nondrinker to conform to the behavior and excessive drinking practices of the other Indian members. So if we operate under the premise that the only good Indian is a drunken Indian, then, "good" Indians or drinking groups internalize their own norms, values, and tend to scorn, ridicule, and ostracize deviants and nonconformists, who in this case are the nondrinkers.

Ferguson (1970:901) states that the Navajos have a "... culture where excessive drinking is sporadically engaged in by many men as an expression of social solidarity...." Navajo informal leadership is such that when it is exerted, it is the kind in which cultural ideals are epitomized by the person who takes the lead and whose humor or silent disdain are the implements by which authority is enforced. Such leadership is powerful because of the emotional involvement with the leader and the willing participating of the group in his use of informal social controls on a recalcitrant member (pp. 911–12).

Ferguson goes on to say that such a leader, by being in contact with his followers, somehow conforms to their needs. She states that "this kind of authority was well illustrated in the phenomenon of a nondrinking peer group of former alcoholics coalescing around project interpreters who had been their drinking companions before enlistment in the treatment program" (Ferguson 1970:912). This kind of informal leadership could be put to good use whenever any kind of treatment and rehabilitative programs are to be implemented for Indians. The use of recovered or ex-alcoholics in any treatment program has been proven to be very effective. Using this type of leadership may be especially useful in a social environment where many basic attitudes toward drinking have to be changed, and particularly in a culture where drinking is not considered a problem by many people.

The Forest Potawatomi are another group who do not consider drinking as a bad activity. Hamer (1965:291) has set down what he says are typical responses from this community: "Most people don't feel guilty about drinking; they say they are going to quit when they have a hangover, but they never do." "Hardly anyone doesn't drink here. I don't think people consider it a problem. People don't feel that it is wrong to drink; like to have a good time." A great deal of heavy drinking is the norm for this community, and drinking has become a form of recreation, perhaps because there are no other alternatives as satisfying and enjoyable as the drinking parties. Hamer (1965:301) summarizes the drinking of this community by saying,

Among contemporary North American Indian societies the Potawatomi of White Horse may be considered as representing the extreme and chiefly negative consequences of drinking as a way of life. Nevertheless, the adaptive aspects of heavy and frequent consumption of alcohol are recognized by these people as out-weighing the social costs.

Another common example of heavy or excessive drinking being tolerated in an Indian community is provided by Honigmann (1945:591). He says that in this particular Indian community, there seem to be no guilt feelings associated with drinking after a drinking bout. He notes that "an Indian is never severely criticized for being drunk." In short, for this Indian community, "drunkenness is tolerated," and "extreme drunken behavior ... is smiled at so long as it does not threaten anyone." In this community, as well as other surrounding ones, solitary drinkers are rare, and persons who have started to drink will almost never refuse a drink when it is offered. "Even very drunk individuals will continue drinking, and reluctance to accept a drink is always beaten down with vigorous urging" (Honigmann 1945:590). Situations such as these are common among many Indian drinking groups. Obviously, the social-culture milieu has a great influence on the rate of excessive and problem drinking.

Whittaker (1963:84) has set forth Bale's three suggestions as to how culture can affect rates of alcoholism:

> The first is the degree to which the culture operates to bring about acute needs for adjustment or inner tensions in its members; the second is the degree to which the culture provides suitable substitute means of satisfaction; and the third is the sort of attitudes toward drinking which the culture produces in its members.

In Whittaker's research among the Sioux Indians, Bale's suggestions have closely agreed with Whittaker's findings. Thus, he concludes that "the generally permissive character of Sioux culture contributes in a significant way to the high incidence of alcoholism since social sanctions against the heavy drinker or alcoholic are virtually nonexistent" (Whittaker 1963:90). In a social environment where excessive alcohol consumption is generally permitted and tolerated, the most obvious fruitful inquiry as to why American Indians drink to excess would be to investigate the social functions of drinking.

THE SOCIAL FUNCTIONS OF DRINKING: THE YAQUIS AND THE PAPAGOS

In order to examine the social functions of drinking, it is necessary to work with a model of Indian excessive drinkers that would be fairly representative of American Indians in this country. I have chosen for this model two Indian groups who inhabit the city of Tucson, Arizona, and who are familiar to me. My familiarity with these two tribes stems from the fact that I have spent my life in Tucson, in excess of thirty years, as a member of one of them. I am a former excessive drinker, and am presently engaged in working with the Indian excessive drinker and alcoholic as a counselor. The tribes are the two largest ones in Tucson, the Papagos and the Yaquis. The majority of the Papago and Yaqui people are very low on the socioeconomic stratification ladder, well below the Mexican Americans and the blacks who comprise the remaining ethnic minorities of Tucson.

Tucson presently has over 300,000 inhabitants of which over 2,000 are Papago Indians and close to 3,000 are Yaqui Indians (see Figure 6.1). For the majority of Papagos and Yaquis, life generally revolves around their own respective people. Although these tribes normally do not mix together in social intercourse, they tolerate each other, each going about its own business. The majority of both Yaqui and Papago males are engaged in casual labor jobs, construction work, yard work, and various other unskilled jobs. In formal schooling, Papagos and Yaquis as a whole are not highly educated. They do not actively engage in political activities, nor do they participate in Anglo political battles. Both tribes are mainly affiliated with the Catholic religion, but each has its own set of beliefs regarding this religion. And neither the Yaquis nor the Papagos actively participate in non-Indian social and recreational organizations.

One of the distinguishing legal characteristics between these tribes is that the Yaquis are not considered American Indians by the federal government.[1] But as far as alcohol consumption is concerned, the pattern of excessive drinking and attendant drinking problems among the Yaqui Indians of Arizona in general and the Yaqui Indians of Pascua Village (Tucson) in particular are no different from the Papagos' or from those of the rest of the American Indians. However, the Yaquis are in a unique position from that of the other American Indian tribes. Willard (1970:31) notes that "these Yaqui residents of Tucson are in the unusual position of being both American Indians and Mexican Americans, with, perhaps the disadvantages of both, and the advantages of neither group." Willard further states that Yaquis are "as much Indian as any other Native American group in North America ..." (p. 7). However, because the Yaquis emigrated from Mexico to the United States beginning about 1880 and continuing on into the 20th century, the U.S. Congressional Act of 2 June 1924, which declared Indians as citizens, was not applicable to the Yaquis. As a result of this act, Yaquis are not legally considered an American Indian tribe. Therefore, Yaquis are not eligible for federal funds generally available to other American Indians, and for a long time Yaquis have been excluded from federal services available through the Indian Division, United States Public Health

---

[1] In October 1978, after this fieldwork was completed, one group of Tucson Yaquis was formally recognized as an American Indian tribe by the federal government (Edward H. Spicer 1979: personal communication).

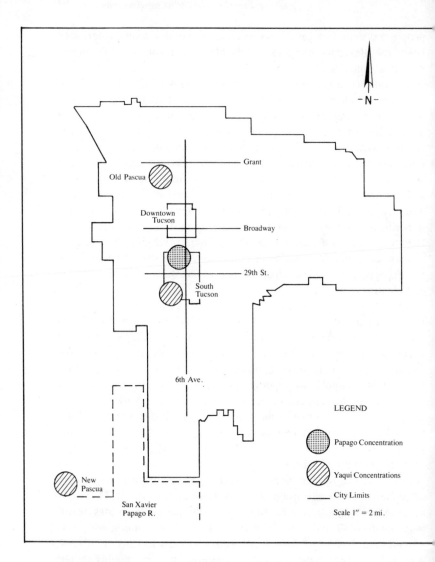

Figure 6.1 Tucson, showing main neighborhoods of Yaqui and Papago Indians

Service, and the Bureau of Indian Affairs. Until 1964, the Yaqui Indians did not receive financial aid specifically ear-marked for them from the federal government. However, a special act of Congress provided 200 acres of federal land to the Yaquis for the purpose of building new homes. This project was designed specifically as a training program to train Yaqui Indians in the housing construction trade and at the same time to build low-cost housing for the Yaquis. For many Yaquis, this project could lead to a better future because the majority of Yaquis in Tucson and elsewhere have lived in a very poor physical environment.

A neighborhood that is in many ways representative of the living conditions of the Yaquis is old Pascua Village. This village is located on the northwest side of Tucson in the vicinity of West Grant Road and Miracle Mile. Nearly 250 Yaquis reside in Pascua Village, which covers an area of 40 acres. From its earliest beginning around 1922, there have been few if any physical changes in the old Pascua Village. The village remains pretty much unchanged from Spicer's 1937 description, as cited by Willard:

> A casual inspection of the cluster of non-descript shacks at the northwest corner of the city of Tucson, Arizona, gives little indication of the cultural gulf which separates the inhabitants of the area from the rest of the people of Tucson. The houses are made of crumbling adobe bricks, wattle and daub, or odds and ends of old sheet metal and wood from the city dumps (Willard 1970:40).

In the late 1970s Pascua Village was within the designated "model cities" area, a project intended to bring about major environmental changes in the village and other slum-type regions of the city of Tucson.

The low socioeconomic status and other deprivations faced by the Yaquis seem to indicate that excessive drinking and problem drinking are the main contributors to all the other problems of the Yaquis, and all of these factors feed into a vicious self-perpetuating cycle. While excessive drinking is nothing new to the Yaquis, it seems that the amount of participation in such activities, with all its attendant problems, is increasing. Drinking has been part of Yaqui culture for a long time. A former school teacher at Pascua Village has noted the recreational character of wine drinking and small talk: "Intoxication on Friday and Saturday night is a form of recreation for those who can afford it" (Nevitt 1951:48). She goes on to say that "Yaquis are overly indulgent in their consumption of alcoholic drinks, especially of wine and whiskey" (p. 59). Barber (1952:47) states that the men congregate to drink beer and wine, and no one refuses whiskey. He says that the main cause of trouble with the law among the Yaquis is liquor: "speeding and other traffic offenses seem less important than being drunk or getting into a fight while drunk" (p. 49). He believes that a few of the older men could be "mild alcoholics."

> ... the drinking of the young men in most cases though heavy, is not compulsive. However, this makes no difference as far as being arrested for drunkenness or attendant rowdiness goes, and probably half of the men have been taken in at least once for this (Barber 1952:49).

Although heavy drinking is not normally accepted today within the Yaqui community, a large quantity of liquor is consumed by male residents who drink because they are sad, happy, or for no other reason than that a ready supply is available to them. Social drinking is found at dances, parties, weddings, fiestas, baptismals, wakes, and spontaneous informal gatherings. From personal observation, I would say that the consumption of alcohol pervades many formal and informal gatherings within the Yaqui community. Excessive drinking should be viewed as a form of "social lubricant" rather than escapism; drinking within this community establishes a degree of group cohesiveness. It becomes difficult for an individual to avoid the social context of drinking within the Yaqui community; group pressures upon the individual are intolerable, forcing conformity. This peer-group pressure to conform to the norm of group drinking supports the hypothesis being tested in this chapter: the greater the pressure upon the individual to drink as a member of the group, the more likely he is to conform to peer-group norms. Peer-group pressure in this situation forces an individual to find his identity as a member of the group.

Examples of peer-group pressure for individual conformity are offered in support of my hypothesis. One Yaqui man said: "I did not drink for six months and I was so sad and unhappy because I did not have friends anymore so I started to drink again." Another, ready to leave the hospital, mentioned: "If I want to stay sober, I will have to live away from the village because I have so many friends who come to the house with their bottles and I don't want to offend them by not accepting their drinks." A young Yaqui did not get out of the car in front of his house because friends were hanging around and they would make fun of him because he was not drinking. He stated that his friends became angry at him for not drinking, calling him names such as: "Who the hell do you think you are anyway, a Christian or some good guy who doesn't want to drink with us anymore?" One man was threatened physically if he did not drink with his friends. His friends said, "If you don't take my drink, you are not my friend anymore. You think you are better than us because you don't drink any more, now you look down on your friends." These are just some examples of the daily pressures upon individuals for conformity within the Yaqui community that result in excessive drinking. It is my opinion that this kind of peer pressure upon the individual is greater than the efforts for rehabilitation from outside of the Yaqui community.

The arrest rate for drunkenness among the Indian population of Tucson exceeds that of other minority groups and the general population. The South Tucson police arrest records for the month of June 1971 show there were 210 arrests for drunkenness. Over half of these arrests where Indians, including 100 Papagos, 13 Yaquis, and 14 other Indians. The remainder were 60 Mexican Americans, 13 Anglos, and 10 blacks. An Indian statistical report released by the Tucson Police Department revealed that for the fiscal year 1968–69, 1,336 Indians were arrested for minor alcohol-related offenses, which in the majority of cases included multiple arrests for drunkenness. Of those 1,336 arrested, at least 35 were Yaqui Indians from Pascua Village. For the year 1969–70, 758 Indians were arrested, 15 of whom were Yaquis.

Even though the arrest figures for Yaqui Indians appear insignificant as compared to the other arrests, these numbers do not reflect the true incidence of excessive drinking among the Yaqui. According to Willard (1970:8), Yaqui males "are employed irregularly and during only a few months of the year in the usual casual labor pattern. A third or more of the males are chronically drunk or under the influence of drugs." The problem of excessive drinking among Yaquis today is revealed by the construction supervisor of the Pascua Yaqui Association Housing Project. He states that of all trainees that he had to fire, 99% were dismissed because of a high absentee rate caused by drinking. He said that few of the men were fired for reasons other than drinking.

Most of the 2,000 Tucson Papagos reside in the area bounded on the east side by South Fourth Avenue, on the north by 17th Street, on the west by Interstate 10 and 19, and on the south by Irvington Road. South Tucson, a separate municipality, is where the majority of Papagos concentrate their socializing and drinking (see Figure 6.1).

Papagos used to get drunk on cactus fruit wine for ceremonial purposes. Waddell (1971:1) states that "ceremonial drunkenness to produce much needed rain has been a sacred activity among the Papagos with social bonding a pragmatic outcome of this communal ritual." According to Waddell, there is no "uniform Papago cultural experience," yet the usual daily social life consists of a relaxed, slow, nonaggressive style, and for a great number of Papagos, drinking in one way or another dominates the social life. He notes that "it does not take long to be impressed by the extent to which, for a sizable number, drinking is a dominant mode of activity" (Waddell 1971:8).

Drinking often occurs at such social events as dances, feast days, wakes, weddings or other particular occasions. It need not be confined to special social events and frequently occurs within peer groups made up of others of one's own age and close friends. There is drinking in bars, streets, parks, homes, and alleys. Papago drinking and drunkenness is a social group phenomenon: "I am very impressed with how intensely social most Papago drinking is ... Papagos seem to intimidate each other into making their drinking, even their drunkenness, a social experience" (Waddell 1971:10).

The majority of Papagos engaging in this type of drinking know where to find drinking companions, and, although Papagos drink primarily in groups, most of them are arrested alone. Papagos have the highest rate for drunkenness of any other Indian tribe in Tucson. Incarceration for drunkenness does not seem to be a deterrent to drinking. Therefore, if any rehabilitative program is to be implemented for the Indian population, consideration must be given to the social consequences of drinking. In this regard, Waddell (1971:13–14) mentions some pertinent considerations:

> Remedial programs with therapeutic inventions must take into consideration: 1) the cultural premises and underlying values and attitudes about drinking and drunkenness which Papagos have; 2) the social realities of everyday life in which these individuals have been and are being socialized; 3) the structure and intensity of the social contexts in which so much of their drinking occurs; 4) the different attitudes, expectations and societal responses to their particular drinking styles; 5) the unique events in individual lives which cohere into particular styles of drinking behavior and which are expressed in the predominant social contexts observed; and finally, 6) the physiological repercussions of habitual alcohol ingestion.

Since drinking among the Papago, Yaqui, and other American Indians provides such an intense social bonding among the participants, it is extremely difficult to successfully rehabilitate any large number of Indian excessive drinkers. The social function of Indian drinking has an overwhelming positive function for its participants, overweighing the negative consequences.

CONCLUSION

In the analysis of the social functions of excessive Indian drinking, I conclude that the type of social cultural environment is directly related to the rate of excessive drinking. In a more detailed examination of the social functions of drinking, I have borrowed part of the Jessor et al. (1968) theoretical framework and applied it to the excessive drinking habits of the American Indian. It is felt that the excessive drinking behavior of the American Indians can be defined within the sociocultural system and its three substructures, which are: the "opportunity structure," the "normative structure," and the "social control structure."

These authors say that "the term 'opportunity structure' is . . . that set of socially structured and institutionally legitimate channels of access to the achievement of goals emphasized or valued by the American culture" (Jessor et al. 1968:55). Applying this definition to the sociocultural system of the American Indian would mean that, "location in the opportunity structure . . . identifies a person or group with respect to degree of access to culturally valued goals presently obtaining and/or likely to obtain in the future" (p. 55). What this means in terms of American Indian excessive drinking is simply that drinking is socially acceptable and institutionalized, and therefore, it is legitimate for an Indian to drink to excess within the bounds or tolerance limits set for that particular Indian community. The cultural definition of appropriate drinking is, for the majority of Indian drinkers, excessive drinking.

Jessor et al. (1968:59) define the "normative structure" as "shared definitions or institutionalized expectations about acceptable behavior, and which includes consequential implications for unacceptable behavior. . . ." This structure applies to Indian drinking in that Indian drinking communities share nonverbal definitions or expectations about drinking, and excessive drinking is generally acceptable. The consequential implications for unacceptable behavior would be name calling, threats of physical abuse, and ridicule directed against the nondrinker.

Lastly, the "social control structure" consists of "socially patterned opportunities for learning and for performing deviant behaviors and to the nature and operation of sanction systems for encouraging conformity and discouraging deviance" (Jessor et al. 1968:66). What this means in relation to Indian drinking is that Indians have an overabundance of opportunities for learning and for performing "drinking" behaviors. But in this case excessive drinking would not be deviant behavior. It would conform to the expected modes of excessive drinking and the undesirability of nondrinking.

American Indian drinking points out a number of social functions. It is a form of recreation, a means of easing social intercourse. For some Indians, it is a way to let off steam by engaging in fights. It provides for sexual adventures, and offers forms of relaxation by drinking in bars, cars, alleys, streets, and homes. And for the majority of Indians, excessive drinking is not seen as pathological or abnormal behavior. With the relative absence of sanction networks against excessive drinking and with the general tolerance of drinking among Indians, it would seem that if anyone had rehabilitative intentions for the Indian who drinks in excess, Waddell's (1971:16) pertinent and crucial question must be considered: "How do we manipulate this environment to alter lifestyles and what kinds of new social environments and social bonds can be created that will help to build a new social bond, a new ritual, and a new language?"

Both a review of the literature on Indian drinking and my personal observations offer evidence relating to the hypothesis that the greater the degree of group pressure, the greater will be the degree of excessive drinking. Even though scientific research is lacking in this area, it is still reasonable to conclude that the data that are available suggest there is definite support for the hypothesis. This chapter is by no means complete. Other variables relative to Indian excessive drinking need to be considered, and the problem of culturally meaningful and effective treatment and rehabilitation must be confronted. It is hoped that, in the future, research will be done on these aspects of the problem of Indian drinking, adding to the knowledge painfully neglected and sorely needed by American Indians.

REFERENCES CITED

Barber, C. G.
    1952   Trilingualism in Pascua: The Social Functions of Language in an Arizona Yaqui Village. MS, Master's Thesis, University of Arizona, Tucson.
Curley, R. T.
    1967   Drinking Patterns of the Mescalero Apache. *Quarterly Journal of Studies on Alcohol* **28**:116–31.
Devereux, G.
    1948   The Function of Alcohol in Mohave Society. *Quarterly Journal of Studies on Alcohol* **9**:207–51.

Dozier, E. P.
   1966   Problem Drinking Among American Indians: The Role of Socio-
           cultural Deprivation. *Quarterly Journal of Studies on Alcohol*
           27:72–87.
DuToit, B. M.
   1964   Substitution, A Process in Culture Change. *Human Organization*
           23:16–23.
Ferguson, F. N.
   1970   A Treatment Program for Navaho Alcoholics: Results After Four
           Years. *Quarterly Journal of Studies on Alcohol* **31**:898–919.
Hamer, J. H.
   1965   Acculturation Stress and the Functions of Alcohol Among the
           Forest Potawatomi. *Quarterly Journal of Studies on Alcohol*
           26:285–302.
Heath, D. B.
   1964   Prohibition and Post-Repeal Drinking Patterns Among the Navajo.
           Quarterly Journal of Studies on Alcohol **25**:119–36.
Homans, G. C.
   1958   *Social Behavior as Exchange.* The Bobbs-Merrill Reprint Series in
           the Social Sciences, S-122. Indianapolis, Indiana.
Honigmann, J. J.
   1945   Drinking in an Indian-White Community. *Quarterly Journal of
           Studies on Alcohol* **5**:575–619.
Jessor, R., T. D. Graves, R. C. Hanson, and S. L. Jessor
   1968   *Society, Personality, and Deviant Behavior.* New York: Holt,
           Rinehart, and Winston.
Lemert, E. M.
   1958   The Use of Alcohol in Three Salish Indian Tribes. *Quarterly Jour-
           nal of Studies on Alcohol* **19**:90–107.
Merton, R. K.
   1938   *Social Structure and Anomie.* The Bobbs-Merrill Reprint Series in
           the Social Sciences, S-194. Indianapolis, Indiana.
Moss, F. E.
   1970   Definitions of Alcoholism. MS, Graduate School of Social Work,
           University of Utah, Salt Lake City.
Nevitt, F. M.
   1951   Educational Implications Derived from a Survey of Pascua Village
           and Adelanto Addition. MS, Masters Thesis, University of
           Arizona, Tucson.
Savard, R. J.
   1968   Effects of Disulfiram Therapy on Relationships Within the Navajo
           Drinking Group. *Quarterly Journal of Studies on Alcohol* **29**:909–
           16.
Waddell, J. O.
   1971   "Drink, Friend!" Social Contexts of Convivial Drinking and
           Drunkenness Among Papago Indians in an Urban Setting. MS,
           Purdue University, Lafayette.

Whittaker, J. O.
    1963   Alcohol and Standing Rock Sioux Tribe, II. Psycho-Dynamic and Culture Factors in Drinking. *Quarterly Journal of Studies on Alcohol* **24**:80–90.
Willard, W.
    1970   The Community Development Worker in an Arizona Yaqui Project. MS, Doctoral Dissertation, University of Arizona, Tucson.

7

Community Programs for Native Americans

ALCOHOLISM PROGRAMS

Richard Cooley

The first thing that needs to be done in attempting to discuss the Indian alcoholism program experience in the Southwest is to try to establish what it is that we are actually talking about. There is a great deal of confusion about the definition of the term "Indian." For example, the Bureau of Indian Affairs (BIA) says that anyone who is subject to tribal law and is an enrolled member of any Indian tribe in the United States is to be considered an Indian. Thus, in organizations like the Congress of American Indians and in the American Indian Movement, which is perhaps a little more militant than some of the other Indian organizations, there are a great many persons who for all intents and purposes are Anglos in general attitudes, language, emotions, value systems, and appearance, and yet have the required quarter Indian blood. Indian militants, of course, have different objectives, goals, techniques, and motives for their political activities than those involved in Indian alcoholism programs in various local communities.

For purposes of this discussion, an Indian in the southwestern group of tribes is one who is significantly dependent upon, or who relies upon,

---

Richard Cooley, before his untimely death in 1976, was active for the U.S. Public Health Service in training Native Americans as health workers in Indian alcoholism programs.

the older cultural forms for economic, political, social, cultural, and personal security, comfort, or belonging. In other words, an individual conforming to this definition of Indian would perceive everything in Anglo society as threatening, hostile, potentially hostile, or at least strange and alien enough so that constant association with and reliance upon it, as a major factor in his life, makes him uneasy, insecure, uncomfortable and not hopeful of producing a situation in which he can live in peace and with some degree of prosperity.

In some tribes, these individuals constitute the overwhelming majority of the membership. They have not retained all of the values of their earlier culture. They have adopted some of the Anglo material things that they use in their daily lives. (For example, a high priority item in these families would be a pickup truck and a horse trailer, probably somewhere in priority above shoes for the children.) They are not openly competitive with each other, or with anyone else. They hold back from taking the initiative in matters, and they also tend to wait until a consensus is arrived at or a unanimous decision is made before they proceed with whatever undertaking they have in mind.

Moreover, the older cultural forms in most tribes seem to pretty much confine activities, decision making, togetherness, and reciprocal obligations, etc. to the extended family, and they are not necessarily binding or in any way connected with the neighboring extended family. This system obviously indicates that in pre-Columbian days there probably was no tribal government, but rather a loose alliance or association of extended families. For example, the Navajo call these "outfits," like the Martinez outfit, the Jones outfit, and so on.

The cultural appreciation for some of these older systems of problem solving and decision making will have a very profound effect on feelings and attitudes expressed by Indian health workers. It will help to answer the ancient philosophical question, "Am I my brother's keeper?" It will provide the thrust, aim, and direction required to make the Indian alcoholism program successful and equally applicable to all people regardless of their clan affiliation, particular local history, political persuasion, or past behavior. In other words, there must develop an idea and ideal orientation rather than a person-oriented approach, as is strongly suggested by the older decision-making systems.

For the discussion which follows, I have consulted a few of my trainees. The trainee seminar was made up of Hopi, Papago, Navajo, and Apache participants. At this level or depth of inquiry the trainees from the different tribes showed very few differences in orientation; their comments and inputs coincided closely with mine.

The first question that we considered is whether an Indian alcoholism program, in relation to non-Indian programs, is a program plus something or a program minus something. Is it similar in its organization, aims, techniques, and methods to non-Indian programs? The answer is, of course, yes, with the probable difference being, perhaps, the strangeness of some of the assumptions. Methods, treatment suggestions, and so on are probably a little bit alien and hard to understand; or they may not be believed by some groups in some areas. The non-Indian concept of mental health and disease origin, the things that are perceived as ''bad'' in many cultures, may or may not be fully embraced by Indians as a culturally meaningful description of what actually happens to bring about human problems.

The consensus among the trainees seems to be that it is a little more difficult for Indians to organize, administer, and get a program into the production stage if they feel the program to be even slightly alien. Sometimes this feeling runs all the way through, directed toward the U.S. Public Health Service, the BIA, and various other agencies that have introduced a particular medical viewpoint or proposition based on their own cultural assumptions. For years, of course, native people have all been familiar with the attempts of these agencies to be of service to Indian people. In the remoter areas, these agencies have not been too successful in developing Indian faith and trust, nor in obtaining the participation of the people in the community who are seeking help. This is one of the main reasons why Indians are being trained in these areas. Indian trainees, once they learn the viewpoints and propositions guiding the agencies, are able to communicate the intentions of the agencies better to other Indians than are their non-Indian counterparts.

The tribe-to-tribe variation in language and culture does not seem to completely do away with the possibility of a kind of Indian view toward these things. The trainees feel more comfortable in dealing with people of Indian ancestry even though they are of different tribes. This is true even when the English language, which carries with it certain cultural values, must be used in framing questions or providing instructions.

Of course, with one's own tribe the answers are obvious. Trainees feel closer to individuals from their own tribes. They are more respectful to suggestions from their own tribal members but they do not, however, gracefully accept supervision in these programs from their own tribal members. The response may be, ''Who the hell is he? He was born in the same village, and groveled in the same gutters as I did. Now he's trying to tell me what to do.'' Nevertheless, they do feel a little closer in terms of help-seeking and help-giving relationships.

Of the three groups, that is, one's own tribe, another tribe, or a non-Indian, the non-Indian is the one with whom it is most difficult to feel comfortable. The non-Indian seems to ask the most embarrassing questions and at the strangest times. Indians invariably presume that non-Indians feel superior to the Indians and their cultures, viewing Indians as low people or "valueless." The non-Indian person is more difficult to communicate with because Indians feel that whites think and show a certain amount of contempt toward Indians. This is thought to be the traditional attitude in Anglo communities around reservations and, while it may not be part of the general population's view, the neighboring Anglos are the people Indians see more of and with whom they have more daily contact.

There is a general notion that the Indian trainee has a harder, more difficult job in alcoholism programs than in other programs because he has to learn and master fairly well both the techniques and the academic knowledge that make up program guidelines. The concept of counseling and the discussion of personal problems are especially difficult. Group therapy, for example, involves public confession before women and others, people with whom some matters should not normally be discussed. Revealing wrongdoing and weakness, or accepting the idea of being a victim of disease are prima facie evidence of wrongdoing somewhere in one's past. These are often seen as punishment by supernatural powers for misdeeds committed against the supernatural forces that abound.

All these factors and others have produced some readily discernible problems in some of the more remote areas and some not quite so apparent ones in the urban areas, where large groups of Indians are caught up in the urban time-scheme. The tempo of life is slower in some of the isolated places. Time is not budgeted carefully nor is it considered vital to the increased productivity or the health-giving role that the program intends to provide. This is, of course, a very common criticism that non-Indians have of Indian people, namely, that their conception of the role of time in the affairs of men leaves a lot to be desired in the fast-paced, tension-ridden atmosphere that characterizes the broader spectrum of modern American society. Indians still seem to be able to breathe and relax and think things over in a relatively remote, quiet atmosphere. This gives the impression of indolence, apathy, and idleness, whereas Indians may feel that they are going as rapidly as conscience and prudence would dictate.

The following analogy might serve as a general comment on the basic differences between Indian and Anglo alcohol programs. Suppose that you had never heard of baseball and had never played it before. Someone in the next town had challenged you or your town to a baseball game. The Indian alcoholism trainees feel pretty much as those in the town might who had never played baseball, who did not know when to run, how to count the score, when to cease and desist, when to put on the pressure, etc. The contrast is between teams that have played all the time and those that are just learning how to play the game. The feeling of the trainees is, "let's learn how to play the game and learn a few of the rules before we accept the competitive role of people who have been doing these things for many years."

Indians have a prevalent idea that the degree of acceptance of the whole bag of knowledge on alcoholism generated in Anglo circles over a period of many years carries with it an obligation to move toward acculturation, toward using the devices of the dominant culture to solve problems of Indian people who may not be totally and emotionally committed to being a part of that culture. Once the trainees start on their training course, they have to disregard a lot of their earlier feelings about alcoholism and view it cheek-by-jowl with Anglo professionals who have defined it. Thus, Indian people begin using the disease concept, seeing alcoholism as a treatable disease. They then go ahead on these assumptions to do something about the problems of alcoholism among Indian people.

This brings us to the question of whether Indian drinkers are somehow different from non-Indian drinkers. The answer to this question is very simple: I do not know. But there are undetermined factors that I do not think we know enough about. How is culture transmitted from one generation to another and how are vestigial aspects of the culture transmitted in the present day? We do know that there is a very profound difference in world view between the people of reservation cultures and of the population in general. Wherever there is a great difference in this general outlook there would be a difference in attitudes toward alcoholism and the possibilities of treatment and recovery.

I feel, for example, that those of the warrior societies, with histories as raiders or the hunters, are more frustrated and more prone to alcoholism than members of the more sedentary, agriculturally based cultures. The former seem to have a stronger degree of frustration and appear to be in more open conflict with the adversity they see around them. The feeling of powerlessness is stronger in these proud warrior types. They do not find it easy to condescend nor to surrender to the point where they can see the value in the purposeful expression of feelings. This is the kind of stoical, stone-faced visage that the warrior or proud soldier turns to the world, with very little tendency to engage in what he perceives as maudlin weakness. To confess that he has all these feelings of insecurity, anxiety, uncertainty, and despair (which he would probably call cowardice) is simply unacceptable.

Thus, the difficulty of an Indian drinker participating successfully in a non-Indian alcoholism program is pretty much connected to the degree of his acculturation and the degree of his comprehension of the whole body of knowledge that has been thrown together about alcoholism. The more closely he understands this, the greater the possibility for gainful participation in a non-Indian program.

On the other hand, it is possible that problem drinking is much the same in all societies. An Indian drinker does quite often drink socially in the sense that any nonalcoholic drinks socially. The problem drinker has many of the same characteristics in any culture—he is one who has problems from drinking. This means anyone who might be arrested for DWI (Driving While Intoxicated) or any of the other drinking-related social problems. The person uses alcohol, in other words, as a kind of problem solver, which turns out to be more often than not a problem evader.

The alcoholic, on the other hand, is an addict. He usually becomes psychologically as well as physically dependent upon alcohol and he usually experiences severe withdrawal syndromes when deprived of alcohol. His system has a total reliance on alcohol and may insist on the presence of alcohol in order to feel like getting out of bed. The difference between the problem drinker and an alcoholic is that the alcoholic shows a very definite interference and deterioration of his bodily functioning. There is physical, emotional, and mental debility because of the toxic, long-term effects of alcohol.

However, Indian culture can be used in Indian alcoholism programs, either in place of or in addition to standard western psychological and pyschiatric techniques. Since religious organizations, the Indian Bureau, and the military began their occupation of the various reservations in Arizona 75–85 years ago, a concentrated effort has been made to eliminate the medicine man, or shaman. These native diagnosticians and curers were both psychiatrists and psychologists in a very real sense. The prolonged and concentrated efforts of various agents of white society to ridicule, put down, and eliminate these valuable practitioners from society has left most tribes with no traditional help-giver to alleviate psycho-emotional problems. This has forced Indians to accept Anglo standards and techniques whether or not they have understood them or wanted them.

This issue is still charged with emotional content for many people, and I imagine it will continue to be a matter of speculation and controversy for some time. My own mind is still open on the validity of each approach. I think it is necessary, though, to continue on with the western body of knowledge in making suggestions and providing the guidelines for Indian alcoholism programs. The non-Indian's notion is that Indians are different; but they are still human, and alcoholism is a human problem. Therefore, if a technique or treatment form is effective for some Italians, there is no reason why it should not, at this level of concentration, be effective for some Indians as well.

Another important consideration for alcoholism programs is that Indians, often former problem drinkers, are recruited as program workers. Early in 1970 and 1971, there was a lot of concentration on and a deliberate effort in getting recovering or stabilized alcoholics into some of the jobs in Indian alcoholism programs. This has not been discontinued or put down by anyone in the field, but there was in the late 1970s a trend toward utilizing younger people and more women in alcoholism programs as trainees and counselors. This suggests that mature men might occasionally prefer to get out of the job because alcoholism and mental health problems are equated with insanity. Adult men would like to get into more culturally acceptable pursuits, such as becoming horsemen, cow punchers, or into other manly lines of endeavor, leaving alcoholism programs to the old men and perhaps the women. Younger people coming into the health field are more acculturated and better educated. They are apt to be more interested in learning the body of knowledge and technology on which the programs are based.

The people working in Indian alcohol programs cover a pretty broad spectrum as far as age, sex, drinking history, and drinking habits are concerned. It is not much of an issue one way or another whether the reformed alcoholic or the adjusting alcoholic is given precedence over anyone else. I think the main criterion is to have an individual with a stable personality, a person with a good perspective, one who can keep his cool and be capable of communicating to others without being hampered by too many emotional problems of his own.

Quite often, we find that many who live in the rural areas or on the most isolated reservation areas either lack job experience or lack perspective as to what constitutes a priority while they are on the job. It is important to be able to forget personal problems for a while and to give some amount of time and responsible thought to what the job requires. This is particularly a problem in the more isolated reservation areas, where rivalries among factions in the community may go on continuously, creating all kinds of preoccupying personal problems. Generally speaking, if the reformed alcoholic remains reformed and the controlled drinker maintains control, neither would necessarily be as important a worker as the person who has a degree of stability, intelligence, or favorable job attitude.

Whatever the trainee's background, the notion is to teach Indian alcoholism counselors the concepts or the idea behind the particular program. For example, in counseling, the first interviews must work toward the individualization of the client, that is, toward finding out exactly where the client's head is and trying to individualize him. This means getting out all the generalities that go with notions of alcoholism and getting down to the specifics of the client's personal feelings, attitudes, and emotions. This is basic, and I think that this approach is presently being modified and used advantageously to fit local circumstances and local values.

After the individualizing of the client, the technique goes on to allow the client a meaningful expression of feelings, the assurance of confidentiality, and all the other factors that make up a relationship of trust and friendly understanding between the client and counselor. This approach allows the counselor to offer suggestions and provide alternatives and options, always making sure that the client himself has a chance to take a big part in planning the recovery program that he feels is most favorable for him. Finally, the client begins to accept the notion that he is suffering from some kind of identifiable thing, that alcohol is not all good, and that perhaps he should try, with help, to avoid the pitfalls that bring him back into the cycle—the jail, the hospital, and detox ward, and back to the jail again. This seems to be the lot of so many people in contemporary reservation society.

Perhaps the most important factor relevant to Indian alcoholism programs is that the majority of such programs are almost totally dependent upon outside funding, principally from the National Institute on Alcohol Abuse and Alcoholism (NIAAA) and other government agencies. The thinking is that in time the effectiveness and value of local Indian alcoholism programs will be proven in the Indian community and that they will then be able to get funding from their local governments or from county and state governments. I think this is also the intent of NIAAA. The possibility of adequate funding is all in the future, which is difficult to foresee. The programs that are effective, through merit and achievement in this general area, will be funded by the communities in which they operate. Those which are not successful will have to re-model or redirect their efforts, mainly toward public education. It is a broad and heavy question whether or not community attitudes towards these ancient problems can be changed so as to provide a climate in which people are more amenable to suggestions. These have been, after all, problems that have been viewed for centuries as personal and private and of no concern to other people in the community or to outsiders.

MENTAL HEALTH PROGRAMS

Maurice W. Miller and Don Ostendorf

Native Americans have had few opportunities to participate in the development of their own mental health programs. In most Indian communities these services have been provided by the federal government in the same manner as other health services or by off-reservation programs serving primarily non-Indian populations. Although there have been efforts to involve Indians in the planning and staffing of these programs, direct tribal or community-based control has been noticeably absent.

Ideally, each community and cultural group should arrive at its own definition of mental health. This is especially true among Native Americans where cultural and environmental factors play such an important role in shaping the behavior of the individual. A fundamental role of mental health programs serving these groups must be to assist the Indian community in reaching its own definition of mental health. Services should then be developed that are consistent with this definition. Given the circumstances within most Indian communities, mental health

Maurice Miller became Executive Director of the Northern Arizona Comprehensive Guidance Center in 1971. The agency provides community mental health, alcoholism, and drug abuse services for the five northern Arizona counties.

Don Ostendorf became Executive Director of the West Yavapai Guidance Clinic in 1976. The agency provides community mental health, alcoholism, and drug abuse services for West Yavapai County, Arizona.

programs would be active in eliminating external factors (poverty, inadequate housing, unemployment, and discrimination) as well as providing services geared to the psychological needs of the individual.

A mental health program for any group should be oriented to the particular needs of that group and should be culturally specific. For example, an Indian program for Indians in San Francisco would need to be much different than an Indian program on a closed reservation or for Indians in a border-town situation. The mental health program should present the expertise and knowledge of general mental health to persons from the community so that a local definition of mental health and illness for that particular group can be constructed. Then appropriate kinds of services, programs, and facilities can be clearly specified.

Everything that is done or carried out in a mental health program for Indian communities should reflect cultural awareness. Mental health workers should show sensitivity to and awareness of the way local people handle problems personally, with the family, and within their social network. These workers need to be aware of what kinds of things are talked about, what taboos are in effect, and what cultural factors can be mobilized to strengthen the individual. All social action programs should be related to the specific needs and cultural patterns of the local people.

It is important that Indian people participate with Anglo people in developing mental health programs, an experience that can be growth-enhancing for all concerned. We disagree with the statement that only an Indian can understand another Indian. But mental health programs need to be specific to the community involved, and one method of accomplishing this is the hiring of local people as counselors. They are better acquainted with the culture, language, problems, and resources of their community. It is not Indianness or non-Indianness but the sensitivities and capabilities of the people themselves that will determine their success and potency.

Many Anglos relate effectively and do productive mental health counseling cross-culturally with Indian clients, and there are Indians who are effective therapists with Anglo clients. Programs composed of Anglo and Indian staff are most successful in an atmosphere that identifies the strengths and limitations of both groups and finds ways for each to complement the other.

A primary criticism of some Indian mental health and social action programs (like the Office of Economic Opportunity) has been that their only function is to provide jobs for local Indian people. When this has occurred, the programs have done a disservice to the people and certainly have not contributed to anyone's self-esteem and ability to function. Indians certainly see through the business of hiring someone just to give him money, and they take this into account when they think about asking the local mental health program for assistance. By hiring people who are not competent to perform their jobs, we communicate to the employee and the Indian people that 1) we are really not sincere about providing quality mental health services and 2) "in Indian mental health programs you really don't need to be competent."

To avoid this problem, training and general skill development in mental health intervention are necessary. The development of well-trained Native Americans, at various skill levels, is critical to the future of mental health services for Indian people. Some ascribe to the notion that "Indianness" is a therapeutic quality in and of itself. Others have gone so far as to say that traditional mental health training will somehow interfere with the Indian's rapport and effectiveness with his community. It seems to us, on the contrary, that the effectiveness of any mental health worker in *any* setting depends upon his ability to apply proven methods and skills to the individualized needs of clients and communities.

Too often mental health training programs for Native Americans have emphasized Indianness rather than skill development. In extreme instances these programs have conveyed to their students a generalized attitude that traditional mental health methods do not work among Native Americans. Mental health training programs should emphasize proven skills and techniques, whether they have proven valuable in Indian or non-Indian settings. The Indian mental health worker can then adapt these methods to local needs and complement them through integration of their unique heritage, cultural orientation, and knowledge. In doing so the community will reap the benefits of trained Indian personnel and can begin to build skills and methods appropriate to its problems and resources. The value of professional training for Indian people as an answer to Indian control of programs and provision of effective mental health services should not be underestimated. This makes sense in terms of the realities of funding, accountability, and the reliance upon credentials as measures of competence and credibility. In addition, Indians have always placed value on professionalism. Traditionally, native practitioners only became accepted and respected when they met "professional standards": a body of knowledge, a training/apprenticeship experience, ethics, and demonstrated skill. The most effective programs relating to Indian communities have been those in which Anglo people approached Indian people with honesty and forthrightness, using their skill and knowledge in the mental health professions. They engage in a dialogue with local people and do not try to become overly Indian or try to impose an outside model on the community.

When tribes operate their own mental health programs, they communicate to tribal members an acknowledgment that mental health problems exist, that the tribe takes responsibility for alleviating these problems and, most importantly, that solutions can come from within the tribal group. This process combats the powerlessness and dependency that are so frequently seen as being at the root of Indian mental health problems. Programs that are not tribally owned or sponsored in some manner always leave an out for the tribe or the local people to place the blame for the effectiveness or lack of effectiveness of the program on the outside agency rather than dealing with it themselves.

Evaluation of mental health programs should be based upon the effectiveness of services as experienced by the Indian client and the community. For example, is the program meeting the needs of the community as defined by the community? Do the people use the services? Do they benefit from them? Proven mental health evaluation methodologies and techniques can be utilized in the evaluation of "Indian Mental Health Programs" as long as these evaluation efforts are based on locally defined criteria.

We believe that any mental health program should be culturally specific and related to the local community. The program should be owned by the community and not by an outside group and needs to develop people well trained and knowledgeable in the mental health area. Emphasis should be on dialogue between skilled staff and the community toward the definition of a mental health program of services to meet the specific needs of that community. The program should give careful attention to the selection of local people for jobs with the selection based primarily on the ability of the people to perform the functions desired.

Tribal ownership of mental health programs is seen as fundamental to reversing the effects of the powerlessness and dependency currently experienced by Native Americans and is consistent with the current trend toward self-determination.

URBAN ALCOHOLISM PROGRAMS

Ron Wood

An urban Native American alcoholism program must be planned and implemented carefully because the native alcoholic and alcohol abuser present a different set of problems than those encountered with Anglo clients. These different problems require different solutions, which are often unique to the individual and his tribal group.

An urban Native American alcoholic generally has certain drinking patterns that are culture-specific. In addition to this, an urban Native American is generally acculturated to varying degrees. The more acculturated a Native American person is, the more his drinking pattern tends to resemble the Anglo pattern of drinking.

Too often, Native American problem drinking is referred to or treated as an "Indian" problem without sufficient recognition of the fact that there are distinct cultural differences between tribal groups that have to be considered when a treatment plan is formulated. A good example would be the different drinking patterns of a Navajo and a Hopi who live on adjacent reservations. The Navajo drinking pattern is generally of an open, boisterous manner with friends, while the Hopi pattern is generally of a singular, secretive, or less boisterous nature. To be effective, a Native American alcoholism counselor must be aware of these differences among individual clients.

Another unique aspect of urban Native American alcoholism programs is that there is a diversity of Native American clients ranging from the traditional to the "modern" acculturated individual. The traditional Native American drinks in a pattern typical of his tribal pattern, while the acculturated Native American drinking pattern resembles the Anglo pattern. This aspect of Native American clients must be recognized by an effective Native American alcoholism counselor. Most personnel in urban Native American alcoholism programs tend to be acculturated by varying degrees themselves, and this helps them in working with urban Native American clients.

Ron Wood, who holds an M.A. in Public Health from the University of California, Berkeley, became Director of Program Planning, Office of Health Improvement Services for the Navajo Nation in 1977. He is a Navajo.

An urban Native American alcoholism program must be able to work with other Anglo agencies within the community in addition to reservation alcoholism programs when they are nearby. There are often areas of overlapping service or areas where neither the off-reservation nor the reservation program provide services. Rapport within and without the urban community is vitally important since much of the work of an urban program in a border town deals directly with these two programs and often acts as a liaison between on- and off-reservation alcoholism programs.

Anglo border towns have traditionally conducted much business with reservation Native Americans who have to go off reservation for needed services and supplies. The sale of alcoholic beverages has also been a good business for border-town merchants, and many border towns are noted for their abundance of bars. The problem is compounded in many areas by the fact that the possession or use of alcohol on reservations is prohibited. Another factor is that some states (e.g. Arizona) have decriminalized public intoxication and established LARCs (Local Alcoholism Reception Centers). While this law is a positive step toward the treatment of alcoholism as a disease rather than a crime, it has had a negative effect by encouraging some Native Americans to leave their home on the reservation to drink in town where they are guaranteed comradeship and a warm place to sleep without the threat of the law.

Another problem Native Americans encounter in an urban environment is lack of cultural activities where a Native American can meet his Brothers and Sisters. All too often, the only place for social interaction for Native Americans in a border town is in a local "Indian bar." Alternate avenues of social interaction are desperately needed. A major alternative to the "Indian bar" is a well-organized Native American Center where activities would be planned that could offer something for all Native Americans in a nondrinking environment.

For many urban Native Americans the urban environment is too harsh in terms of unemployment and underemployment, substandard housing, cultural isolation, and racial discrimination. The bottle is often used as an escape mechanism and alcohol abuse leads to additional problems. Urban Native American alcoholism counselors generally have a better understanding of the problem because they are usually subjected to many of the same pressures that force many of their Brothers and Sisters to drink.

The operation of a Native American alcoholism program in an urban environment has many pressures placed upon it. The problem of Native American drinking is perceived by the local Anglo community as an

"Indian" problem, not a community problem. This attitude makes it extremely difficult if not impossible for a Native American alcoholism program to generate local supporting funds. The theory of NIAAA (National Institute on Alcohol Abuse and Alcoholism) funding is that a program will demonstrate its usefulness to the community, and the community will assume the financial responsibility after a certain number of years. NIAAA also realizes the problem that Native American programs may have generating this support, so NIAAA will consider funding Native American programs beyond the initial three-year grant period. The approach of NIAAA seems to be to fund Native American alcoholism programs with a minimal amount of strings attached so that they are free to develop to their maximum effectiveness. As can be expected, there have been some very successful, innovative programs and there have been some failures, but the important thing is that Native Americans have had a chance to run Native American programs for Native American clients, and this has been an invaluable experience. NIAAA is to be commended for this approach to the problem. Future funding may require more control and/or conformity to established, successful Native American alcoholism programs.[1] If these requirements become a reality, it is important that specific cultural traits be included in programs, whether they be operated in California or in Florida.

Another problem facing urban Native American alcoholism programs is the pressure of Anglo professionalism, with its emphasis on degrees and credentials. Most Native American counselors do not have the advanced training and degrees that Anglo society considers necessary for an effective alcoholism counseling program. The differences between a Native American alcoholism program and an Anglo program might be described by saying that Native American programs operate more with their heart and Anglo programs operate more with their head. While training in basic counseling techniques is necessary, I do not feel that advanced degrees are essential to being a good counselor. A good example of this is the fact that Alcoholics Anonymous (AA) enjoys a very high success rate in treating alcoholics with AA members who are lay people with very little formal training. AA's success rate is greater

---

[1] Editor's note: In 1978, many of these NIAAA-funded programs were brought under the administration of the Indian Health Service of the United States Public Health Service. There is some concern as to what effect this will have on the innovativeness of existing Indian alcoholism programs, since under the NIAAA, Native Americans were given considerable freedom to develop these programs in terms of local needs.

than that of many expensive Anglo programs that employ highly trained professionals.

The pressure on urban Native American alcoholism programs will increase because more emphasis is being placed on certified counselors and accredited programs. Certification and accreditation are necessary to qualify for third-party payments and to comply with national and state standards being imposed on all programs. As of the late 1970s, reservation Native American programs are not threatened by this as much as are the urban Native American programs. Third-party insurance payments for Native American alcoholism programs do not provide much incentive since few Native Americans carry health insurance.

Competition with counterpart Anglo alcoholism programs also has to be contended with. Some Anglo programs claim to serve all segments of the population, including the Native American population. Their staffs are Anglo dominated and are often insensitive to the needs of Native American clients. The other area of competition is for program monies. Established Anglo agencies may perceive a Native-American-run program as threatening their existence or at least depriving them of additional program monies, which they might use to serve Native American clients themselves. Native American self-determination is professed by all, but when it comes to actual implementation and award of monies to a Native American program, Anglo programs often feel threatened by losing these potential funds.

To be effective, an urban Native American alcoholism program must have two facets to it. On the one hand, the program must have feeling and empathy for Native American clients, while on the other hand, it must maintain an Anglo business sense in order to deal with the Anglo community. The Anglo business world is exacting in terms of finance, formal written commitments, and other related functions. Native American alcoholism programs must not become over-balanced in either direction.

Being "Indian" is not enough qualification to be a successful counselor, nor is the fact that a person is a recovered alcoholic sufficient qualification. A certain amount of technical training is necessary to be a good counselor, but the most important criterion is having a "good heart" and empathy to help fellow Native American Brothers and Sisters. Thus, counseling of Native American clients is not done on a strict time schedule nor in a formal setting. As long as a Native American client is trying to help himself, a Native American counselor will try to help him. We try not to be overly concerned with numbers and statistics, although we realize how important they are. This is where the

Anglo facet of the urban Native American alcoholism program is important. A Native American alcoholism program should keep their counselors free to do their maximum amount of client contact and let the administrative staff worry about the necessary but evil ''paperwork.''

The future of Native American alcoholism programs is uncertain due to the uncertainty of federal funding. The future trend will probably be that more accountability will be necessary in terms of finance and cost-effectiveness of programs. These conditions can be endured as long as it is recognized that Native American programs can best work with Native American clients even though the program might not conform to Anglo program models. We insist upon this.

PART FOUR

The Native Southwest, Native
Americans, and Alcohol Use:
Some Comparative Conclusions

Introduction

This volume was introduced with a number of goals specified and questions raised. Everett pointed out the widely shared concern of Native Americans and non-Native Americans alike over the consequences of alcohol abuse among Native Americans but he also made it clear that the editors of the volume were not intending the book to be just another reminder of this fact. Instead, the emphasis is on the value of culture-specific knowledge about alcohol use and abuse in helping to resolve two central controversies. One issue has to do with whether or not Native American tolerance for and' use of alcohol is really different from that in other populations. The other issue has to do with whether or not cultural variables are crucial for explaining or accounting for behavioral differences instead of or in addition to the commonalities of social structure shared by many ethnic populations. The studies in this collection are not intended to support either side of the issue as to whether there are or are not genetic differences. This is a problem that only the pharmacologists, biochemists, and population geneticists can finally answer. Nor has the approach here sought to contest explanations of alcoholic behavior that look at the structure of contemporary society to see the commonalities among many ethnic and status populations. Our collective effort has been to point out that there are culture-specific realities and cultural bodies of knowledge about alcohol and its use and misuse that are sufficiently different so that rehabilitative and educational programs must not ignore them. In this sense, our main argument is that Indians, where there are cultural frames of reference still viably operative, do behave toward alcohol differently, not only with respect to non-Indian populations but with respect to each other. This final section attempts to evaluate whether or not our studies of a select number of Southwest Native American societies reflect these differences and what might be significant in the cultural perspective to suggest for improvement of culture-specific alcoholism programs among Native Americans.

Similarities and Variations in Alcohol Use in Four Native American Societies in the Southwest

8

Jack O. Waddell

We began this volume by proposing that the unique cultural histories of different Southwestern native populations could provide the broad framework in which to understand cultural similarities and differences in alcohol use. The historical overview (Waddell) attempts to isolate two predominant patterns stemming from aboriginal times, the one pattern being the extensive use of native intoxicants and the other being the absence of them. Some societies used alcohol and integrated it into the agricultural and ritual dimensions of culture, while others made alcohol an important part of social relations. It was shown that some societies had agricultural rituals but did not integrate alcohol into the ritual matrix, while other societies without the agricultural-ritual complex did incorporate alcohol as an important dimension of the social system.

On the basis of these historical variations, four ethnographically well-known native societies were selected to represent some of the variation discussed above. The Papagos, with a long history of ceremonial intoxication and positive valuing of intoxication under controlled cultural conditions, constituted the first study. In contrast, the second study of Taos Pueblo reveals a people who, like the Papagos, had a long history of agricultural ceremonialism but who, unlike the Papago, culturally rejected intoxication as a component of the ritual system. Hence with the Pueblo case there is evidence of a historical negative valuing of intoxication in corporate community life. The Navajos, originating in a hunting, foraging economy but adopting the puebloan agricultural sedentarism, were selected as the third case. While they adopted agriculture, they did not adopt the agricultural-ritual complex, but instead, maintained their unique ceremonial concern with personal health. Alcohol served primarily to integrate social groups and cement social obligations to kinsmen and has not been integrated into ceremony, though it may be used as an accompaniment to it. The fourth case, the Western Apache, was selected to represent a people in closer contact with Mexican native societies where both drinking and agricultural ritual were important. The Apaches, like their relatives the Navajos, used alcohol as a means of binding locally meaningful social groups together and did not incorporate it into agricultural ritual.

Upon this variable aboriginal base, Spanish influence was differentially established among the four tribes in question. Spanish cultural influences probably diffused over the same thoroughfare as did prehispanic Mesoamerican-Southwest cultural contacts. While the general features of the Spanish frontier culture of conquest (Foster 1960) such as mission settlements,' agricultural and animal husbandry extension services, indoctrinal instruction, social regulation using local native government, and visual influence of the military at presidios, etc. were somewhat uniformly spread throughout the Upper Sonoran Province and New Mexico, there are some marked differences in overall impact. The Jesuit extension into the land of the Papago, for instance, was far more gradual and less oppressive of native culture than was that of the Franciscans into the Pueblo country somewhat earlier (Spicer 1954; Dozier 1956).

It could be argued that Pueblo isolation of alcohol from Pueblo culture was a part of the broader pattern of compartmentalizing Spanish and native elements under the generally oppressive conditions. Thus, drinking and drunkenness have never been strong components of corporate Pueblo culture. If aboriginal use of intoxicants had been the pattern, it surely would have remained a part of the ritual life of the Pueblo; hence, this fact alone is the strongest evidence for its absence in pre-European times.

The Papagos, on the other hand, could incorporate or fuse Spanish-derived beverages into their social life as they did many elements of Spanish-Catholic culture, without disrupting the aboriginal ritual matrix. This is not to say that clerics and administrators consciously and willingly opened up drinking to native communities. In fact, they were frequently frustrated in dealing with native intoxication, as was noted in an earlier chapter. But the models for drinking behavior were both aboriginal in origin and available by the increasing presence of Europeans and, eventually, those Mexicans, mestizos, and acculturated natives of the Spanish-Mexican frontier.

Spanish towns and presidios, based on European models, grew up in strategic outpost locations, primarily along river valleys that could provide water for sustaining settlements. In both the Pima and Puebloan areas, these became locations for attracting segments of the native populations on a regular basis. As the frontiers stabilized and as missions declined, native populations lived alongside mestizos and were significantly influenced by them, particularly in the economic and material culture sphere.

Waddell points out how the Papagos developed a long-standing relationship to the Mexican Pueblo of Tucson just as Brown notes the close relationship of Taos Pueblo to the social and economic activities of Don Fernandez de Taos. For both societies, the towns became focal points for economic and secular time-out activities. Obviously, the corporate pueblo with its long history of occupation within just a few miles of the developing Spanish town is structurally a different situation than that of the desert-dwelling Papago amorphously hanging about on the outskirts of a growing town and urban place. For Papagos, "time out" for social drinking and intoxication was ritually and culturally sanctioned; the "time-out" activities revolving around drinking were perceived to be causally related to the sober time-in periods of successful subsistence activity in their desert surroundings. As the aboriginal economic base drastically changed, especially under conditions of rapid acculturation to American inroads into the Tucson area, "time-out" periods were longer in duration as viable economic pursuits were depleted or altered. Nonetheless, there was no negative cultural devaluation of either drinking or drunkenness, as long as inter- and intra-familial obligations were upheld. It was not the drinking that was disruptive but rather the corruption or undermining of the *himdag,* the Papago custom. Drinking and intoxication per se had been integrated into Papago social and ritual life long before European influence. It was only the creation of new social contexts that brought the elements of disruption. Alcohol abuse in Papago life did occasionally occur but its disruptive features could be handled.

As Brown noted, Spanish *aguardiente* and wine were introduced in the Spanish settlements of New Mexico, including limited usage in the church Eucharist. As early as the 17th century, Pueblo and Apache-Navajo Indians were engaging in secular drinking at the Spanish settlements, especially at fairs. In Pueblo communities, generally, ritual controls appear to have operated to restrict usage primarily to those non-Pueblo settings.

In all four societies presented, there is clear evidence that the commercial liquor trade increased both the availability and the incidence of drinking. For Papagos and Pueblos, this appears to have been most intense around the Spanish-Mexican settlements, where people left their home communities and depended heavily on Mexican suppliers. For Apaches and Navajos, these beverages appear to have been utilized in their local reunions for social purposes as well as at the town locations.

The rapidity and intensity of alcohol usage, both in and outside of all four native societies appear to have accelerated in the 20th century, particularly following the economic booms of the frontier growth, the increasing efforts at prohibition to Indians, the access of illegal merchants to once-remote areas, the return of itinerant natives from more urban places, and the social-economic-political transitions brought about by both urban growth and increasing governmental regulation of reservation political economics. Following World War II, up to the late 1970s, the pervasiveness of drinking in all four societies plus the growing concern of administrative sectors to do something about it have helped to provide a common social definition of alcohol as a problem.

The major concern, then, has been to sort out the common social dimensions and the similarities in historical process from those particular cultural factors that still stand as the measure of difference among these four groups.

Perhaps what is significant is neither the drinking of intoxicants nor the pervasiveness of intoxication but the conditions or contexts in which they occur in each of the four societies. It is a question of determining the extent to which various social contexts do or do not allow for the articulation of meaningful cultural behaviors. Waddell notes that for Papagos in the urban contexts as well as for those in rural-reservation settings, there are still viable ways of behaving customarily (*himdag*). Some drinking is *himdag* when it articulates the cultural value of meeting reciprocal obligations; it is *pi-himdag*, not the people's way, if drinking is solitary, niggardly, possessive, or individually ostentatious or flamboyant. These models for collaborative drinking were provided for individuals within the Papago communities themselves on special occasions. Contrary to this, Brown points out that in Taos Pueblo, it is appropriate for village residents to proclaim that while drinking goes on, it did not originate in the pueblo but is a product of the outside. At Taos, social heavy drinking at picnics, celebrations and feast days does take place, perhaps a carry-over from the fair-like patterns of earlier days. This is acknowledged to be of outside origin. Topper makes it quite clear that drinking in outside contexts (e.g. bars) is full of ambivalence for many Navajos, yet he points out that there are many environments in which appropriate action decisions regarding the kind of drinking called for are learned. To engage in risks, not to be bound by firm moral constraints, to make amends for those transgressions for which he may be found out, and to try avoiding any behavior that would disrupt the life of his family, etc. are indications that much Navajo conduct is directed by social encouragement and social constraint operating within the community. Hence, Navajos do not seem prone to place the responsibility for drinking on non-Navajos as the Taos Pueblo people are prone to do.

It is possible to abuse alcohol. As with the Papago case, a Navajo is a problem drinker not so much by how much or how often he drinks but the extent to which he is a lone, selfish, unsharing drinker. Brown also noted that individual solitary drinking is regarded as the most culturally deviant form of drinking in Pueblo society. A solitary drinker makes decisions to drink outside of social contexts or events where social norms, appropriate to age and sex, are operative. Wherever a considerable amount of neglect of others is the product of selfish drinking, it is defined as the problem. Social events set the norms for drinking.

Everett, in the Western Apache example, similarly argues that dealing with intoxicants and intoxicated behavior has a lengthy social precedent. Native corn beer or *tulpai* has been used for a long time when groups of kinsmen come together for social purposes, including curing ceremonies. The models for drinking behavior are attributable to the social group, not to the outside, non-Apache community. Only after World War II is there clear indication that drinking models from the outside, often defined as disruptive, are attributed to the alarming increase and differences in drinking habits among all four groups. Whether this necessarily is a real index of rapid change in both pattern and incidence is not that clear, since pervasive social drinking for all four societies has been around for over a century.

The most significant change seems to be related to the growth of non-Indian bureaucratic and service institutions in reservation areas, where appropriate behavior for functioning in these institutions calls for nontraditional criteria in defining what kinds of drinking are problematic. The conflict produced by the differing ideologies regarding what may or may not be appropriate is unquestionably more intense than in former years. Where more Indians conform or aspire to the roles and ideologies of the supervening institutions, whether health, occupational, law and order, etc., the more likely it will be that the conventional environments and their norms will be negatively defined.

Certain drinks such as Mexican- and American-derived beers, Mexican tequila, and grain-based whiskeys or liquors among the Papagos, and cold beers, *tułpai,* and "home brew" among the Western Apaches, are still important in domestic and festive events. These beverages, long used and socially integrated in domestic and festive life, will continue to be important to large numbers of people. The sweet, cheap, commercial wines (the most popular form used in binge drinking in towns and urban areas) and the far less-used hard commercial liquors (exorbitant in price and attributable to white man's high-class drinking) are more likely to be perceived as the source of any problems. All four studies seem to suggest this.

All four societies classify drinking in terms of the kind that is appropriate and the kind that is inappropriate. Papagos, Navajos and Apaches all have a range of social situations where it is appropriate to drink. While the incidence of alcohol use is relatively high among the Taos Pueblo people, it is more difficult to find a range of domestic events in which it is given wide-scale social approval. For Papagos, there are those who are *s-i'imk,* those who have uncontrollable cravings for alcohol—in contrast to one who is just drunk, *s-naumk;* for the people of Taos Pueblo, there is the heavy drinker, *chuna,* usually of middle-age, largely influenced by white culture, who indulges heavily alone and who does so away from the village; for Navajos, there are also the antisocial heavy drinkers, *yeego da'adlą́ą́nii,* or alcoholics; and for Apaches, there are those who are the *tii bigan diskit* or "camels" who drink everywhere and whenever, usually in large amounts. The camels need not be instigators of trouble, but drinking can become problematic if it leads to bad talk, fighting, suicide, and murder. A situation where a large number of unrelated people are present and where *betnawodizigiz* or drunkenness prevails is apt to yield the largest amount of trouble. Hence, in all four societies drinking behavior is monitored, according to context, and can be categorized as either appropriate to or deviant from the expected behavior.

Another noticeable feature of drinking in all four societies, reflecting traditional social norms, are the age and sex distinctions in appropriate drinking behavior. While there are occasions for all ages and both sexes to mingle and, perchance, to drink, many events are age-limited and the standards and expectations vary. Old people generally see themselves and are seen by others as drinking differently. There seems to be cultural acknowledgment that old people are, and always have been, more tranquil drinkers, while the young, especially adolescents and young adults, are more ribald, more verbally aggressive, more boisterous, etc., characteristic of those who are still trying out life, not yet maturely experienced. The age distinctions are so significant in behavioral terms that the old, as Everett particularly points out in the Apache case, are frequently intimidated by younger people's styles of drinking, often to the point of fear.

While there are heavy drinkers among females and older women comparable to the heavy, even solitary patterns of problem-drinking males, all four societies seem to define drinking behavior in categorically different ways along sex lines. Waddell suggests that verbal bantering, even aggressiveness among Papagos may be expected, while such behavior among Apaches might be perceived as trouble, in the form of bad talk. For Papagos and Apaches as well as for Taos Puebloans and Navajos, physical abuse, suicide, and homicide are clearly indicative of violation of social standards and should be avoided. Such behavior or events are threatening to domestic social stability and when they occur, they are traumatic.

Papagos, according to Waddell, would probably intimidate and pressure a teetotaller; but Apaches, according to Everett, would find it inappropriate to drink around abstainers or nondrinkers. Brown points out that the Pueblo people are also selective in that they become *chu'puyena,* drinking buddies. Outside of family festive social drinking, one is likely to drink with these select friends and, like the solitary drinker, is more apt to do so outside the pueblo. Therefore, intimidating drinking is out of character with Pueblo life, yet one who does not drink at social gatherings would lose friends. When there is ceremonial responsibility or responsibility to family among the Taos people, even the heavy drinker may abstain. Given the importance of demonstrating manliness, Topper points out that Navajos use drinking and risk taking as means to this end; hence, like the Papagos, they use social pressure to persuade friends and relatives, even abstainers, to drink with them.

Topper's study is focused specifically on young Navajo males, the contexts in which they drink, and the meanings they attach to them. The young males have followed adult models since they were very young and, when they became young men, it was socially expected that they would use alcohol to both discover and demonstrate their manhood.

Drinking becomes established as a pleasurable venture with peers, where risk taking, bravado, experimental sexuality, and independence are asserted. Everett likewise points out that Apache adolescent or youthful drinking is different from the adult models before them. Peer-group settings provide different social environments than those occupied by adults. Youthful peer groups may even be hostile toward adult interference. We see the same risk-taking, aggressive behavior among Western Apache youthful peer groups that Topper notes for the Navajo. Brown does not tell us much about the youthful drinkers at Taos other than the fact that young people may seek to alleviate boredom in the pueblo by going off to drink with a few friends. Papagos, as Waddell notes, drink in age- and sex-restricted groups in some contexts. In actual urban situations it was not uncommon to see people of several ages drinking together, but the more prevalent pattern was for younger men to seek each other out, and middle-aged and older men to drink together. The younger men were more apt to engage in risk-taking, aggressive behavior.

Navajo and Apache youthful risk taking and daring are carry-overs from earlier cultural values, while any risk-taking and adolescent bravado in age-peer collectivities among Papagos and Taos Puebloans are a by-product of contemporary reservation social life. In all four cases, however, the elderly are seen to both drink differently and to have different expectations made of them. Where youthful indulgence and frequent social drinking binges are the expectation for the adolescent unmarried, all four groups called for the assumption of family responsibility, appropriate political or ceremonial participation in community life, and greater control over the contexts where drinking might be taking place. Problem drinking, nonetheless, as cases from all four groups show, spreads out over all age ranges. Brown and Waddell both point up the fact that the greatest incidence of heavy drinking appears in the middle-age group, the forties and fifties, for Puebloans and Papagos. Everett and Topper, on the other hand, point to the problematic character of youthful styles of drinking for Apaches and Navajos. Given the addictive quality of alcohol, it should not be surprising that the greater incidence of chronicity among all four groups would be among those of middle age. Youthful binge drinkers may or may not, upon assuming new responsibilities, carry heavy drinking over into their later years. Important to keep in mind are the significant roles that military life and industrial wage work have played in altering the traditional contexts and their controls.

Perhaps the most significant contribution of all four studies is their identification of the specific social contexts in which drinking takes place. They emphasize that it is more than drinkers versus nondrinkers; different kinds of drinking take place in different contexts. Drinking *is* context-related, not something that takes place in a vacuum.

Papagos drink at the *nawait* or wine feast as well as at large collective feasts celebrating saints' days or commemorative events. They drink at the border on special days when Mexican merchants come to meet them. If beer is available, it may be regularly drunk at family meals. They also seek out special bars in cities and towns, or may congregate in public places with friends and relatives. Or they may gather in the homes of friends living in the towns or cities, to drink socially. Taos Puebloans do their heavy social drinking at family gatherings or go to the neighboring town, since obvious drinking is defined as disruptive within the pueblo. While it does occur in the latter, there is still a strong corporate sanction against this. For Navajos there are a variety of very specific environments ranging from young men drinking at stomp dances to the drinking that goes on at a squaw dance, where the patrolling behavior of the police as well as the different environments call for different drinking patterns. And barroom drinking away from the reservation is of another character altogether. Western Apaches drink at dances, parties, wakes, and in homes, each form regulated by the norms operating in such social gatherings. These differ from roving adolescent gangs and from ''camels'' going anywhere and everywhere.

Another important dimension of these studies is that of recognizing variations within each group. Not only do social contexts vary but individual personalities respond differently to these situations. There is an often overlooked clinical dimension to Native American drinking; that is, that unique personalities have different kinds of responses to similarly structured social events. It is not enough to beg that culture is operative or that different cultures share common structural situations. While these are factual statements, appealing only to cultural and social facts and ignoring personality variables will obviate any meaningful efforts to solve problems. There is greater need for clinical observations in order to sort out how persons realize their cultural personalities differently. There needs to be greater exploration of the development of individual styles, the attrition of particular anxieties and tensions, the coping with unique crisis events that all individual human beings must handle. These four studies suggest that individual perceptions of events are as significant as identifying common cultural events.

Where concern is on the practical side, that is, on the development of effective rehabilitative or problem-solving strategies, the four studies share some basic perspectives. Waddell and Everett both suggest that non-natives are culturally and conceptually confused within their own normative framework, hence may be in a poor position to define themselves as custodians over the welfare of those who claim a differing normative framework. As Everett particularly emphasizes, non-native institutions and models usually take precedence, even when they have not proven effective. Priorities in decision making as well as in the critical matter of funding frequently are in control of non-Indian benefactors, as Ron Wood also points out. Some of the ambiguity and confusion of Richard Cooley's Hopi (Pueblo), Papago, Navajo, and Apache trainees could well be as much due to non-Indian ambiguity as due to their own perceptual difficulties. Yet, in most cross-cultural communication problems, the benefactor usually presumes his program to be clear and the recipient the one who is confused. There is nothing intrinsic to our programs of mental health or our culture in general that makes them stand out as obviously workable. For instance, Wood points out that less formal techniques and therapies frequently have better success than highly professional strategies. If our culture had produced a totally successful way of dealing with alcohol problems, there would be no need to argue over alternate therapies or to so frequently change our programs. Our own normative culture, including our understanding of alcohol problems and ways to deal with them, has variability and ambiguity, yet non-Indians dominate most programs and frequently control funding decisions as if they knew best what to do. In spite of the ambiguity in non-native culture, Topper's suggestion that Navajos be consciously taught how to negotiate Anglo culture is sound and could be extended to all of the groups discussed. The same may be said for the more difficult task of educating whites about the real world of Indians. Cooley, Miller and Ostendorf, and Wood concur on this point.

A second important common element in all four studies and that of Escalante is that many of the problems revolving around alcohol management are taxonomic or conceptual. The selections by the four practitioners in Part Three argue the significance of the point as well. There are cultural meanings attached to certain behaviors and these are not cross-culturally shared. Topper reminds us that there are different, opposing moral systems, a point which should be clear by looking at our own Western European varieties. This should have significant implications for the variety of moralistic programs found in Native American communities today, wherever non-Indian institutions have proliferated. The implications of this fact are evident in Cooley's observations of his Indian trainees. All of the studies in this volume point to existing cultural realities, the different moral systems that are still active. Rehabilitative programs are ill-fated that fail to discover what these are or fail to make use of them once they are understood.

Native concepts and definitions of problems must be given higher priority. Certainly contemporary Native American communities should not be totally dominated by non-Indian realities. Perhaps, as Everett suggests, there should be a thoughtful reduction in the extent to which we perpetuate non-native institutions and models of health care at the expense of culturally meaningful institutions and models. A local community's conceptualization of problems and their solutions rather than total commitment to outside frames of reference are in order. A major source of conflict stems from the juxtaposition of outside programs to local ingenuity. Priorities in decision making should be allowed to those decision-making bodies that locally exist, as Brown argues. This commitment to local priorities, supported also by Cooley, Miller and Ostendorf, and Wood, does not necessarily mean a rejection of Anglo therapy technologies and ideas. It does call for more genuine cross-cultural communication in addressing commonly perceived social problems such as alcohol abuse.

There are, of course, the language and skill problems and the need to open up the opportunity structure for economic betterment. So it is not only a matter of attacking alcohol abuse but also a matter of addressing ourselves to broader social and economic issues. And, indeed, as Brown and Topper argue, prohibition is not the answer. Answers will come when culturally meaningful plans of action can be established with a minimum of outside institutional management, always keeping foremost the priorities and needs as formulated by Native Americans themselves. There is still too much "firsthand hurt" being experienced by Native Americans today.

REFERENCES CITED

Dozier, E.
   1956   Two Examples of Linguistic Acculturation, The Yaqui of Sonora-Arizona and Tewa of New Mexico. *Language* **32**:146–57.
Foster, G.
   1960   *Culture and Conquest: America's Spanish Heritage.* Viking Fund Publications in Anthropology, No. 27.
Spicer, E.
   1954   Spanish-Indian Acculturation in the Southwest. *American Anthropologist* **56**:663–78.

EPIGRAPH

Anthros

Well, yes, I been studying anthros
and according to their surveys,
now I know:
why I'm sitting in this bar polishing
this stolen 30-30 Winchester
(I'll probably kill somebody, I'm assured)
And why I'm going to get drunker and drunker
and probably get in a fight and go to jail
(to which I'm bound to return time after time)
but while I'm getting drunk I'll
think of my wife and family and cry because
I'm underprivileged, uneducated, re-located,
as-yet-un-assimilated, deprived, depraved,
and bound for hell if I don't go to church
even though I can really do Indian dances that
all the good white people like
and, hey, I can really do "crafts,"
maybe I should go to Hollywood
and learn the Tonto Stomp or something
or maybe write a letter to Mr. Anthro Survey
and ask him about heartache
and hungry little children
as I walk through these angry ghettos
getting first hand hurt.

from *Akwesasne Notes*

Index

246   *Index*

Papago: (*Continued*)
234; variations in drinking, 44, 45,
233; veterans, 39; work habits, 41,
195. *See also* Ceremonial
intoxication; Alcoholism,
conceptual problems with;
Intoxicated
Party (*daiyąą́*), 158–60
Pasqua Yaqui Association Housing
Project, 199
Personal tragedies from drinking,
54, 79
Peyote, xvii, 16, 19, 20, 86, 91,
100, 143
Phoenix, 38, 56, 60, 61, 142
Pimans, x, 3, 6, 7, 15, 18, 20, 28
Plants for preparing fermented
beverages, 9, 11
Police, 48, 134, 137, 138, 184, 234
Power (*gewkdag*), 43
Problem drinking, xvii, 90, 126, 140,
146, 149, 170, 173, 176, 185, 197,
210, 218, 219, 229, 230, 233. *See
also* Alcohol, problems with
Prohibition of drinking, xxviii, 54,
87, 98–100, 115, 117, 119, 138, 157,
158, 229, 236
Proxemics of drinking group, 136, 137
Public confession, 208
Public intoxication, 157. *See also*
Drunkenness
Pueblo Boy Scout Troup, 92; Council,
84, 86, 87, 91, 98, 99; drinking,
228, 230, 234; 4-H, 92
Pueblos: disavowal of intoxicants in
ritual, 22, 95, 100, 227; One Spring
Time ceremony, 22; rain and
growth ceremonies, 3, 21, 28,
29, 226
Pulque (*Ochtli*), 4, 5, 18

Queer (*uwikwuad*), 52

Racial prejudice, 135, 136
Rainmaking ceremonies. *See*
Agricultural-ceremonial complex,
intoxication as feature of;
Intoxicants in agricultural ritual

Reciprocal drinking, 51–53, 64,
75, 76
Recovered Indian drinkers, xvii, 207,
211, 220
Rehabilitation strategies, xvi, 200,
202, 219, 234, 236
Relict region. *See* Cultural sink
Rio Grande, 20, 21, 83, 84
Ritual intoxication. *See* Ceremonial
intoxication

Sahagún, 5
Sahuaro cactus fruit, 7, 26. *See also*
Ceremonial beverages
Sanctions regulating intoxication, 9,
11, 15, 62, 138, 174, 187, 229, 234
Santa Cruz River, 38
Sells, Arizona, 49, 50, 52, 63, 70
Sex roles: changes in, 68, 69, 71, 72;
tensions in, 67, 68, 70–72, 74. *See
also* Cross-sex antagonisms
Sexual frustrations, 139, 140
Shaman. *See* Medicine man
Sharing drinks and food, 59, 65,
75–77, 188
Sibling (*wehnag*), 48
Sobriety, 67, 69, 110, 166
Social drinking, 28, 52, 56, 61,
63–65, 77, 187, 229. *See also*
Drinking of alcohol, social bonds
Social margin, xxvii, xxviii, xxix
Social pathology, 78, 167. *See also*
Drinking of alcohol, deviant
behavior
Social pressures to drink, 51–54, 75,
76, 139, 189–92, 198, 199,
218, 232
Sonoran Province, 3, 7, 12, 15, 227
Southern Athapascan territory, 150
South Tuba, Arizona, 132
South Tucson, 52, 55, 58–60;
police, 199
Southwest Indian, definition,
205, 206
Spanish influence, 38, 39, 59, 84,
149, 227–29
Squaw Dance (Navajo). *See* Enemy
Way Ceremony (Navajo)